THE AUTHORITY
OF THE SAINTS

The Authority
Of the Saints

Drawing on the Theology
of Hans Urs von Balthasar

PAULINE DIMECH
Foreword by Dominic Robinson

PICKWICK *Publications* · Eugene, Oregon

THE AUTHORITY OF THE SAINTS
Drawing on the Theology of Hans Urs von Balthasar

Pickwick Publications
An Imprint of Wipf and Stock Publishers
199 W. 8th Ave., Suite 3
Eugene, OR 97401

www.wipfandstock.com

PAPERBACK ISBN: 978-1-5326-0403-4
HARDCOVER ISBN: 978-1-5326-0405-8
EBOOK ISBN: 978-1-5326-0404-1

Cataloguing-in-Publication data:

Names: Dimech, Pauline, author. | Robinson, Dominic, foreword.

Title: Book title : The authority of the saints : drawing on the theology of Hans Urs von Balthasar / by Pauline Dimech ; foreword by Dominic Robinson.

Description: Eugene, OR : Pickwick Publications, 2017 | Includes bibliographical references.

Identifiers: ISBN 978-1-5326-0403-4 (paperback) | ISBN 978-1-5326-0405-8 (hardcover) | ISBN 978-1-5326-0404-1 (ebook)

Subjects: LCSH: Balthasar, Hans Urs von, 1905–1988. | Christian saints—Cult—History of doctrines.

Classification: BX4705.B163 D52 2017 (paperback) | BX4705.B163 D52 (ebook)

Manufactured in the U.S.A.   05/03/17

Permission to quote the following publications by Ignatius Press has been sought and granted:

Balthasar, Hans Urs von, *The Christian State of Life*. Translated by Sr Mary Frances Mc-Carthy. San Francisco: Ignatius,1983.

Balthasar, Hans Urs von, *The Glory of the Lord: A Theological Aesthetics, I, Seeing the Form*. Edited by Joseph Fessio and John Riches. Translated by Erasmo Leiva-Meri-kakis. San Francisco: Ignatius, 1982.

Balthasar, Hans Urs von, *The Office of Peter and the Structure of the Church*. Translated by Andrée Emery. San Francisco: Ignatius, 2007.

Balthasar, Hans Urs von, *Theo-Logic: Theological Logical Theory, III, The Spirit of Truth*. Translated by Graham Harrison. San Francisco: Ignatius, 2005.

Balthasar, Hans Urs von, *Two Sisters in the Spirit. Thérèse of Lisieux & Elizabeth of the Trinity*. San Francisco: Ignatius, 1992. *Thérèse von* Lisieux: Translated by Donald Nichols and Anne Englund Nash. *Elisabeth von Dijon*: Translated by Dennis Martin.

To all the Saints

"We are slowly returning to the realization that those of the faithful who stand out by the way in which they live the Church's faith, who used to be called 'saints' (whether they were canonized or not), are the people in whose hands lies the whole destiny of the Church of today and tomorrow and who will determine whether or not the Church will achieve recognition in the world. It is by no means necessary that such 'saints' as these should be exceptional individuals. Some have such a calling, but they are few and far between, and these are often only the spark that kindles a group, be it great or small, which does the work of spreading the new light that shone in its founder in the scattered places of the world . . . And such authentic Christianity will give the world a great deal more to worry about than the towering edifices of the hierarchy."

HANS URS VON BALTHASAR, *ENGAGEMENT WITH GOD*, 95–96.

Contents

List of Diagrams | ix
Foreword by Dominic Robinson | xi
Preface | xv
Acknowledgments | xvii
Abbreviations | xviii

CHAPTER 1
The Problem of Saintly Authority | 1

CHAPTER 2
Theoretical Insights | 51

Chapter 3
The Existential Dimension | 85

Chapter 4
The Epistemological Dimension | 119

CHAPTER 5
The Ecclesiological Dimension | 165

CHAPTER 6
General Conclusion | 209

Bibliography | 229

Diagrams

Diagram 01. The *Communio Sanctorum* | 12

Diagram 02. Experience | 136

Diagram 03. Mysticism | 150

Diagram 04. The Teaching Authority of the Church | 155

Diagram 05. The Marian Church | 166

Diagram 06. Offices within the Church | 173

Diagram 07. Office and Charism | 188

Diagram 08. The Charismatic Dimension | 188

Diagram 09. Petrine Office and Marian Holiness | 199

Diagram 10. The Baptized and the Saints | 220

Foreword

IT IS A GREAT pleasure and privilege to introduce this exciting book by Pauline Dimech. The subject of this work is a much under-researched and underestimated aspect of Hans Urs von Balthasar's thought. As such it is to be welcomed as a significant contribution to contemporary studies of this important theological figure. In turn the research carried out is a springboard for reflection on wider issues surrounding our understanding of theology and church emerging from the ongoing interpretation of such a key figure in post-Vatican II theology. Balthasar's legacy is surely being served well as this complex and seminal thinker has the fruits of his labour digested through diverse interpretations shaping our understanding of Catholic theology and the nature of the church herself in the post-Vatican II era. This book is part of that process of digestion, reception and continued debate. It is fitting then that this work started its life as a doctoral thesis at the Centre of Catholic Studies at the University of Durham.

Pauline Dimech has chosen a contentious topic which lies at the heart of the post-Vatican II debate. She has developed a convincing argument for the increased significance of the communion of the saints in Balthasar's theology and shown how this impacts on theology as a whole. It is, she boldly argues, implicit in Balthasar's thought that theological statements derive no small authority from those who in the Christian and Catholic tradition we regard as saints. If this is so—and that is surely the big question—this has an impact on how Balthasar, one of the seminal post conciliar giants of Catholic theology, understands how we do theology in the Catholic tradition.

Dimech proceeds to lay out carefully Balthasar's understanding of the official and unofficial "communio sanctorum" and places this in the context of his ecclesiology and theological anthropology. This is the result of a survey of a wide range of secondary literature which draws out mainly implicit as well as explicit views on the weight Balthasar gives to certain "figures" regarded as authoritative. The wide-ranging scope here of both secondary and primary literature is impressive. The critique of the material is searching, taking in different strands of opinion on Balthasar. The critique of Karen Kilby in particular, it must be said, is daring and provocative but it is balanced. As such it introduces an interesting and crucial debate on what Balthasar intended for his theology. Does this complex thinker fall foul at times of making sweeping "dogmatic" statements, as Kilby suggests? There may be a good argument for taking this view which, sadly, might in fact lead to an undervaluing of the contribution Balthasar has made or, worse, dismissing him as a valid bearer of post-Vatican II thought on theology and church. Or, as Dimech suggests, does he often legitimately present perspectives emerging from a radiating constellation of figures who patch together a tapestry of pictures of God and God's dealings with humanity?

Here we can see how Dimech's research raises questions on the wider horizon relating to the nature of Balthasar's theology as a whole, and the impact it may have on contemporary theology. What is "dogma" for Balthasar? This is surely a key question to explore still further for scholars of Balthasar. What does he learn from aesthetics, from the medium of drama, from Ignatian spirituality? How does he marry a firm belief in revealed truth with a receptive paradigm of learning from the other, from the diversity of responses to God's revelation as he shows his glory in encounter with humanity who are expressed in the broader constellations of discipleship in the church?

Dimech's response to another important recent work on Balthasar, Lyra Pitstick's *Hans Urs von Balthasar and the Descent into Hell* is fascinating. Dimech shows how Pitstick, for all her searching and revolutionary work on the Descent into Hell, misses important points about the nature of the theological task as emerging from "figures" like Adrienne von Speyr as well as from the magisterium. Pitstick's view is valid from the point of view of her full and careful research into the tradition on the Descent but Dimech has begun to ask questions about the nature of Balthasar's statements. Is it permissible to mix the mystical with dogma? Or are these more eastern ways of doing theology to be avoided? This is again contentious and daring to argue but it is a fascinating suggestion to throw out to new scholars of Balthasar to debate. Not much has been written critically on this since the Pitstick–Oates debate ended when Edward Oakes sadly died in 2013. So it is timely.

Students of Balthasar, be they Catholic or not, in leadership positions in the church, in ministry, following the baptismal call of the faithful, will find this book challenging. Dimech's work stirs up the pot already brewing through contemporary debates on Balthasar.

I am delighted then to introduce this engaging, provocative work on one of the seminal theologians of the post-Vatican II era and whom we are still trying to understand. This book daringly advances an important area of research in Balthasar studies which it is hoped will stimulate much more debate and discussion in the academy and church as a whole.

Dominic Robinson, SJ

Preface

As a Catholic, a Religious Educator, a Catechist, and a member of the Society of Christian Doctrine, the commemoration of the saints has always been a part of my life. As a member of the Society of Christian Doctrine, I also followed closely the process whereby the Founder of my Society—a Catholic priest by the name of Fr. George Preca (1880–1962)—was beatified in 2001 and then canonized in 2007. Since I have known and often spoken to people who knew Fr. Preca personally during his lifetime, and who were, literally, mesmerized by him, the influence of the saints—on other people and in the church—has always fascinated me. I would say that it has fascinated many other theologians and philosophers besides myself. Max Scheler's "value persons," Nietzsche's "übermenschen," Hegel's "great men of history," Johann Baptiste Metz's "classics," can all be interpreted as attempts to understand why and how some have authority over the rest.

On the other hand, this book is also a product of my frustration with my own sinfulness and that of the church. History is full of examples of individuals who held positions of authority, which they would not have deserved either spiritually or morally. Their position put them at an advantage over the saints, who may not have held such positions, and whose life may even have been completely hidden from the world. My concern throughout has been pastoral as well as dogmatic. Not only do I ask whether and to what extent we may attribute authority to the saints but also how may we ensure that it is the saints and not the scoundrels whose influence persists and whose memory endures.

As a Catholic priest and theologian, and an ex-Jesuit, Hans Urs von Balthasar (1905–1988) was also captivated by the saints and by their writings. Moreover, he personally knew, and collaborated closely with, the Swiss theologian and mystic Adrienne von Speyr (1902–1967), whom he met in 1940. All things considered, I became convinced that Balthasar would help me clarify the issues surrounding authority and particularly the authority of the saints. Although Balthasar did not develop a full-blown doctrine of the authority of the saints, I believe that his work can be used as a resource to navigate the way through such a doctrine, if theologians were to seriously seek to develop it. I have often asked myself whether the theme of the authority of the saints is one example were "popular religion" has progressed at a faster pace than the reflection upon it.[1] This book is an application of Balthasar's theology to a subject that has fascinated me personally for many years. I have also been propelled by it. Reading the lives of individual saints, I have been made uncomfortable by the complexity with which the status of the saints fluctuated, both within the community and vis-à-vis the church hierarchy. I have also been captivated by the fact that the devotion towards the saints oscillates so rapidly because of contemporary philosophical and theological trends, which have an impact both on the process leading to the canonization of the individual saint, but also on the perpetuation of the veneration, or of the esteem, towards that same saint. It is a subject which, it seems to me, Balthasar also struggled with. He strove to bring the Fathers of the church back to living memory, to promote a more accurate depiction of saints like Thérèse of Lisieux and of Elizabeth of the Trinity, to integrate Adrienne von Speyr within the church.

Besides establishing Balthasar's involvement with the enterprise, what this book tries to do is establish the theological foundations upon which any authority of the saints would have to be based in theory, and possibly has implicitly been based in practice, using Balthasar's theology. The focus is on the theological anthropology (the existential), theological epistemology (the epistemological) and the theology of the church (the ecclesiological).

This book will not answer all the questions, but I hope that it will stimulate thought and motivate further research.

1. Rahner, "The Relation between Theology and Popular Religion," 140–47.

Acknowledgments

THIS STUDY WAS INITIALLY a thesis submitted in fulfillment of the requirements for the degree of Doctor of Theology at the University of Durham, under the supervision of Prof Mark Allen McIntosh and Prof Paul Murray. I am immensely grateful to them both for their guidance and mentorship. There are also many friends and colleagues who supported me during the past years, as I did my Master's Degree at Heythrop College, London, and then my PhD at Durham University, UK, and in the first years of my academic career. I would especially like to thank my friends and mentors Rev. Prof Louis Caruana, SJ, Rev. Dr. Charles Delia, SJ. Rev. Dr. Joe Inguanez, and Rev. Dr. Arthur Vella, SJ. I would also very much like to express my gratitude to the Dean of the Faculty of Theology at the University of Malta, Rev. Prof. Emmanuel Agius, as well as to all my colleagues. They provided stimulating theological conversation, which though often unrelated to my research interests, reinforced my vocation as a theologian, a Religious Educator, and a Catechist. I am especially grateful to the late Rev. Dr. Isidore Bonabom, SJ for his kindness, his profound wisdom and his support. I am also grateful to Dr. Eddie Fenech Adami and to the late Rev. Prof. Peter Serracino Inglott, who also believed in me and acted as my Referees for the initial MGSS scholarship which enabled me to do my PhD. Finally, all the members of my family have been especially supportive, particularly my mother. Although she herself never received a tertiary education, she is one of the wisest people I know, and I am truly grateful for her generosity, understanding and encouragement.

Abbreviations

TA1: *The Glory of the Lord: A Theological Aesthetics, I, Seeing the Form*

TA2: *The Glory of the Lord: A Theological Aesthetics, II, Studies in Theological Style: Clerical Styles*

TA3: *The Glory of the Lord: A Theological Aesthetics, III, Studies in Theological Style: Lay Styles*

TA4: *The Glory of the Lord: A Theological Aesthetics, IV, The Realm of Metaphysics in Antiquity*

TA5: *The Glory of the Lord: A Theological Aesthetics, V, The Realm of Metaphysics in the Modern Age*

TA6: *The Glory of the Lord: A Theological Aesthetics, VI, Theology: The Old Covenant*

TA7: *The Glory of the Lord: A Theological Aesthetics, VII: Theology: The New Covenant*

TD1: *Theo-Drama: Theological Dramatic Theory, I, Prologomena*

TD2: *Theo-Drama: Theological Dramatic Theory, II: Dramatis Personae: Man in God*

TD3: *Theo-Drama: Theological Dramatic Theory, III, The Dramatis Personae: The Person in Christ Personae: The Person in Christ*

TD4: *Theo-Drama: Theological Dramatic Theory, IV, The Dramatis Personae: The Action. Personae: The Action*

TD5: *Theo-Drama: Theological Dramatic Theory, V, The Last Act*

TL1: *Theo-Logic: Theological Logical Theory, I, Truth of the World*

TL2: *Theo-Logic: Theological Logical Theory, II, Truth of God*

TL3: *Theo-Logic: Theological Logical Theory, III, The Spirit of Truth*

Chapter 1

The Problem of Saintly Authority

INTRODUCTION

MY THESIS IS THAT Hans Urs von Balthasar manifests remarkable interest in the saints, expresses huge respect for the theology of each saint, and develops a generic theology of the saint, that is, a broad description of the inherent features, the characteristics, the essence of the saint, as well as provides an account of the features and the characteristics which are typical of the theology of the saints. Balthasar regards the life of the saints and their theology as crucial to the task of writing significant theology—not just his own, but also that of others—and to the task of building the church. He makes various remarkable connections, which in turn can serve to ground the authority of the saints in the eyes of others, particularly in the eyes of practicing theologians, but also in the eyes of the church. One such connection is that between theology and life, a link which Balthasar defends and validates in a particularly notable manner. It is clear that Balthasar attributes an authority to the saints (in the case of the link between theology and life, an existential authority) that is analogical to that of the Pope and the bishops.

Within a Catholic context, the term "Magisterium," first introduced into papal declarations by Gregory XVI, has developed multiple meanings. It could refer to "the wide range of authoritative teaching activities of bishops, and, especially, popes."[1] However, it often carries a more personalistic meaning, referring to those whose office puts them in a position of

---

1. Hellemans, "The Magisterium," 55 and 57.

authority. In this case, the term would refer specifically to the person of the Pope and the bishops. However, the term "Magisterium" also has a more conceptual meaning. Here, it refers to the authority which lays down what is the authentic teaching of the church, without making a direct reference to the authority holders. This distinction is important, because it will allow me to speak of the authority of the saints as analogical to that of the Magisterium, or even to speak of the Magisterium of the saints.

A word must also be said about the word "authority." Although the term, used within an ecclesiastical context, generally evokes images of prelates, judgments, verdicts, dogmas, and *imprimaturs*, the term authority here will signify more a kind of propelling quality. Victor Lee Austin, a priest and theologian in the Episcopal Church, has said that an authority always has "*something to convey to us,*" always has "*a place to lead us toward,*" always embodies "a sense of what the human good is" and always "exist[s] to help us flourish in [that human good]."[2] It is in this sense that we may speak of the saints as being authoritative.

My reading of Balthasar has convinced me that there is no reason why we should restrict the term "Magisterium" (that is the term which refers to the authority that lays down what is the authentic teaching of the church) to the Popes and the Bishops. There is no reason why we should not say that the saints too have authority, that they too are a Magisterium. Perhaps it should be stated that the saints, more than anyone else, lay down what the authentic teaching of the church is. This authority (which is manifested in the saints and which is attributed to the saints) has at least another two dimensions besides the existential. These are: the epistemological, and the ecclesiological. All three dimensions represent the different grounds for the authority of the saints, as well as the different settings in which the saints function authoritatively.

The study of the authority of the saints may seem unusable. Some may even consider it an unnecessary endeavour, because the saint's authority is already recognized. The Catechism claims that "The saints are the light bearers of the *sensus fidei*."[3] The great majority would agree that they were outstanding witnesses of the *sensus fidei* in their own time and for all times, in their own place and for all places. Others would think such a theme provocative because authority has always been associated with the Magisterium, that is, with the official teaching authority, and not with

---

2. Austin, *Up with Authority*, 7.

3. International Theological Commission, "*Sensus Fidei* in the Life of the Church," par. 100.

the saints.[4] The crux of the matter is that theology without the authority of the saints is simply unimaginable. So is the church *per se*. To conceive of a church that does not uphold the authority of the saints is a *contradictio in terminis*. The scientist and philosopher Michael Polanyi (1891–1976) once said that "[t]he curious thing is that we have no clear knowledge of what our presuppositions are and when we try to formulate them they appear quite unconvincing."[5] The issue becomes all the more clear when one asks the following questions, the first dealing specifically with Balthasar, and the second dealing with theology generally. What would Balthasar's theology have been like, had Balthasar not trusted the saints? And, secondly, what would theology and the church be like if they rejected the authority of the saints? That would possibly be an *argumentum ad absurdum*. The fact is that the authority of the saints is presupposed, and yet, formulating this presupposition proves to be extremely awkward. This book is an exploration into the nature, the sources and the limits of the authority of the saints. Balthasar does not set out consciously intending to investigate the matter. Like other theologians, he seems to take the authority of the saints for granted. And yet, I use Balthasar's theology of the saints to help me navigate through a theology of the authority of the saints. This means that there are times when I take it upon myself to articulate Balthasar's thoughts, to flesh out Balthasar's underlying views and concepts. There are times when Balthasar does shed more light on the issue of the authority of the saints. It is for this reason that I decided to use Balthasar as a guide and a resource as we reflect on the issue.

THE SAINTS AND HAGIOGRAPHY

Before we delve more deeply into Balthasar's theology, in order to emphasize the importance of the theology of the saints in that context, we should say something about Balthasar as a hagiographer, or rather, about Balthasar's non-typical hagiography. Traditionally, hagiography contained accounts of the discovery or relocation of relics, bulls of canonization, investigations held into the life of a candidate for canonization, legends associated with the saint, as well as descriptions of sermons, visions, and other extraordinary

4. Sullivan has pointed out that the word *Magisterium* refers to that group within the church who is responsible for "providing ecclesiastical teaching that is *magisterium authenticum*." The Latin adjective *authenticum* should be translated as *authoritative* (in the sense of bearing the force of a teaching that is consistent with the Scriptures), and not as *authentic* (as opposed to inauthentic). See Fahey, "Church," 200.

5. Polanyi, *Personal Knowledge*, 62.

phenomena. The typical hagiographer would consider the saint as a thau-
maturge, an "epitome of . . . ethical excellence,"[6] a romantic hero, an exces-
sive ascetic, someone who deserves to be admired for having withdrawn
from the world, or for having performed strange deeds. Historians, particularly medievalists, and liturgists would typically focus on verification and
authentication of the evidence. None of this is to be found in Balthasar's
explorations of the saints. Balthasar's is certainly not a romantic hagiography. Neither is it a modern rationalist account that reduces truth-theory to
verification.[7] What concerns Balthasar is the theological content of hagiography. What concerns him is that the saints are "rich in suggestions that
theologians only need to expand in order to bring out their lasting value,"[8]
and that "their sheer existence proves to be a theological manifestation that
contains most fruitful and opportune doctrine" not only for theologians,
but for "the whole Church," and "for all Christians."[9] With Balthasar, the
individual theologian, and the church as a whole, must look to the saints
(even more than to the Pope and the Bishops). More specifically, the role
of the theologian is to expand the suggestions of the saints (rather than to
elucidate the documents of the members of the official Magisterium).

Let us, for a moment, delve into the concept of the saint as depicted
by Balthasar, that is, explore who the saint is, and who the saints are in
Balthasar's view. If we were to take a segment of Balthasar's work—let us
say, that between the early fifties and the early seventies—we would be able
to see that the perception, the hermeneutics of the saints, remains constant,
even when different images are used or different emphases are made. The
saint is always much more than a patron who offers protection and security,
one who acts as a mediator between God and ourselves.[10] In *Two Sisters*
the saints are those who "lift" the world, by having God as their "fulcrum,"
and prayer as their "lever."[11] They are "a new type of conformity to Christ
. . . a new illustration of how the Gospel is to be lived."[12] In his *Das Betrach-
tende Gebet*, the saint is "an almost inexhaustible storehouse of light and
love, providing strength and nourishment for centuries."[13] In *Theologie der
Geschichte*, the saint is

6. Heffernan, *Sacred Biography*, 221–22.

7. Nichols, *Say It Is Pentecost*, 11.

8. Balthasar, *Two Sisters*, 150.

9. Ibid., 25.

10. Ibid.

11. Ibid., 199.

12. Ibid., 25.

13. Balthasar, *Prayer*, 106.

a presentation to his own age of the message that heaven is send-
ing to it, a man who is, here and now, the right and relevant
interpretation of the Gospel, who is given to this particular age
as its way to approach to the perennial truth of Christ.[14]

In the first volume of the *Aesthetics*, the Christian saint is the one "who
has made the deep-rooted act of faith and obedience to God's inner light
the norm of his whole existence,"[15] the figure who is "characterized by the
Christ form."[16] In his *Einfaltungen*, the saints are the ones who represent the
glory of God's justice and mercy. They are those who "let themselves be expropriated into Christ's personified 'justice of God', to stand in the authority
of Christ as his 'ambassadors' in the 'ministry of reconciliation'."[17] In *Engagement with God*, the saints are individuals who are "specially chosen,"[18] individuals "who tower above the rest."[19] In his essay on Matthias Claudius, the
saints are depicted as more perceptive, more responsive, more alert, than
the typical Christian. They are the ones who clarify things for the church.
They are those who trust God "to perform the greatest work," those who
"sense falsehood."[20] And so on, and so forth. These seemingly insignificant
descriptions of the identity, the essence, the characteristics, the function
of the saints are, in fact, very suggestive, on three levels. First of all, with
Balthasar, the focus is on the saints' message "from God to the Church,"[21]
rather than on the comfort which the saints provide to us when we become
aware of their similarity to ourselves, or on their role as facilitators when
there is something that we would like God to grant us, as with most spiritual writings about the saints. Secondly, Balthasar clearly attributes to the
saints an eminence, an authority that the Magisterium has traditionally
attributed to itself. He grounds the authority of the saints there, were the
Magisterium is generally expected to be authoritative. Thirdly, it is clear
that Balthasar intends to revive the familiarity with the "saints" as peda-
gogues and interpreters, presenting them as adept and skillful, as unique
and exceptional guides. Interestingly, Balthasar does not depict the saints
as perfect, or their theology as necessarily inerrant.[22] "Even true saints often

14. Balthasar, *A Theology of History*, 110.

15. Balthasar, *Seeing the Form (TA1),* 165.

16. Ibid., 36.

17. Balthasar, *Convergences,* 20–21.

18. Balthasar, *Engagement with God,* 19.

19. Ibid., 20.

20. Balthasar, "A Verse of Matthias Claudius," 17.

21. Balthasar, *Two Sisters,* 27.

22. According to Balthasar, "perfection is not in itself self-sufficient and purpose-
ful." See Balthasar, *The Christian State of Life*, 82.

have faults."[23] After all, as Austin has pointed out, authority may not always be right.[24] Rodney Howsare grants that, in Balthasar, even those saints who would generally be considered more important may be wrong sometimes.[25] John of the cross is criticized for his unrelenting reductionism, for discarding all forms and figures, for his attitude toward Christian art. Howsare himself identifies instances when Balthasar critiques the Church Fathers. Most specifically, Balthasar criticizes the Fathers for adopting the Christian message to the egress/regress metaphysics of the ancient philosophers and for over-emphasizing the ineffability of God.[26] Authority would naturally be lost if that individual holding it was generally wrong, or wrong in something that was considered substantial, but one would assume that this would not be the case with the more important saints whose theology is more cogent, and, possibly by virtue of that, more authoritative. Howsare has suggested that what Balthasar does is to discern between the "better" and the "weaker" moments of the saints. He attempts to identify the "better" moments when Christ "shines through" and to correct the "weaker" ones, when the Gospel is being obscured. Howsare's is a fair assessment of what Balthasar does.[27] But one wonders whether the argument as a whole can be sustained. One would have to say that everybody has his better and weaker movements, but finding precise criteria to distinguish the two is not straightforward, and forgiving errors as simply moments of weakness is not always defensible. I would agree with Howsare that an essential part of Balthasar's project requires the "retrieval of past Christian thought," which will always involve a process of discernment.[28] It is very significant that, in Balthasar, this past thought is always closely coupled to its thinker. Balthasar goes beyond Blondel's emphasis that tradition was a living reality, through which dogma developed.[29] On his part, Balthasar does not just think and analyze thoughts or examine the development of dogma, as if dogma could be disconnected from its human source. Balthasar would rather analyze the individuals who fabricated these thoughts. It is the thinkers whom he discerns, rather than the thoughts. In Balthasar, the theology of the saints (that is, the theology produced by saints) is not to be detached from the saints.

23. Balthasar, *First Glance*, 73.

24. Austin, *Up with Authority*, 3.

25. Howsare refers to Balthasar's criticism of Augustine's theory of predestination and to Aquinas's doctrine on the immaculate conception, and to the torture of heretics. See Howsare, *A Guide for the Perplexed*, 161.

26. Howsare, *Hans Urs von Balthasar and Protestantism*, 114.

27. Howsare, *A Guide for the Perplexed*, 34.

28. Ibid.

29. Boersma, "Sacramental Ontology," 248.

WHICH SAINTS?

Yves Tourenne once said that "[o]ne way to enter into Balthasar's thought process is to note the proper names he cites, to compile an index, and to try to understand why certain names appear in certain passages or alongside certain other names."[30] I am sure we would all agree that Balthasar's theology was not fortuitous. Rather, it involved a whole process of discernment concerning which saints to use in a particular context. It is certainly necessary to evaluate this process of discernment if we are to understand Balthasar's work. Aidan Nichols argues that Balthasar would have voluntarily chosen those saints who had a lot to contribute to the contemporary church.[31] While agreeing with this sensible supposition, I feel that it is only partially accurate. I would say that Balthasar's decisions were based on five criteria. First of all: there were the saints who were especially alluring to him personally, those whom he came to know spiritually, who most fascinated and inspired him in his own religious life, those who influenced him spiritually and theologically. Ignatius of Loyola (1491–1556) would fall into this group. Secondly, there were the already established saints, whom all worthy theologians quoted, and whom everyone considered authoritative, like Augustine and Aquinas. Thirdly, there were those saints whose wisdom he had discovered, but who were no longer known to the Western world. According to him, the Fathers of the church—like Gregory and Maximus— would fall in this group. Ben Quash has identified what Balthasar admires in the Church Fathers: their mystical warmth, their rhetorical power, and so on.[32] Fourthly, there were then the saints whose import was yet to be discovered. Thérèse of Lisieux would fall among this group. Balthasar believed that Thérèse could be presented as a paradigm, and he wanted to divulge her wisdom, and to make her theology known. I actually think that, if it were up to Balthasar, he would also include Adrienne in this fourth group. She was a saint and a mystic whose wisdom and import was yet to be discovered. Finally, there were those "saints" who were not generally recognized as holy, because they were associated more with philosophy and literature than with theology. These were those philosophical and literary figures whose work manifested the glory of the Lord, who had contributed to the philosophical and theological arena, even if their connection with the church may have been partially or totally invisible.

---

30. Tourenne, "Foreword," 17.

31. Nichols, *Divine Fruitfulness,* 3.

32. Quash, "Hans Urs von Balthasar," 107.

Needless to say, Balthasar makes innumerable references to saints throughout the whole of his work. He is especially attracted by the Fathers of the church, the contemplatives, and the productive theologians. In the *Theo-Aesthetics*, it is the constellation of Christ, or the fourfold tradition of archetypal experience in the church that takes precedence. In Balthasar, Christ is the archetype and the prototype *par excellence*. However, those who experienced Christ first hand are also designated as archetypes because of the universal significance of their experience. In terms of their theological fruitfulness, it is the four archetypal figures in the Gospels who are most favored: John and Peter in particular, but also Paul, and especially Mary.[33] According to him, it is Mary "who presents to us the highest paradigm of what is meant by the 'art of God,' and by 'well-structured sanctity.'"[34] As Lucy Gardner has said, the "hermeneutic of theological-personal significance," particularly where Mary is concerned, is indubitable.[35] In *The Office of Peter*, Balthasar also gives prominence to the "constellation" of Jesus, but he now widens the circle, including other figures besides the four archetypes: the Twelve, John the Baptist, Joseph, Mary Magdalen, Martha, Mary, Simon of Cyrene, Nicodemus, Joseph of Arimathea, Judas Iscariot—whom no Christian would consider a saint—and the constellation in the Acts of the Apostles. For Balthasar, these saints were not just dead figures from history, narrative material for catechesis, or resources for dogmatic announcements. They were the chief sources for the theological enterprise, and the primary prototypes for the configuration of the church. Balthasar claims that all the members of the constellation were made "structural principles" of the church.[36]

The monographs dealing with the individual saints: Maximus the Confessor, Gregory of Nyssa, Thérèse of Lisieux, and Elizabeth of the Trinity, written in the first two decades of his theological career, are an important part of Balthasar's theological corpus. So were the anthologies and translations of select texts from Irenaeus, Basil of Caesarea, and Augustine, which Balthasar provided in the early years. The list of saints mentioned by Balthasar is endless, covering not only figures from the Scriptures and from the early Church Fathers, but also the medieval mystics (most of whom were never canonized), the founders of the mendicant orders, and the French mystics of the Grand Siécle. One finds in his work continuous

---

33. Balthasar describes Jesus' relationship with Mary as "a primary, all-embracing relationship." *The Office of Peter*, 145.

34. Balthasar, *Seeing the Form (TA1)*, 36.

35. Gardner, "Balthasar and the figure of Mary," 67, 72.

36. Balthasar, *The Office of Peter*, 243–44.

references to "the Great Tradition of Western Theology."[37] There are also a considerable number of women saints featuring alongside Augustine, Anselm, Bonaventure, Ignatius of Loyola, Francis of Assisi, the Curé of Ars, Bernard of Clairvaux, John of the Cross, Francis Xavier, de Caussade, and Peter Canisius. Balthasar manifests remarkable sensitivity to the theology of the saints. His sensitivity to the wealth and the vibrancy of the theology of the saints is especially evident in the inter-saintly debate Balthasar creates in his book *Dare we Hope "That All Men be Saved?"*[38] Here, Balthasar brings forward the testimony of the mystics who indicate that "hope for all men is permitted" (Mechtild of Hackeborn, Juliana of Norwich, Angela of Foligno, Mechtild of Magdeburg, and Adrienne von Speyr) against that of Augustine, Gregory the Great, Anselm, Bonaventure, Aquinas, John Henry Newman, and so on, who maintain that there are, *de facto*, humans who are or will be eternally damned.

Clearly, Balthasar's preferred saints were theologians, saints who, however humble, left behind autobiographical reflections, letters, treatises, in short, a record of their insights documented in what would generally be considered authentically authored texts. He maintained that the saints live out what they know in a dramatic existence, and consequently become the best interpreters of theodrama.[39] Gregory of Nyssa is a case in point. Balthasar states that it is the contradictions one finds in him, and which create the drama, that makes him so effective.[40] The trilogy is testimony to the fact that the saints whom Balthasar selects are the ones whom he considers to have been strategic, having provided estimable aesthetic, dramatic or insightful interpretations of Christian existence and of Christian wisdom. Steffen Lösel has accused Balthasar of a "tendency to offer an elitist view of the Christian existence," as well as that he has a "monastic (in the larger sense of the word) perspective."[41] This may be true. But then, as Balthasar himself remarked "[t]he vast majority of canonized saints have been members of religious orders or persons who shared by vow in the form of that life." He states that "[o]nly in exceptional instances (Thomas More, Anna Maria Taigi) have married persons been canonized."[42] One may wish to explain this as an issue of politics on the part of the church authorities,

37. See O'Donaghue, "A Theology of Beauty," 7.

38. Balthasar, *Dare We Hope*.

39. Balthasar, *Truth of God (TL2)*, 14. See also *Prolegomena (TD1)*, 25–50, 122, 125–31.

40. Balthasar, *Presence and Thought*, 16–18.

41. See Lösel, "Conciliar, Not Conciliatory," 41–42.

42. Balthasar, *Christian State of Life*, 377–78. On the politics of canonization, see Woodward, *Making Saints*.

or as a narrow interpretation of what holiness represents. Balthasar himself claims that the evangelical state "is normative for all states of life within the Church," and that the evangelical state and the lay state are necessary complements.[43] This means that Balthasar never restricted sainthood to those in religious life.

The case of Adrienne von Speyr is more complicated. Not only are her insights considered by Balthasar to be as splendid as some of those associated with the major saints, Balthasar even relies on Adrienne when she claims that she experiences the saints and communicates with them, even when some of what she professes in this regard seems to be far-fetched. In addition, there is enough evidence that she is herself counted by Balthasar to be among the saints. We are not quite sure as to how much of Balthasar's theology of the saints rests on the visions and transports which drew her into "the *turba magna* of the saints."[44] What we know is that Balthasar transcribed many of her visions and mystical commentaries,[45] and that he claims his general indebtedness to her, stating that she was the source of much that is original in his theological reflections.[46] Considering that his treatment of the saints is significantly original, there is no reason to doubt that her theology concerning the saints was influential and even authoritative for him.

Adrienne's case provides evidence that Balthasar does not feel constrained to use the more typical saints to initiate or enliven his arguments, or to substantiate his claims. He also uses individuals whom he deemed to be pertinent for Christian thought: philosophers, poets, novelists, and dramatists, and it sometimes seems as if these are as commendable and as reliable as the saints, and their theological contribution to be taken just as seriously.[47] He claims that the two criteria that assisted him in volumes II and III of his *Herrlichkeit* were "intrinsic excellence and historical efficacy."[48] These two criteria are central. In Balthasar, any work that exhibits the qualities of "intrinsic excellence and historical efficacy," whether from the fields of philosophy, drama, or literature is worth preserving. But a more theological reason for valuing such work is that, in Balthasar, everyone—and, therefore, even the lay figure—is already involved in the christological drama,

43. Ibid., 19–20.

44. Balthasar, *First Glance*, 33–34.

45. Wigley, *Balthasar's Trilogy*, 22.

46. Adrienne tells Balthasar that it was because of his relationship with Mary, that "the question of the other saints also became acute" for her for the first time. Balthasar, *First Glance*, 179–80.

47. Contributors include "writers and poets, mystics and philosophers, old and new, Christians of all persuasion." Kilby, *Balthasar*, 31, 151.

48. Nichols, "Balthasar's Aims," 116.

whether they like it or not. David S. Yeago's avowal is not too far-fetched in this regard: "[W]hat von Balthasar writes of the philosopher can be said equally well of the poet, the novelist, or the playwright."[49] And what does Balthasar write about the philosopher? In a nutshell, he says that the philosopher could also be a theologian. More precisely, he says,

> Insofar as the philosopher knows nothing of revelation (of God's Word) and looks out on a cosmos that is noetically and ontically saturated with moments of the supernatural, he will *also* be, at the very least—without knowing it—a crypto-theologian. The outlook of his reason will not be the outlook of a *ratio pura* but of a reason that already stands within the teleology of faith or unbelief.[50]

Balthasar often treats these philosophers, and literary figures, in the same way as he does the "saints," that is, as authoritative figures—though this happens only in selected contexts. It is also possible that he wants the term "saint" to be used more widely, so that it includes contemporary saints like Adrienne and early writers like Origen and Plotinus,[51] who were never canonized, and the lay "theologians," whom he discusses in volume III of his *Theological Aesthetics*.[52]

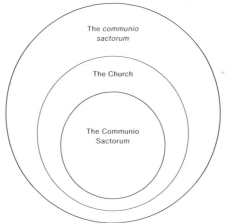

Diagram 01. The *Communio Sanctorum*

49. Yeago, "Literature in the Drama of Nature and Grace," 101.

50. Balthasar, *The Theology of Karl Barth*, 101.

51. Concerning the importance of Plotinus, see Henrici, "The Philosophy of Hans Urs von Balthasar," 156.

52. Balthasar wrote about Dante, Pascal, Hamann, Soloviev, Hopkins, Péguy, as well as—in the Klosterberg collection—about Goethe, Novalis, Nietzsche, Claudel, Bernanos, and Mauriac. See Howsare, *Balthasar: A Guide for the Perplexed*, 5.

Because of what at first sight seems like a lack of clarity on Balthasar's part, I have become ever more convinced that Balthasar's ecclesiology is best described as a series of concentric circles: the church is the middle circle, the *communio sanctorum* (all of humanity) is in the outer circle, whereas the *Communio Sanctorum* (in capital letters, referring to the saints in the narrow sense) is in the inner circle. Here, Balthasar's scheme is marked by a dialectic between the maximalist and the minimalist position: the saints in the narrow sense, and the saints in the wide sense. Furthermore, it seems to me that, in the order of redemption, Balthasar takes an inclusivist approach. He wants to emphasize the inclusiveness of salvation (as opposed to exclusivism and pluralism). In this way, according to Balthasar, Ishmael, Esau, the Pharoah, and Israel, could be saved alongside, Isaac, Jacob, Moses, and the church. According to him, there is already an element of sanctification in the order of creation, as a consequence of the incarnation. Balthasar thus takes an inclusivist approach where the order of creation is concerned: human nature is graced. The same goes for the order of redemption. We do know that, throughout the centuries, the question has often arisen as to whether it is in the action of "*justificatio,*" or that of "*deificatio*" that we are reconstituted. With Augustine, and with Barth, "*deificatio*" is contained in "*justificatio.*"[53] Balthasar fluctuates between associating sanctification with the order of creation and associating it with the order of redemption. At times, deification is a higher form of reconstitution, a higher form of "justification," so to speak, limited to the few. Balthasar also fluctuates between an inclusivist and an exclusivist position. There are times when, speaking of the order of creation and of the order of redemption, Balthasar seems more disposed to include all of humanity in the "deification" process. Both where creation and where redemption is concerned, Balthasar takes an inclusivist approach: everyone is made holy. However, Balthasar's position is not as well-defined where sanctification is treated as a trait that is over and above the order of creation or of redemption. Here, his position is more exclusivist.

In the earlier work—in the early 50s—Balthasar restricts sanctification to membership within the church. He claims that the church is the only place where the subjective sanctity of the members can be realized,[54] and therefore asserts that no subjective sanctity is possible outside the church. A few years later, in *A Theology of History,* he narrows it down even more. *Sentire cum Spirito Sancto* (what I will translate as holiness) requires a closeness to the church: a "thinking with the Church, and hence the thinking of

---

53. See Robinson, *Understanding the "Imago Dei,"* 102–3.

54. Balthasar, *Two Sisters,* 19.

the Church."[55] Writing about objective and subjective holiness, Balthasar claims that the model of authentic sanctification must be sought not simply in the church, but in the heart of the church. It

> must be sought where it really exists: namely, not in the aver-
> age views of the mass of sinners that populates the Church, but
> rather where, according to the Church's prayer, the *forma Christi*
> best comes to prevail and best becomes impressed on the form
> of the Church—in Mary, in the saints, in all those who have con-
> sciously made their own form to wane so as to yield the primacy
> in themselves to the form of the Church.[56]

For Balthasar it is possible to have philosophers and literary figures being part of the *Communio Sanctorum* (in the inner circle). I have already stated that Balthasar sometimes treats these philosophers and literary figures in the same way as he does the "saints," that is, as authoritative figures whose theological contribution is authentic. Certainly, in treating them as members of the *communio sanctorum* (the outer circle), Balthasar wants to establish that *sentire Spiritus Sancti* (the thinking *of* the Holy Spirit (my Italics) is wider that the *sentire ecclesiae* (the thinking of the church), and is the foundation for the thinking with the church. This unity he sees between the order of creation and the order of redemption will allow him to include individuals whom he believes to be an "intimation of Christ," and "a highway for the divine" within the inner circle. However, Balthasar's awareness of the distinction (though never the separation) between the order of redemption and the order of sanctification will not allow him to *automatically* include individuals like Socrates, Buddha, and Lao Tzu, although he believes them to be an "intimation of Christ," and "a highway for the divine," among the saints.[57] His category of the "saints" (in the narrow sense) does not include every man whose doctrine describes a beneficial and effective way of salvation for an individual. But neither does Balthasar rule out the possibility of having someone from "outside" the ecclesial circle become authoritative on the inside: it is possible for "the keenest discernment of spirits" to have us include more unusual specimens into the category.[58]

We would have to say, here, that Karl Rahner's concept of the "anonymous Christian" can arise even among the saints. We do know that Balthasar did not approve of the Rahnerian concept of anonymous Christianity.[59]

55. Balthasar, *A Theology of History*, 104.
56. Balthasar, *Seeing the Form (TA1)*, 256.
57. Ibid., 184.
58. Ibid., 185.
59. Balthasar, *Engagement with God*, 5.

Balthasar attacked Rahner for blurring the distinction between men and women's apprehension of the divine and divine revelation. For Balthasar, the spiritual dynamism is not inherent or natural. In spite of his criticism of Rahner (1904–1984), Balthasar was not willing to dismiss the possibility— even if he does not approve of the terminology—of having a non-Christian expressing the essence of Christianity and appealing to other Christians. Balthasar probably disapproved of Rahner simply because he found the notions of *Fides Implicita* and of *Baptismus in Voto* to be sufficient.[60] Balthasar claimed that to dismiss the possibility of having God becoming "visible in one privileged existent" is either to fall "below the level of ('natural') religion or [to dissolve] that possibility in a scholastic, rationalistic manner."[61] Therefore, he saw the possibility of having non-Christians manifesting God's attributes, but also insisted that "this borderline case of natural religion demands from Christians the keenest discernment of spirits." He stated that this discernment presupposes, besides its "No", also "a possible Yes."[62] This is in agreement with a whole series of other theologians (Augustine, some of the Fathers and Henri de Lubac himself).[63] It is also in keeping with common (popular) practice. Few would question the continuing influence, and even holiness, of individuals such as Nelson Mandela (1918–2013) and even Mohandas Gandhi (1869–1948); although these individuals do not fit into the conservative definition of the saint, and may never receive official recognition by the church hierarchy. My conviction is that it is Balthasar's sacramental theology of revelation which allows him to acknowledge the possibility that "God's true light" also falls "upon figures of the human imagination (myths) and speculation (philosophies), and that this light can lead through them and their partial truth to the God of revelation."[64] This would explain Balthasar's own respect, not only for the saint and theologian, but also for philosophers and literary figures like Georges Bernanos, Charles Péguy, and Paul Claudel. Péguy's influence is especially pervasive. De Lubac (1896–1991) had already identified the sacramental order of reality as that which draws humanity to a deeper participation in divine life.[65] In this regard, Balthasar is following his lead. Also on account of his sacramental theology of revelation, not only does the *communio sanctorum* in Balthasar's

60. Scola, *Test Everything*, 39.

61. Balthasar, *Seeing the Form (TA1)*, 185.

62. Ibid.

63. De Lubac writes, "We willingly allow . . . that divine mercy was always at work among all peoples, and that even the pagans have had their 'hidden saints' and their prophets." De Lubac, *Catholicism*, 108.

64. Balthasar, *Seeing the Form (TA1)*, 156.

65. Boersma, "Sacramental Ontology," 245.

theology include writers and poets, philosophers and mystics, ancients and moderns, and Christians of all denominations,[66] but Balthasar seems to consider the poetry, drama, and fiction of these literary figures, as authentic lay theology. In his *Aesthetics*, Balthasar states quite clearly that, "anything which reflects, mediates, and helps us to perceive . . . beauty becomes legitimate theological material."[67] Balthasar seems to be saying that the theology of Dante Alighieri (1265–1321), Blaise Pascal (1623–1662), Vladimir Soloviev (1853–1900), Gerald Manley Hopkins (1844–1889), Charles Péguy (1873–1914), Johann Wolfgang von Goethe (1749–1832), Georg von Hardenberg, better known as Novalis (1772–1801), Friedrich Nietzsche (1844–1900), Paul Claudel (1868–1955), Georges Bernanos (1888–1948) could be as pertinent as that of Thomas, if it sheds light on God's glory. For Balthasar, not only does Christian existence (in what seems like an automatic manner) lead to authentic theology, but authentic theology proceeds (in what seems like an automatic manner) from authentic Christian existence. Moreover, Balthasar is also implying that cultivation of the capacity to perceive artistic beauty and to express it is analogous to the contemplative discipline of the saints and their theology. The vocations of the Christian poets, dramatists and writers serve the *communio sanctorum* through artistic representation. As Nichols puts it, "[i]n the genealogy of theological beauty, the poets belong to the legitimate line for they are its witness."[68]

While agreeing that, within Balthasar's scheme, everything and everyone seems to have theological import because—through Christ's humanity—everything and everyone has become sacramental, the question then becomes, are we then to discard the distinction between the theological and the non-theological and between the Christian saint and the non-Christian saint? Are we to consider everyone on a par? Balthasar hints at a reply to this matter in his essay on "Martyrdom and Mission." In this essay, Balthasar asserts that the martyrs whom the "crowd" venerates could very well "be called Scholl or Stauffenberg just as well as Delp or Bonhoeffer or Kolbe." Balthasar is arguing that, from the outside, Christian martyrdom "is perceived as," looks like, human martyrdom. However, there is an important difference. The two differ in the "motive" that triggers the martyrdom.[69]

---

66. De Lubac quoted in Sicari, "Hans Urs von Balthasar: Theology and Holiness," 127.

67. Beauty is conceived of transcendentally. Therefore its definition is derived from God himself. God's self-revelation in history and in the incarnation becomes for us "the very apex and archetype of beauty in the world, whether men see it or not." Balthasar, *Seeing the Form* (*TA1*), 69. See also Kilby, *Balthasar*, 54.

68. Nichols, *The Word Has Been Abroad*, 126.

69. Balthasar, "Martyrdom and Mission," 285–86. Sophia Scholl and her brother

This is precisely what St Augustine had said: "Not the injury, but the cause makes martyrs."[70] Thus, whereas Balthasar would attribute an instructive character to all martyrdom, the two martyrdoms are different in essence. We could find the terminology of sacramentality helpful in attempting to explain the difference between the two. We use the word "sacramental" both adjectivally, referring to the authentic sacrament, and nominally, referring to an object, a gesture, or a rite which resembles the sacrament but is not instrumental in bestowing grace. Human martyrdom could be compared to the latter, and Christian martyrdom to the former. We could use the same terminology to clarify the issue of authority where the saints are concerned. In all dimensions—the existential, epistemological, and ecclesiological—the "motive" is an important element to consider where the authority of the saints is concerned, that is, it is their motive which appeals to their devotees, which makes the memory of the life and works of the saints worth conserving, which enables the authoritativeness of the doings and sayings of the saints to function authoritatively. In the meantime, it is very clear that Balthasar's theology of the saints is anthropocentric, not in the sense that it is not Christocentric, but in the sense that it respects the ascending movement of man. As a consequence, in spite of the fact that his concept of sacramentality extends to all of creation, the saints are limited to human-kind. Holiness is not attributed to other creatures. Moreover, whenever his theology deals with the saints, it is restricted to what (we would presume) would be a small group of humans, or rather, that it does not extend to the whole of humanity.

A word should be said about the terms we are using. As we know, there is a vagueness concerning the meaning of the term "saints." What postmodernity has deconstructed is really the narrow concept of the saint as pious, devoted and one-dimensional. The deconstruction of the very concept is significant because it allows for the multi-dimensionality of the individual saint. It is clear that, even within this deconstructive approach, there is a pressing demand for clarifying the terminology, particularly in view of the French Postmodern literary sense of the term "saint," which though using the term "saints," often canonizes the scoundrels.[71] In short, here, the saints often include the not so saintly, and this does not help. Nowhere does Balthasar contrast his own theology concerning the saints with

---

Hans were two nonviolent opponents to the Nazis, killed in 1943, Colonel Claus von Stauffenberg was a Roman Catholic aristocrat, involved in the July conspiracy against Hitler organized by the civilian side of the German Resistance. He was executed in 1944. Fr. Alfred Delp was a Jesuit, arrested by the Gestapo in 1944, and killed in 1945.

70. Pieper, *The Four Cardinal Virtues*, 125.

71. See, for example, Dickinson, "Jean Genet versus Saint Genet."

postmodern representations of sainthood, but the dissimilarity between the two is enough to beg description. First of all, postmodern saints are taken from a context which is different to that of the "real" saints. The Postmodern saints are generally taken from literary texts (e.g. Henry James's *The Wings of the Dove* or Jean Genet's *Our Lady of the Flowers*), from writings which deconstructed literary texts. They are more often than not fictitious figures. At other times, the saints are taken from the musical scene, from the film industry—actors or movie characters—from the world of politics, or even from everyday life.[72] Balthasar's saints are generally taken from the Scriptures and from the Catholic tradition, they are historical figures—often theologians of some importance—and they all play an important part in his theology. Having said that, Balthasar expresses deep appreciation for the work of literary figures such as Bernanos and Claudel whose work includes saintly figures, and he does utilize, an apocryphal young girl saint (Cordula) in his "The Moment of Christian Witness."[73] Balthasar does not seem to mind using non-historical figures, but he will not confuse the saint with the scoundrel, or the good with the holy. As with John Henry Newman, Balthasar would grant that the cultivated intellect can form the ethical character apart from the religious principle, but the *beau ideal* of the world is not to be confused with holiness.[74]

Moreover, within the postmodern scheme of things, because otherness and difference is critical,[75] practically anyone who offers an alternative vision for the world, could conveniently be promoted to sainthood. For Balthasar, originality—or even shockingly scandalous behaviour or thought—is far from enough. Neither is one's importance to be measured by the radical challenge he or she generates in the spectators. Balthasar prefers to emphasize and explore that which grounds the saint, rather than to focus on the outrageousness of that which can be perceived, or on the adulation of the one who perceives. This is in contrast to that which we observe in celebrity culture, and this has consequences on the issue of authoritativeness. Referring to Philip Rieff, Victor Lee Austin has said that the "amoral (thus shallow and false) charisma of what is called 'celebrity culture'" reflects "[o]

72. Matzko McCarthy, "Desirous Saints," 305.

73. Balthasar, *The Moment of Christian Witness*, 76–78. Translated from the German original: *Cordula oder der Ernstfall* (1966). See also Endean, "Von Balthasar, Rahner, and the Commissar," 34. Concerning Balthasar's use of poetry, narrative, and drama for his purposes, see Block's essay on "Balthasar's literary Criticism."

74. Newman's comparison of Basil and Julian, fellow students at the schools of Athens makes this evident. See Newman, Discourse VII(i). Quoted in Meilaender, *The Theory and Practice of Virtue*, 148.

75. Matzko, "Postmodernism, Saints and Scoundrels," 26.

ur culture's inability to understand authority."[76] A comparison of Balthasar's concept of the saint to that of postmodernity would only be useful if it could ultimately be used as a corrective to it.

THE FUNCTION OF THE SAINTS IN BALTHASAR'S THEOLOGY

Before we can insist on a theology concerning the authority of the saints, we ought to establish the place of the saints within the Balthasarian corpus, as well as ascertain that, in Balthasar's view, the life of the saints and their theology are crucial to the task of writing significant theology and of building the church. We have already pointed out that the saints are an inspiration to Balthasar's own spiritual journey as a Christian. But he is particularly fascinated by saints as a theologian. He wishes to be guided by the "vision, this way of looking at things and this way of thinking common to the saints."[77] He wishes his own theology *of* the saints (i.e. *concerning* the saints) to be based on the theology *of* the saints (i.e. *belonging to* the saints). In *The Office of Peter*, Balthasar states that the word "saint," like the term "holy" (*heilig*), is an analogical concept, and adds that one cannot speak of all "saints" in a univocal sense.[78] This may seem to denounce the very idea which I am working with here, namely, of a generic "theology of the saints" (*concerning* the saints). However, despite what Balthasar said here, it is possible to accumulate a body of knowledge which provides an overall view of what Balthasar claims about the saints in general. As a matter of fact, scholars persist in writing about Balthasar's theology of the saints or in making a reference to such a theology. It is also possible to speak about the totality of their theology, that is, of the theology of the saints (that is, which belongs to the *saints*) as a whole, rather than as individual parts unearthed at different historical moments, and, likewise, it is possible to refer to Balthasar's portrayal of the theology which belongs to the saints as a group, or more precisely, as a community. While granting that the "character of the saints' view of the world" may be "temporally conditioned," Balthasar asserts that "[o]ne must be careful not to discard as outmoded things which from century to century [the saints] have experienced again and again."[79]

Needless to say, the saints have various functions in Balthasar's work. They stimulate, revitalize, debate, serve as models of reflection and

76. Austin, *Up with Authority*, 39. Referring to Rieff, *Charisma*.

77. Balthasar, *Elucidations*, 17.

78. Balthasar, *The Office of Peter*, 343–44.

79. Balthasar, "Tradition," 125–26.

creativity, synthesize.[80] As David Moss puts it, Balthasar advocates and promotes, endorses and recommends the saints "as a resource for investigation
and employment."[81] At this stage, it would be best to explore Balthasar's use
of the saints in his own theology, to point out how and why he uses them,
what it is that they allow him to see, how they help him theologize, and the
various ways in which the saints function as authorities of both content and
form (in the sense of method).[82] What I would like to argue is, firstly, that
Balthasar manifests remarkable sensibility to the theology of each saint and
of saints overall. Secondly, that the theology of the saints—in both senses
distinguished above—is integral to Balthasar's theology, and that, thirdly, in
Balthasar's case, if one were to discard all references to the saints or to their
work, very little of substance would remain.

To begin with, the saints function as a means for animating, enliven-
ing and invigorating Balthasar's own theology. They are situated within his
theological discourse, making his writing more vivid and exciting. Already
in the early stages of his theological career, he had claimed "that few things
are so likely to *vitalize* and *rejuvenate* theology, and therefore the whole of
Christian life, as a blood transfusion from hagiography."[83] Balthasar puts
this principle into practice in his own theology, so that the saints are intimately connected with Balthasar's method of doing theology, acting as a
means of rejuvenation and revitalisation, but also as a resource. The records
of the real-life events and sayings, the letters, the autobiographical descriptions and the reflections, act as Balthasar's primary resource. Balthasar is
not concerned with biographical exactness as most hagiographers would be,
but with the account of the theological meaning of the message which the
saint him or herself embodies, or which is embodied in the text produced
by the saint. In a way, Balthasar's method is similar to that of medieval theology, particularly Aquinas's, where one had to reconcile the authorities.[84]
But, whereas, in medieval theology, it is reason that takes precedence, it
is the rational mind which brings the different authorities to bear on that
particular question, with Balthasar, the ideas are never detached from their
source, and it is the saints, not the ideas that are being reconciled to each
other.[85]

80. See, for example, Daley, "Balthasar's reading of the Church Fathers," 189.

81. Moss, "The Saints," 84.

82. Like Karl Barth, Balthasar puts a lot of emphasis on the relation between the
form and the content of theology. See Kilby, *Balthasar*, 25.

83. Balthasar, *Two Sisters*, 39.

84. See Austin, *Up with Authority*, 37.

85. Writing about St. Francis, Balthasar states that he is not an "idea," but a "reality."
Scola, *Test Everything*, 83.

More importantly, Balthasar is not concerned with establishing the importance of individual saints, as much as with emphasizing the importance of individual saints for the whole of the tradition. The theological and the ecclesial communion are always a priority. In *The Office of Peter*, Balthasar insists on the "*mitmenschlichen Konstellation*," that is, the communal nature of our identity. He maintains that "[a]ll men are interrelated in a human constellation," and "[o]ne sole human being would be a contradiction in terms, inconceivable even in the abstract, because to be human means to be with others."[86] Balthasar also emphasized that, in order "to be able to function meaningfully, the individual must find his particular place in the social body."[87] These two perspectives are reflected in his theology of the saints. Balthasar emphasizes that the "massive achievements" of the saints must not be rejected, but that one should see saints "alongside" each other, and in "relationship to the others, both past and future."[88] For example, according to von Balthasar, Pascal's theology of the poor makes up for the less socially conscious mysticism of John of the Cross.[89] An isolated saint does not really seem right to him. Saints are always part of the *communio sanctorum*.[90] Quite early on, Balthasar warns against allowing "the subjective limitations of one person's experience" to be taken "as the measure for the objective truths of revelation."[91] Saints have to be placed within the context of a constellation, an ecclesial or a religious community, in order to be understood. The method which Balthasar employs is precisely that of listening to the saints as they shed light on theological matters, and as they share their own particular contribution with the rest of the community. While appreciating the contribution of each one of the saints, Balthasar does not commit himself to any of them, and recommends that other theologians do the same,[92] that is, appreciate each one only for what it gives to the rest. Despite the

86. Balthasar, *The Office of Peter*, 142–43, as well as "The Communion of Saints," 98. The social character of Catholicism was emphasized by de Lubac, in *Catholicism*, and defended by Alfred Loisy against Adolf von Harnack. For the latter, the essence of Christianity was the relationship between individual and God, making an organized church a largely unnecessary creation. Loisy maintained that it was necessary and inevitable for the Catholic Church to form as it did, and that God had intended this. See Boersma, "Sacramental Ontology," 246; and Boersma, *Nouvelle Théologie*, 19.

87. Balthasar, *The Office of Peter*, 4–5.

88. Balthasar, *Cosmic Liturgy*, 35.

89. Nichols, *The Word Has Been abroad*, 112.

90. As already pointed out, Balthasar's lack of clarity requires that we distinguish between the *communio sanctorum*, which is wide enough to incorporate all those called to holiness, and the *Communio Sanctorum*, which consists of those who are holy.

91. Balthasar, *Two Sisters*, 65.

92. Balthasar, "Tradition," 123.

Vatican's publicity in the encyclicals *Aeterni Patris* of 1879 and the *Studiorum Duce* of 1923,[93] Balthasar upholds that one need not commit oneself to the view that Augustine is the "Father of the West," or to the view that Aquinas is "the unsurpassable climax of theology."[94] These expressions must have sounded scandalous at the time when they were stated, but, clearly, Augustine and Aquinas are only two among the many saints and scholars whom Balthasar commends. The reason is not that their contribution is no longer relevant, but that, according to him, even Augustine and Aquinas can only be comprehended within the context of a community consisting of other saints. In this regard, Balthasar shows himself to be typically post-liberal. As with Lindbeck's cultural-linguistic model of religion, the intratextual intelligibility of the individual saints rests on the wider comprehension of the community of saints,[95] rather than on the extraordinariness of the sole individual saint. This has implications not just on the amount of authority which is attributed to the particular saint but also on the prolongation over time of such authoritativeness.

Significantly, Balthasar defines tradition in psychological terms: as a "consciousness" and a "memory," but his model of tradition is, above all, personalistic, one which emphasizes the value of persons, rather than of the contents of tradition or the processes involved in its transmission. Here individual persons "succeed in keeping the 'sacred deposit' alive and intact in an incredibly diverse panoply of situations."[96] This model of tradition, complemented by a doctrine of mission, makes Balthasar especially sensitive to the theology of the saints not as a static reality in one historical moment, but as an actuality that is constantly on the move throughout the ages. For example, in Balthasar, Maximus the Confessor's task "was to carry the spirit of the Areopagite into the heart of [scholastic theology's] academic distinctions . . . it was to strike mystical and spiritual sparks out of the rough scholastic lint" which one associates with scholasticism.[97] In Balthasar's work, "[t]here are connections and dialogues to be had" between saints wherever you look.[98] According to him, Origenist spirituality made its way into the Eastern tradition, through Maximus, and it found a home

---

93. *Aeterni Patris*, given by Leo XIII and promulgated on 4 August 1879 and *Studiorum Duce*, given by Pius XI and promulgated on June 29, 1923.

94. Balthasar, "Tradition," 123.

95. Lindbeck, *The Nature of* Doctrine, 34, 114.

96. Balthasar, *Presence and Thought*, 11.

97. Balthasar, *Cosmic Liturgy*, 51.

98. Kilby, *Balthasar*, 88.

in the West, thanks to Jerome, Ambrose, and Cassian.[99] Maximus is heir to both the Cappadocians and the school of Alexandria (Evagrius, Pseudo-Dionysius and Origen.[100] Dialogue with Plato, with Greek tragedy and "with Asian metaphysical ways" becomes possible only through Meister Eckhart (c.1260–c.1328). The idea of "man never measuring up," held by Blessed John of Ruysbroeck (c.1293–1381), will continue in the Idealists and Neo-Kantians.[101] And so on and so forth. Balthasar is always on the lookout to point out these synchronic and diachronic connections. The authoritativeness of the saints comes mostly from the role which they play within the historical tradition, a role which surpasses their life-span. As Nussberger puts it, "Balthasar's project never sees the end of this movement between multiple encounters with epochs and figures in the tradition and contextual understanding of these meetings."[102] In Balthasar, each and every individual saint is a juncture, an instant, where other theologies come together. Every great thinker is at the confluence of diverse tendencies. Aquinas, he says, is "the fruit of the meeting between Augustinianism and Aristotelianism," and Kant benefitted from the conflict between Gottfried Wilhelm von Leibniz (1646–1716) and David Hume (1711–1776).[103] Balthasar describes how saints point to each other, complement each other and, so to speak, create each other. For example, according to him, Thérèse of Lisieux and Elizabeth of the Trinity should not be weighed "against each other," but they ought to be allowed to "confront" each other.[104] Balthasar claims that the motive behind this confrontation of the saints is definitive. It is not done out of "a snobbish liberal pose, but out of responsibility to the Church." Balthasar even feels duty bound to facilitate this process by taking "hold once again of material that had been lost" and by making "the central results of that dialogue [his] own."[105] In agreement with Henri de Lubac (1896–1991), Balthasar believes that, as soon as the work of "the great minds" is "surpassed" it is "already misunderstood."[106] For this reason, his in-depth exploration of the saints is almost compulsive. Moreover, in his theology, the saints themselves function as a means of approving or disapproving "corrections" that were made to tradition over the centuries. Balthasar may use one saint to defend and

---

99. Balthasar, *Cosmic Liturgy*, 27.

100. Ibid., 98.

101. Balthasar, *The Realm of Metaphysics in the Modern Age (TA5)*, 69, 72–73.

102. Nussberger, "Review Symposium," 95.

103. Balthasar, *Presence and Thought*, 17.

104. Balthasar, *Two Sisters*, 11.

105. Balthasar, *Cosmic Liturgy*, 35.

106. Balthasar, *The Theology of Henri de Lubac*, 92.

clarify another saint's theology, to express approval when some forgotten element within tradition has been restored, or disapproval when something significant has been ignored, or to endorse saints or traditions whose credibility had been put into question. Does Balthasar have a right to do this? The answer is "yes," if we see Balthasar as part and parcel of this tradition, which is how he sees himself. It seems to me that Balthasar does not do what he does out of conceit, but out of a conviction (was this pretentiousness?) that his clarification of their position, and his defense or criticism of them could validate the saints once again, or rectify things, and thus be of service to theology and ecclesiology as a whole. Likewise, because of the personalistic model of tradition, it is possible to have saints promoting other saints who represent specific theological traditions. Balthasar points out that Maximus designates Gregory of Nyssa as "the Universal Doctor," that Gregory was confirmed "Father of the Fathers" by Nicaea II, and that Scotus Erigena quoted Gregory more than he quoted Augustine.[107] In all of this, I believe that Balthasar transcends the level of doctrinal polemics. He uses Maximus to project a view of the Christian truth not as an "anti-heresy," but as "a synthetic whole."[108] This synthetic method is something which he admires in the saints, and it is clear that this is one of the characteristics which he attributes to all the saints whom he admires. It is a method which he also attempts in his own theology.

To recapitulate: It should by now be clear that how and why Balthasar uses the theology of the saints—in both senses distinguished above—is integral to Balthasar's theology, and that the Balthasarian corpus would be reduced to a skeleton, if all references to the saints or to their work were removed. It is also clear that Balthasar theologizes through the saints. Balthasar's use of the saints to theologize could be interpreted as a dishonest endeavour. This is because his choice of saints is selective. He uses those saints who can act as advocates, as apologists for his own theology. He uses them as the authority which not only assists his theological enterprise but authorizes his venture. But, in fact, Balthasar often gives valid reasons for eliminating the saints whose position he rejects. In using the saints in the way he does, he applies the synthetic method which he admires so much in the saints themselves.

By insisting on Balthasar's sensibility to the saints, I am not stating that Balthasar is alone in *emphasizing* the saints in his theological enterprise. Nicholas M.Healy confirms that Scripture and tradition provide us with these "debate partners" with whom "we can engage" and from whom we can

---

107. Balthasar, *Presence and Thought*, 15.

108. Balthasar, *Cosmic Liturgy*, 30. See also Daley, "Translator's Foreword," 17–18.

learn.[109] But Balthasar is unique, at least among contemporary theologians, in theologizing *through* the saints. What could be seen as a flaw is in fact an asset. Balthasar's project was to depict and to promote a model of theology as a "collaborative enterprise," to use Rowan Williams' expression,[110] and an image of the church as a "*colloquium*" or "conversational community," to use Francis Sullivan's.[111] Although the latter terms are not Balthasar's, Balthasar held that "our need for one another as debate partners . . . our need for genuine others who can challenge us and thereby help us to receive and embody truth more adequately" unifies us "in our diverse activities."[112] Not only is it possible, but also necessary for us to have "a genuine intellectual dialogue . . . with an earlier author."[113] Here, Balthasar adopts the theme from dialogical philosophy, where *communio* involves letting the other be other. Furthermore, whereas Modernism is characterized by a break with the past, and therefore, by a break with authority, Balthasar seeks to have the saints function as links to previous "concrete and unique situation[s]" in the past, in order to create connections with the past. In Balthasar's theology, the saints inform the present.[114] Thus, writing about his study of the Greek Fathers: Gregory, Origen, and Maximus, Balthasar states that

> [w]e should like rather to penetrate right to those vital well-springs of their spirit, right to that fundamental and hidden intuition that directs every expression of their thought and that reveals to us one of the great possibilities of attitude and approach that theology has adopted in a concrete and unique situation. [115]

Balthasar does not just—effortlessly—transfer chunks of past history into the present and pretend that that was sufficient. According to him, the rejuvenation of the thought of the Fathers requires "a total critique."[116] The implication is that even if the thought may not provide much "support to the task of the theologian today," yet it is important that the church keeps

---

109. Healy, *Church, World and the Christian Life*, 105.

110. Rowan Williams, "Theological Integrity," 9.

111. See Sullivan's examination of the twelve theses on "The Ecclesiastical Magisterium and Theology" in *Magisterium*, 174–218. Cited by Stagaman, *Authority within the Church*, xii.

112. Healy, *Church, World and the Christian Life*, 153. See also 125.

113. Balthasar, *Cosmic Liturgy*, 35

114. Balthasar, *Presence and Thought*, 13.

115. Ibid.

116. Ibid.

the memory alive,[117] even if it does so by critiquing it, because only then will the whole of the theological substance be grasped. Balthasar's theological approach is thus evidently pro-dramatic, enabling him to highlight the interactions—even the disagreements—between the saints within tradition over time. The dramatic method enables him to embrace theological differences which he would otherwise not have been able to embrace. In fact, there is a proliferation of drama on account of the saints. In Balthasar, truth is "symphonic," and, to the extent that our views "contain truth partially," we are contributing "to the living organism of unity," when we contribute our own share.[118] On account of his dramatic concept of truth, Balthasar can explain "contradictions" away, as possibly being "the simple and necessary expression" of a dramatic vision, or as "[t]he outlines of a system of thought that is in progress."[119] Through this "dramatic" perspective, not only is Balthasar able to explain away the contradictions pertaining to individual saints, but also those pertaining to tradition. Balthasar harbours the hope that "these contradistinctions" may one day "be harmonized and diminished in a 'synthetic' outlook that embraces all the winding, sinuous turns of thought that have been traversed."[120] For the time being, however, "the form of theology must. . .remain unconcluded, because only the *Kyrios* has the full vision of the final form of revelation."[121]

It is only on account of Balthasar's model of theology as a collaborative enterprise, involving discernment, of his model of the church as a colloquium or conversational community, and of his model of the structure of the truth as dramatic, that Balthasar is able to pose "modern questions" which are "set by the peculiar situation of French and German Catholic theology in the mid-twentieth century" to saints long-departed.[122] As Howsare has stated, the concerns which Balthasar has are typically modern: "individuality, difference, personhood, historicity, event, freedom."[123] There are clear examples where the saints function as an instrument in Balthasar's hands in order to elucidate these modern philosophical and theological issues. The saints act as a medium which provides new insights on familiar material, providing a different standpoint on the subject under discussion.

---

117. Balthasar, *Presence and Thought*, 11.

118. Balthasar considers "antithesis," as Möhler had taught it, to be a "fruitful" method. See Balthasar, *The Office of Peter*, 247.

119. Balthasar, *Presence and Thought*, 18.

120. Ibid.

121. Balthasar, *Convergences*, 73.

122. Daley, "Translator's Foreword," 11–21.

123. Howsare, *Balthasar: A Guide for the Perplexed*, 68.

Two examples of this should suffice. Let us first take the example of freedom: Balthasar was very much aware that the "one great anxiety" of the Modernists was "to find a way of conciliation between the authority of the Church and the liberty of believers."[124] Balthasar therefore uses the saints to try and reconcile the two. His proposal in this regard will be a much more active form of Eckhart's and of Heidegger's "*Gelassenheit.*"[125] A second example would be that of "modern evolutionism," which Balthasar describes in *Engagement with God*. Balthasar uses the saints to argue that a world based on the principles of the "aggressiveness of the strong and the destruction of the weak," on "exploitation" and "suppression" is "quite unacceptable for us Christians."[126] In contrast, Balthasar uses the saints to emphasize the paradox that the greatest power is to be found in powerlessness.

To recapitulate: we have so far argued that, in Balthasar's theology, the saints stimulate, revitalize theology. They synthesize, clarify misunderstandings, elucidate specific theological issues, and so on. We have not as yet answered the question concerning the authority of the saints but we have been exploring Balthasar's use of the saints as an authoritative source of knowledge and language. Patrick Sherry once said that the task of theology is not simply to use the saints to teach people the meaning of "theory laden theological terms." Its task is rather to be able to create a theological language using the saints' lives.[127] Balthasar's sensitivity to the theology of the saints has made available to him a whole miscellanea of theological terms. The saints function as an authority for him both where theological content and where theological language is concerned.

Sometimes, perhaps too often, the saints function as validation for Balthasar's own theological positions. In this sense, they are the authority to which he refers when his arguments are not yet sufficiently convincing. Howsare has said that Balthasar's method of doing theology actually requires that he "point out a whole list of people to defend his cause."[128] Saints are used to substantiate and authenticate his claims. Balthasar uses the saints to corroborate, to demonstrate, and to verify his own assertions. He seeks support in them. He uses them to confirm beliefs that either have already been established through his use of other sources, or else simply to sanction his own beliefs. In this case, the saints do not really add much to what has already been said. Some work has been done on the hagiographer and his

124. *Pascendi Dominici Gregis*, Encyclical promulgated by Pope Pius X, 23.

125. Löser, "The Ignatian Exercises," 108.

126. Balthasar, *Engagement with God*, 7.

127. See Sherry, "Philosophy and the Saints," 33–34.

128. Howsare, *Balthasar: A Guide for the Perplexed*, 146.

or her use of the saints. The use of hagiographic material as a vehicle for affirming the writer's authority has been explored and legitimated.[129] In this sense, Balthasar's use of the saints to support his work is legitimate. Karen Kilby claims that Balthasar inverts the process. He arrives at his case in the process of presenting the various contributions of his figures, rather than refers to these figures to substantiate a case that he would like to defend.[130] My problem with this objection is that it does not emphasize enough the value of having chosen the contributors, which choice would have been made before the actual presentation, so that it is in itself significant and integral to the case that is being put forward.

In Balthasar, the saints also function as an excuse for experimenting with new methods. The method which Balthasar proposes for the study of the saints is what he calls "a sort of supernatural phenomenology" of the mission of the saints, or what he calls, "a hagiography 'from above.'"[131] The term "phenomenology" usually refers to any system of thought that has to do with appearance. In Husserl's conception, phenomenology is primarily concerned with the systematic reflection on the structures of consciousness and the phenomena that appear in acts of consciousness, and with the study of such structures and phenomena. Balthasar suggests "a sort of supernatural phenomenology" of the mission of the saints. Balthasar is not really interested in arguing that all reality is directly or reflectively present to consciousness, or that the only knowledge we can have is that of phenomena. He is not interested in denying the thing in itself. Neither is he interested in rejecting the possibility of knowledge of the substance of a thing in the metaphysical sense. Balthasar is suggesting phenomenology as a method. He is suggesting "a purely descriptive approach to that which appears to us, without bringing in theory or explanations," and one which "focuses on the manner in which the subject structures, or 'constitutes' the world differently, on the basis of different experiences and cultural backgrounds, but also on the basis of adaptation to other subjects through interaction and communication."[132] It is a descriptive science of consciousness, a science that describes the structure of intentional experience, and hence of experience itself. The phenomenological method claims to be relatively unadulterated, since it prefers pure description to explanation and interpretation. It is a descriptive theory of the essence of pure experiences and, therefore, as

129. See, for example, Watson, "The Authority of Saints and their Makers."
130. Kilby, Balthasar, 35.
131. Balthasar, Two Sisters, 26.
132. Føllesdall, "Phenomenology," 483–84.

a method, it is certainly suited for a theology about the saints.[133] We could say that Edmund Husserl (1859–1938) gives Balthasar a method to describe phenomena as observed *by* the saints, and as observed *in* the saints through the eyes of God, as well as the license to do it. The method is especially helpful because, here, the form, the shape of consciousness is not a private item. It is public, and it can be shared. Husserl's intentional realism would have suited Balthasar: we are not trapped in our own mind. Balthasar would have wanted to bracket out unexamined assumptions so that the phenomena could speak for themselves. What is interesting is that Balthasar is not concerned with the paranormal or the blatant extrasensory phenomena sought out by the inquisitive. His objective is strictly to try and identify, understand, and describe, the structures of consciousness of the saint, and the distinctive, but typical phenomena, that appear in the acts of consciousness of a saint, who abandons him or herself to God.

I do not think anyone can coherently argue that Balthasar provides his readers with a full-blown phenomenology of the consciousness of the saints, but he does use the method of phenomenology to shed some light on the consciousness of the saints. Nichols has said that Balthasar's phenomenology of the saints is particular in that, unlike late nineteenth and early mid-twentieth century phenomenology, his phenomenology is at the service of Christian ontology. Balthasar's is not the positivistic phenomenalism of Hegel, nor the noumenalism of Kant.[134] The phenomenological approach seems to allow Balthasar to identify and describe the "structure of anticipations" which the saints experience, the *noema* (the object or content of the thought, judgment, or perception)—to use Husserl's terminology—without, in the process, ignoring the object which they experience, that is, God. This is what Balthasar does in *Wahrheit der Welt* (*TL1*), but instances of this are also evident in his hagiography. There is also, in Balthasar, an attempt at an interpretive phenomenology, and not just a descriptive one. He is as concerned with meanings, as he is with phenomena.

Significantly, Balthasar also uses the saints to handle ecumenical issues, insisting, in the process, that the saints are authoritative in this regard, and that both the ecumenical movement and academic theology have a lot to learn from the saints. He claims that the differences between denominations "can only be handled by living organisms which have a capacity to

133. Among other things, phenomenology can describe how experience as consciousness can give or contact an object and how experiences can be mutually legitimated or corrected by means of each other, and not merely replace each other or conform. Husserl, "Philosophy as Rigorous Science," in *Phenomenology and the Crisis of Philosophy*.

134. Nichols, *Say it is Pentecost*, 12.

meet and understand each other, only because they all can be animated by just *one* life: that of God in Christ."[135] Clearly, abstract dogmatics are not sufficient, for in their abstraction they are not capable of resolving the differences. It is not surprising that Balthasar sees a saint (Thérèse) as the solution to the dogmatic issues of the Reformation,[136] just as he sees Maximus's Christocentric Cosmology as the evangelical answer to Hegel.[137] Balthasar used her to teach "Catholic integration,"[138] and claimed that she could help resolve various other issues:

> the rejection of Old Testament justification by works; the demolition of one's own ideal of perfection to leave room for God's perfection in man; the transcendent note in the act of faith . . . the existential fulfillment of the act of faith; and, finally, disregard for one's own failings . . . [139]

This exploration of the multiple ways in which the saints function in Balthasar's theology is certainly not comprehensive, but it should be enough to demonstrate that, in his own theology, Balthasar takes the saints and their theology very seriously. The saints are his models, his guides, his resources, even his sources. In his work, the authority of the saints is evoked and articulated in a variety ways. Balthasar articulates their authoritativeness by praising their achievements, and by endlessly referring to them in his writings. In the way in which Balthasar uses the saints, and in his references to them, Balthasar attributes to them an authority that, though difficult to describe, is undeniable. The rest of this chapter will help us to determine the importance which Balthasar attributes to the saints within theology in general, and within the church, as well as to clarify what it is that we understand by authority where the saints are concerned.

135. Balthasar, *Convergences*, 45.

136. Balthasar writes that "[o]ne would have to be blind not to see that Thérèse's doctrine of the little way answers point by point the program outlined by the Reformers and that she presents the Church's bold, irrefutable answer to Protestant spirituality." *Two Sisters*, 283.

137. Nichols, *The Word Has Been Abroad*, 115.

138. Schönborn, "Hans Urs von Balthasar's Contribution to Ecumenism," 261.

139. Balthasar, *Two Sisters*, 283–84.

BALTHASAR ON THE FUNCTION OF THE SAINTS IN THEOLOGY

We have just seen that the "authority of the saints" as we are using the phrase refers primarily to the accreditation which Balthasar gives them, that is, to the authority which he attributes to them, simply by using their work recurrently, by mentioning their name, by praising their theological contribution, and by attributing to them a critical function in his theology. Writing about expertise as argument, Zoltan P. Majdik and William M. Keith have claimed that "broadening expertise beyond the bounds of accreditation" is risky, because it "renders expertise completely relativistic, and reduces its democratic potential to individual subjective opinion."[140] In this book, the phrase "authority of the saints" refers to the explicit recommendation of the saints as competent and worth considering, even when specific arguments put forward by the saints may be wrong. The phrase refers to an endorsement by individuals, by theology, or by the church, of the saints' life and teachings. The implication is that any theology that is built on that of the saints may also be regarded as authoritative. I would agree with Kilby that "there is no real suggestion . . . that Balthasar would want to point to his own saintliness, to his own sanctity, as in any way a guarantee for his theology."[141] But Balthasar would certainly want to point to his dependence on the theology of the saints as a guarantee for his theology. Balthasar regarded the life of the saints and their theology as crucial to the task of writing significant theology. In this respect, Balthasar considered his own method of doing theology as exemplary. He maintained, not only that theology should contemplate the saints and that authentic theology should use the saints to stimulate it, but, by his example, he also maintained that the primary role of theology is to *serve* the saints by elucidating their accounts of their own encounter with God. Therefore, with Balthasar we have theology *through* the saints and theology *for* the saints (that is, in the service of the saints). Balthasar insisted that the academic distinctions of scholastic theology required "mystical and spiritual sparks"[142] and the saints provided that. The solution to the predicament in which theology had found itself was to be found in the saints, who could counteract the arid style of a theology that was disconnected from life, and who could restore to theology a dynamism that Balthasar believed was essential. According to Balthasar, the saints function

---

140. Majdik and Keith "Expertise as Argument," 375–76.

141. Kilby, *Balthasar*, 156.

142. Balthasar, *Cosmic Liturgy*, 51.

as the way for integrating theology with spirituality,[143] which was why he thought of them as the proper solution to the predicament in which theology often found itself. Balthasar complains that "theologians have tended to treat [the] opinions [of the saints] as a sort of by-product, classifying them as *spiritualité* or, at best, as *théologie spirituelle*."[144] The problem which disturbed Balthasar ultimately concerned the *form* which theology should acquire in order that "spirituality . . . could join with it," as he puts it.[145] Balthasar maintains that the only theologies which "became vitally effective in history" were the ones "which bore their spirituality not as an addition but within themselves, which embodied it in their innermost being."[146] It is only in the saints that this integration has taken place. Spirituality is thus understood as the "subjective side" of dogma.[147] The saints are portrayed as models for genuine theologians, and of authentic theology, thanks to their ability to overcome the "divide" between spiritual theology and dogmatic theology,[148] and between "theoretical and affective theology."[149]

THE ECCLESIAL FUNCTION OF THE SAINTS

For Balthasar, the function of the saints is not restricted to the production of theology and to their contribution to the method of doing theology. The theological importance of the saints extends to the wider ecclesiological domain. Their import must be seen within the context of the whole body of the church. For one thing, as Gerard Mannion has said, the saints "have also helped build up the body of teaching and contributed to the authoritativeness of the Roman Catholic Church's mission and witness in the world."[150] Therefore, Balthasar sees the saints as much more than a resource, or even a

143. In Balthasar, spirituality is not equivalent to "ascetic(-mystical) theology." According to him, the latter "narrows down the personal portrayal in life of the fundamental religious decisions to particular 'practices' and 'experiences.'" Balthasar defines spirituality as "the practical or existential fundamental attitude of a person, the consequence and expression of his religious . . . understanding of existence." See "The Gospel as Norm," 281.

144. Balthasar, *Two Sisters,* 26.

145. Balthasar, *Convergences,* 23–4.

146. Ibid., 30, 43–44.

147. Sachs, Randy, "The Pneumatology and Spirituality of Hans Urs von Balthasar," 40.

148. Howsare, *Balthasar: A Guide for the Perplexed,* 4, 19; Sicari, "Hans Urs Balthasar: Theology and Holiness"; and Balthasar, "Theology and Sanctity."

149. Balthasar, *Convergences,* 34.

150. Mannion et al., *Readings in Church Authority,* 5.

source, for theology. In brief, Balthasar does four things: firstly, he interprets the saints as principal contributors to the authority of the church, so that the Magisterium can only claim authority because of the contribution of the saints. Secondly, he sees the Magisterium (as well as theology) as the mouthpiece of the saints, so that the Magisterium and theology are non-authoritative unless they serve the saints and are in synch with the tradition of the saints. Thirdly, Balthasar correlates the authority of the church with the authority of holiness, so that holiness becomes the more pertinent authoritative element within the church. Finally, Balthasar allies the authority of holiness with the authority of saints, so that the authority claimed by individuals becomes meaningless unless accompanied by holiness, and any authority attributed to the non-holy becomes contradictory.

In Balthasar's theology, the saints have a more pronounced claim to credibility, they are more deserving of respect, they are more qualified at providing instruction to the church, they merit more consideration than the ordinary Christian. Balthasar sees the saints as more capable of challenging the Christian community and more deserving of being heard, remembered, quoted, but also confronted. Balthasar evidently sees their position within the Christian community as a privileged one, although this privileged position is not one assumed by them. Authority may be assigned and attributed to the saints by others, through a conscious decision on their part, in which case it is a kind of *bestowal* of authority, but authority may also be aroused in others without any conscious encouragement either from the saints themselves or from other recognized authorities. In this case, it is more a *recognition* of an authority that has been manifested, rather than a bestowal of it.

Whichever way, any authority that they may have been assigned, or that may become manifest in them, and consequently recognized, is always to be seen within an ecclesial context. It is others within the *communio* who recognize this authority and who ascribe it to them. All the saints are *animae ecclesiasticae*, and it is in the spirit of the church that they are judged. For instance, Maximus is described as "one of the founders of the Middle Ages, even in the Latin West." He is "the philosophical and theological thinker who stands between East and West."[151] He is a "genius," a "biblical theologian," a "philosopher," a "mystic," a "theologian," a "monk," a "man of the Church,"[152] a "martyr of the intellectual life,"[153] "the last great theologian and martyr of the Christological controversies."[154] Similar praise can be located

---

151. Balthasar, *Cosmic Liturgy*, 25.

152. Ibid., 57.

153. Ibid., 37.

154. Ibid., 41. Balthasar uses Erich Caspar's *History of the Popes*.

for other saints whom Balthasar examines. From this ecclesial perspective, Gregory of Nyssa is "the most profound Greek philosopher of the Christian era, a mystic and incomparable poet."[155] Pseudo-Dionysius is "the man who may well be the most profound thinker of the sixth century."[156] Origen is a "man of the Church," a martyr, a great lover of the Scriptures, a "daring theologian" who took that which was good and positive in Hellenism and "put it at the service of Christ's truth."[157] Thomas is the *kairos*, mediating between the ancient and the modern world.[158] John's spiritual doctrine is valid for everyone, although only analogically, not literally.[159] Unless we consider these words to be mere exaggerations or mere rhetoric, we have to take these comments seriously. Balthasar is stating very clearly that the saints are indispensable for the church, that the recognition of their contribution is mandatory, and that their function is authoritative both synchronically and diachronically.

In Balthasar, the saints also function as unifying figures within the community. Yves Simon (1903–61) has argued that a community requires means to unify and to generate its common action.[160] Balthasar once wrote that "we should not underestimate the community-building power" of "the memory of a great dead person."[161] In this respect, the saints resemble Max Scheler (1874–1928)'s "value persons." Memories of them are mandatory, if the community is to survive. We have to remember that community building was an important part of Balthasar's project, and his judgment on all kinds of individuals is based on whether he interprets their experiences as ones which "bound them . . . the more intimately" to the community of faith, rather than which separated them from this community.[162] In actual fact, Balthasar's preoccupation with unity could, paradoxically, become counter-productive to any theology about the authority of the saints. But for the moment, it is sufficient to note the emphasis which Balthasar places on the unifying effect of a commemoration of the saints.

Balthasar may not have stated that the saints have the power or right to give orders, to make decisions, and to enforce obedience, but he does

155. Balthasar, *Presence and Thought*, 15.

156. Balthasar, *Cosmic Liturgy*, 27.

157. Ibid., 33.

158. Balthasar, *Studies in Theological Style: Lay Styles (TA3)*, 356. Concerning the importance of Aquinas, see Howsare, *Balthasar: A Guide for the Perplexed*, 39 and 160, and Henrici, "The Philosophy of Hans Urs von Balthasar," 162–63.

159. Nichols, *The Word Has Been Abroad*, 108.

160. Quoted in Austin, *Up with Authority*, 24.

161. Balthasar, *Seeing the Form (TA1)*, 573.

162. Balthasar, *Seeing the Form (TA1)*, 260–61.

furnish them with an authority that makes demands. In this sense, it is analogical to that of the Magisterium where theological authority is concerned. Balthasar is clearly presenting the saints as a corrective, particularly in challenging situations where official authority becomes distorted. He presents them as a coping mechanism in situations where the sinfulness of the empowered authority requires some kind of regulation, thus acting as the authentic Magisterium.

THE AUTHORITY OF THE SAINTS

Some further clarifications are called for. For instance, what authority do the saints manifest? And what kind of authority does Balthasar attribute to the saints? Furthermore, what response do the saints demand? Or rather, what does Balthasar believe our response to the saints should be? If the right of the church to teach requires the duty of obeisance on the part of the faithful, applying this to the saints becomes problematic. The answer to these questions will be followed by an inquiry into whether the saints can demand any recognition of their authority (or rather, whether Balthasar thinks we can remain indifferent to the saints). We shall take these one at a time, beginning with the first of them: that is, the nature of the authority which the saints manifest.

The "authority" which the saints manifest and which Balthasar attributes to the saints consists primarily in the competency and the credibility of their being, their action and their words. There is something with the saints which makes them worthy of attention, deserving of serious consideration. They inspire, convince, persuade (though not necessarily by means of reasonable arguments). There is something in them, in their actions and in their writings, which makes their statements moving and often irrefutable. Even when they are wrong, they deserve to be considered. The aptitude of such individuals is noteworthy, their contribution always to be taken seriously, and any so-called minor blunders do not affect either their authority, nor the authoritativeness of their judgments.

Balthasar attempts to provide a description of this authority in several of his works. In his *Aesthetics*, Balthasar writes of "the shaping power and the genius of the human spirit" and "the overpowering historical influence" which the human spirit may bequeath.[163] Although he is hereby describing the human spirit in a broad way, these words could easily be applied to the saints. In *The Christian State of Life*, moreover, Balthasar talks about the "imprint," the "mark," which the founder saints may place upon a candidate

---

163. Balthasar, *Seeing the Form (TA1)*, 78.

for the religious life.[164] In his interview with Angelo Scola, Balthasar speaks of "the ecclesial radiance of a person."[165] The implication is that the *anima ecclesiastica*, and particularly the saints, have an appeal, an attraction about them that draws others to their way of life. It is like standing in front of an artistic object and like acting within a drama. You are drawn towards it and into it. Clearly, the authority of the saints which Balthasar is suggesting is more than just moral and cognitive. More precisely, it goes beyond the respect which others express for their good character or knowledge. It is an authority that is derived from the side of the saints themselves, not from the reactions of their devotees to them. In *Theo-Logic*, we are told that the saints can "restore anyone who has fallen."[166] Such a statement on Balthasar's part makes it clear that the authority rests as much with the saints as with their adherents. Is this to be interpreted as an attribution to the saints of the restoration that may only takes place through Christ? It could be interpreted in that way. However, this is actually biblical (1 Cor 6:2). Some translations would speak of "the Lord's people," rather than the saints. Balthasar's own exegesis would go a step further. He understands the *communio sanctorum* to be itself Christ, and consequently competent to share in the restitution which is possible through him.

Let us now attend to the second issue: What authoritativeness do the saints demand? Or rather, what does Balthasar believe our response to the saints should be? How obliged are we to respond to the demands which the saints make? Although to some extent, it is peculiar to write about the saints presuming a response from others, what Balthasar wrote about the saints was partly meant as an appeal to the theologian, to the reader, to the Christian, and to the church, to turn to the saints and to attend to them. Therefore, this issue of the response is one thing we should discuss, even if hypothetically, since there is no authority unless there are those to whom this authority is being addressed and on whom demands are being made to respond or to comply to such demands. Edith Wyschogrod has said that

> [t]he saints' addressees are acutely sensitive to the problem of interpreting hagiography. They believe that understanding hagiography consists not in recounting its meaning, but in being swept by its imperative force. The comprehension of a saint's life understood from within the sphere of hagiography is a *practice*

---

164. Balthasar, *The Christian State of Life*, 483.
165. Scola, *Test Everything*, 82.
166. Balthasar, *The Spirit of Truth (TL3)*, 379.

through which the addressee is gathered into the narrative so as
to extend and elaborate it with her/his own life . . . [167]

With Balthasar, we could then say that the response which we can envisage where the saints are concerned is one of recognition: the saints are to
be recognized as the true eye-witnesses of revelation, to be acknowledged
as types for the church,[168] as a challenge to the way of life of the Christian,
to the way theology is done, to the way the Magisterium makes its decisions or to the way in which it pronounces its statements. The authority
which is envisaged where the saints are concerned—and which ought to
be recognized—is that their role in fraternal correction be accepted, that
their place as role-models for how to be church be recognized. The authority
which is anticipated where the saints are concerned—and which ought to
be conceded—is their propensity to act as sacraments of God, their aptitude
to operate as models for a proper *martyria*, their proficiency for leading us
in *leiturgia*, their adeptness for inspiring our *diakonia*. The authority which
most of them (not Paul!) shunned during their lifetime, is something which
we might suppose that they would expect today—not for themselves, but
for God's sake—namely, that of being listened to and remembered, because
their being, their actions and their words, have made the church, and,
because—since their influence is diachronic and has survived the test of
time—continues to make the church. We also need to establish whether the
recognition of this authority of the saints is indispensable, and if so, whether
it is only indispensable for the lay Christian, or whether it also applies to the
members of the Magisterium, or even to every human being. Are we all to
recognize the authority of the saints, and abide by what they advocate? Or is
their calling merely reserved for one or a few categories within the church?

Finally, we have to inquire whether the saints themselves envisage this
recognition by others, whether they expect it, whether they can request a
recognition of their authority, or rather, whether Balthasar thinks one may
remain indifferent to the saints without losing much. The answers to these
questions will, hopefully, become clearer in the course of our discussion.
But it would be best to say that the saints see themselves as communicators,
not enforcers, of principles and truths. However, this is not to say that their
contribution is not authoritative. Something in the nature and the quality
of their contribution stimulates trust, arouses respect, and claims assent

167. Wyschogrod, xxiii.

168. Yves Simon claims that the importance of the witness lies in matters of truth,
and that the role of the witness is not to give orders or to command obedience, it is to
point. See Austin, *Up with Authority*, 46. With Balthasar, the saint is a pointer, but he or
she is also more than that. The saint also carries, and judges, which is why, in Balthasar,
saints assume, or are furnished with, a leadership role.

almost spontaneously. As Austin has put it, "[a]uthority never functions without drawing forth a response."[169] The saints may not command, but they do provoke, and they do counsel, and a provocation and a counsel can be just as exacting, especially when it is given in a believable manner, as with the authentic saints.

There is another crucial issue. We should determine whether the nature of the authority which Balthasar attributes to the saints is analogous to that which is usually attributed to the Magisterium, and what it is that makes this authority analogous to it. Needless to say, the Magisterium is a political agent, but it is first of all an authority of those who teach theology. The saints are also, for Balthasar, *loci theologici*, although their statements and behaviors have sometimes had political repercussions. In this sense, the two are certainly similar. The authority which is attributed to the saints is not exactly the power of jurisdiction, but it is an authority notwithstanding. The wisdom and holiness of the saints are intrinsically potent, and their force is comparable to the allure, the magnetism and the appeal of a work of art, and it is because of this that the saints become authoritative, commanding and influential. On the part of the observer, this authority is perceived, recognized, and ascribed to the saints, in such a manner that the observer may abide by what they propose without any enforcement being necessary. At the same time, in Balthasar, the authority of the Magisterium is not as unlimited as it may seem. The fundamental truth is that "the ecclesial *magisterium* can represent Christ's truth only from the standpoint of doctrine and not of life."[170] In contrast, the authority of the saints is best described as an authority of both doctrine and life, one that goes even beyond the authority which we associate with the Magisterium. The authority of the saints is one of influence. It is an impression that others will commit to memory, an inspiration that will challenge others to come out of their apathy and act, probably in a deeper way than when faced by the decrees of the Roman Curia. More concisely, what makes the saints' authority analogical to that of the Magisterium is, firstly, that both the authority of the Magisterium and that of the saints point to the good. The final cause of both is to point to the good, so to speak. Both of them are concerned with faith and morals.

Secondly, and this has become more so in postmodernity, both are ultimately based on credibility. Thomas O'Loughlin has written about the challenges which the Catholic Church faces as a public actor.[171] I would say

169. Austin, *Up with Authority*, 54.

170. Balthasar, *Seeing the Form (TA1)*, 212–13.

171. O'Loughlin distinguishes between the challenges to the credibility of faith, of theism, and of the church. He interprets the challenges to the credibility of the church as an invitation to grow in awareness of its true identity. See "The Credibility of the

that, nowadays, the pronouncements of the Magisterium only have force in so much as they are credible. Hannah Arendt once said that authority is not persuasion (in the sense of a reasonable argument) and it is not coercion.[172] In short, it is not invasiveness, nor domination. It is more a kind of transformation that takes place as a consequence of an encounter. Thirdly, what makes the saints' authority analogical to that of the Magisterium is a theological reality.[173] For Balthasar, the Cross is integral to both authorities. According to him, the Cross transforms the saints into a political authority and transforms the members of the Magisterium into saints.

Even once the concept of an authority on the part of the saints is accepted, however, there are still questions which need to be asked: The first concerns the grounding of the authority of the saints: what is it that really makes these saints an authority? What are the sources for this authority of theirs, and which are the different settings in which the saints function authoritatively? Remember that my question is not: what are the indicators of holiness, but what are the grounds for the authoritativeness of the saints? This will be discussed in our third, fourth, and fifth chapters. The second question is just as important: Considering Balthasar's preoccupation with church unity, does Balthasar dare to write openly about the Magisterium of the saints, or about the *Successio Sanctorum*?[174] Or will he simply reiterate what tradition has done, that is, emphasize the authority of the saints, only to then refuse to distinguish the saints from the rest of the Christians?

Balthasar's creative contribution to the theology of the saints is original in that he attributes to the saints an authoritativeness that goes beyond mere mention, citation or recommendation. Would Balthasar consider an official statement, attributing authority to the saints, problematic? Possibly. And yet, there is evidence that Balthasar, along with tradition, considers the saints as an authority for him, for theology, for the church, and for humanity in general. The solution is therefore not to avoid mentioning it, but rather to try and deal with it. In order to define the authoritativeness that is associated with the saints, I think it would help to analyze Balthasar's approach to authority, and to the concept of power.

Catholic Church as Public Actor," 132.

172. Arendt, "What is Authority?," 93.

173. Balthasar is the master of analogies, and to attribute an analogy to him, even one he never fabricated, should not be so appalling.

174. Balthasar came very close to inaugurating a *successio sanctorum* through his emphasis on the Marian and the Johannine principle.

AUTHORITY AND POWER

Power is commonly understood as the ability of a person or a group to influence the beliefs and actions of other people and events. In 1959 and in subsequent years, social psychologists John R. P. French and Bertram H. Raven identified distinct forms and bases of power or influence, calling them Informational, Reward, Coercion, Legitimate, Expertise, and Referent.[175] The "power" of the saints would seem to be most similar to the Informational power, where the saint acts as the influencing agent, to the Referent power, that is, the power of the personality which attracts followers, and to the power of expertise, that is the power of knowledge and competence. Power resides in the person who uses it, and it can flow in any direction. On the other hand, there is authority. Authority flows downwards. It resides in the position or the post and is therefore more strictly official and legitimate. Authority is ordinarily to be understood as the right given to someone to get the things done through others, to take decisions, to give orders. In the light of these definitions, should we associate both power and authority with the saints? Could we perhaps say that the saints start off by exuding power, and then become authoritative once they are canonized, that is, officially recognized as an authority? This is one way of looking at it. My intuition is to stick to the term "authority" throughout, not least because, within the context of ecclesiology, the term "power" is reminiscent of exploitation and manipulation, but, in doing so, my intention is not to deny the presence of power. Rather, it is to acknowledge it, as Balthasar does.

John McDade has said that "the question is not about where 'power' lies in the Church; the question is about how to eliminate the category of 'power' from Church members' attitudes."[176] In this John McDade exemplifies the tendency for the depoliticization found in contemporary thought. But, whether we like it or not, power is an element of all authority, and Balthasar chose to preserve the concept of power and to rework it using a Christian paradigm, rather than to avoid or exclude it. Some insights about what Balthasar means by authority, and its relationship to power may be obtained from passages where Balthasar discusses "power" with reference to Christ. According to Balthasar, Christ speaks and acts as someone who has plenary power (exousia), but this power is something given to him at the same time as it is being requested from him by the Father. Therefore, while Christ does have power, and he does exercise it, he does so in being obedient

175. Reward, Coercion, Legitimate, Expertise, and Referent are bases of power, whereas the Informational is an influence. See Raven, "The Bases of Power and the Power/Interaction Model of Interpersonal Influence," 1, 12.

176. McDade, "Von Balthasar and the Office of Peter in the Church," 112.

to the will of the Father and in the very act of abandonment to the Father.[177] Something similar is repeated in his essay dealing with "Authority."[178]

Balthasar's own understanding of "power" is in agreement with most New Testament exegesis.[179] Here, the legitimacy of authority always comes from the distinct mark that it carries, namely that of the Christ-event.[180]

In *Gottes Einsatz Leben*, written in 1970, Balthasar formulates the principle of the authority of love into a paradoxical principle where love is powerful precisely because it refutes power: "for love does not conquer in the way that power conquers, but wins its victories precisely because it does not resort to power."[181] The same concept is repeated elsewhere, particularly in other works published in the seventies. In the same essay on authority, Balthasar claims that, in its original sense, *auctoritas* means "promoting," "increasing," power. He asserts that, if authority is to be "edifying," it will have to "develop and flower in an interplay with that which is to be 'increased' in a fundamental relationship of trust."[182] This reflects the post-war mentality, which brought about a shift from an understanding of authority in terms of essence to one in terms of relationality, so that authority is to be understood as a relation "constantly in flux" rather than a "fixed essence."[183] The concept of trust is integral to the contemporary investigations of authority.[184] Balthasar seems to think that this concept of authority as a relation does not contradict the concept of authority as an essence (that is, as a gift which comes from above, and which normally accompanies particular roles). My interpretation is that, for Balthasar, both concepts (that of relation and that of essence) are necessary, and that the two concepts are closely interwoven. Without the "fixed essence" of authority, so to speak, the authority that comes from relationality does not hold sway, and vice-versa. What allows Balthasar to combine the two concepts of authority is the fact

177. Balthasar, *A Theology of History*, 33–34. See also Howsare, *Balthasar: A Guide for the Perplexed*, 149–50.

178. Balthasar, "Authority," 137–39.

179. Writing about Matthew, Brown states that "[b]y the standards of other societies the greatest authority or power makes one the greatest figure in the group . . . in Jesus' eyes, not power but a lack of it can make a person great." Brown, *The Churches the Apostles Left Behind*, 140.

180. Balthasar writes, "the will of the Son transmits to the Church the authority he possesses in the Father so that in his name the Church, too, can make unconditional demands on the company of believers." *The Christian State of Life*, 259.

181. Balthasar, *Engagement with God*, 45.

182. Balthasar, "Authority," 128.

183. Stagaman, *Authority within the Church*, 4.

184. See also Austin, *Up with Authority*, 21.

that Balthasar understands relationality in a particular way. With Balthasar, the relationship in question is more specifically theological. With Balthasar, authentic *auctoritas* promotes another, and not itself. It is a power that is *given* to another, and not one that *belongs* to oneself, and, if I understand Balthasar correctly, this "another" is God. Moreover, like Christ, the authentic *auctoritates* have power and exercise it only in obedience to God's will. Their power is entirely governed by [their] receptivity toward the Father.

Der Antirömische Affekt, published in Freiburg in 1974[185] provides us with most of what we know about Balthasar's concept of authority within the church. With regards to authority, Balthasar, openly confronts the criticism that comes from atheistic positivists concerning authority: such as Auguste Comte (1798–1857), and Sigmund Freud (1856–1939), as de Lubac had done, from atheistic existentialists such as Friedrich Nietzsche (1844–1900), as well as from the historical materialists represented by Karl Marx (1818–1843).[186] In *The Office of Peter*, Balthasar indirectly refers to these opponents when he claims that "authority is interpreted as a socially detrimental ideology in pejorative words borrowed from sociology."[187] Secondly, in this work, Balthasar retains his support for authority, without discarding its link with power. This is the first point I would like to make: for Balthasar, *exousia* is not detached from power. He defines *exousia* as "*supreme power* for service" [my italics].[188] Balthasar maintains that service *requires* authority, and that the People of God benefits from a service only when "authority" is effectively present. Balthasar concedes that the *exousia* that Jesus entrusts to the Twelve on *choosing* them can be expressed in Latin only as *potestas*, that, though not exactly power, certainly implies a "fullness of authority."[189] Another point is that, with Balthasar, authority is present in each and every act of the church, not just that of government.[190] Balthasar indicates authentic proclamation, and the administration of the sacraments as two other situations where service is beneficial precisely because of the "authority" with which that service is given.[191] The "full authority" which Jesus gave to his disciples against the demons would be another example

185. Translated and published as *The Office of Peter and the Structure of the Church* in 1986.

186. See Scola, *Test Everything*, 15.

187. Balthasar, *The Office of Peter*, 100.

188. Ibid., 18.

189. Ibid., and *The Christian State of Life*, 147.

190. Where the church's authority to govern is concerned, Balthasar considers it significant that, both in practice and in theory, this authority is called the "*power* of jurisdiction." *The Office of Peter*, 27.

191. Ibid., 134.

of *exousia*.[192] Fourthly, here, Balthasar adopts a Pauline—and therefore pre-Augustinian—position concerning authority.[193] The Pauline model of authority has three distinct characteristics: it is "distinctively marked by the unique Christ-event," it "proceeds in harmony with the community," and it "strives to create *communio*."[194]

In his *Theo-Logic*, there is an emphasis on the fact that this "power" that the Son has is entirely governed by his receptivity toward the Father, so much so that it can even adopt the paradoxical form of the powerlessness of the Cross, where (*sub contrario*) the power to reconcile the world with God, takes on its "perfect form."[195] It is here that Balthasar is most expressive of the paradox of authority. Balthasar maintains that Christ's "power" is best grasped when it is scorned and that "what Christ means by 'power' . . . must bear witness in the face of the world and its different kind of power—and this witness can be most victorious and fruitful when it is rejected and violently suppressed by the world."[196]

Having attended to the nature of authority in Balthasar, the next step is for us to survey the various degrees and holders of authority which he identifies.[197] There is the authority of the bishop who "participates integrally in the fullness of hierarchical power," whose call is to "enlighten" the whole church and to transmit to it the divine graces and powers.[198] There is the authority of the doctors of theology, who are, as it were, chief artificers who inquire and teach how others are to procure the salvation of souls.[199] There is the authority of the clergy,[200] and the authority of the spiritual director.[201] According to Balthasar, the "individual confessor" may not "represent the fullness of the ecclesiastical office, nor is there a guarantee that he can represent God's pure will in each direction he gives,"[202] but his authority is not without its importance. There is also the authority of the religious superiors.[203] Here, Christ's obedience becomes incarnate "in the relationship

---

192. Ibid., 244.

193. Ibid., xiii.

194. Ibid., 154.

195. Balthasar, *The Spirit of Truth (TL3)*, 400.

196. Ibid., 402.

197. Balthasar, "Obedience in the Light of the Gospel," 244.

198. Balthasar, *The Christian State of Life*, 302.

199. Ibid., 304.

200. Balthasar, *The Office of Peter*, 197.

201. Kilby, *Balthasar*, 161.

202. Balthasar, *First Glance*, 69 and 177.

203. Balthasar, *Two Sisters*, 182.

of superior and subject within [what he calls] the supernatural sociology of the evangelical state."[204] Within the monastic framework, authority and office can acquire "a sacramental significance," acting as "the means of coming into direct contact with the divine will."[205] There is also the authority of the contemplative, of the missionary and of the scholar. As in the secular sphere, this is often an official authority, that is one that is strictly coupled with the corporate role that one has.[206]

Balthasar also speaks of the pneumatic, whose authority is more personal, and whose authority is "based on knowledge, ability, maturity."[207] In all of this, as Austin has argued, if we are to understand ecclesial authority and the relation of authority to God, "it is to [the church] that we should look."[208] Express importance must be given to the ecclesiological and the theological dimension. In relating to the diverse practices of authority within the church, Balthasar does precisely that.

Where the ecclesiological dimension is concerned, Balthasar writes of the authority to govern, the power of jurisdiction, or legal authority, which, in Balthasar, is there to uphold "the purity of faith and love,"[209] but which involves the power "to interfere in disciplinary and legal concerns,"[210] and includes both the power to command and the power to impose sanctions on those who fail to obey,[211] both the power to arrive at judgments and that of giving verdicts.[212] Balthasar seeks to emphasize and defend, but also to purify and reform, ecclesial authority. In this he is more in accord with the Pastoral Letters.[213] He does mention the misuse and misdirection of authority, and he does write about people's mistrust of authority. But, rather than

204. Balthasar, *The Christian State of Life*, 157.

205. Balthasar, *Two Sisters*, 181.

206. The authority of the scholarly theologian is not without its problems. Steck has said that nowadays "[t]here exist two forms of moral authority, that of the saint and that of the scholar, neither of which is by itself sufficient as a source of moral wisdom." Steck, "Studying Holy Lives."

207. Balthasar, "Obedience in the Light of the Gospel," 247.

208. Austin, *Up with Authority*, 3.

209. This is evident "in practice and theory in the life of the Church as well as in canon law." See Balthasar, *The Office of Peter*, 27, 174, 182–83.

210. Ibid., 73.

211. Balthasar, *The Christian State of Life*, 264.

212. Balthasar, *The Office of Peter*, 245–46.

213. Brown has compared the ecclesiology of Matthew with that of the Pastoral Letters. According to him, both ecclesiologies are legitimate, although they have a different focus. Brown, *The Churches the Apostles Left Behind*, 136, 145.

criticizing particular structures, he makes use of the archetypes, to suggest ways that would prevent the misuse of authority.

Balthasar sanctions an ecclesial authority which can "intervene in the consciences of individuals," although this only occurs "among those who believe of their own free will."[214] There is then the "educational," or teaching authority,[215] and the *exousia* to cast out demons.[216] There is the pastoral authority, the sacramental authority, which includes the authority to forgive sins,[217] the authority "for the dispensation of grace,"[218] the authority to "arouse," to "prompt," to "train the saints . . . for the execution of their service, for building up the body of Christ,"[219] and so on and so forth. There is also the authority to canonize.[220] This ecclesial practice of authority is charged with controversy. The process of canonization allows for an individual to be examined, for his holiness to be recognized, and for his or her life and work to be promoted as a model for others.[221] If one applies a hermeneutic of suspicion, this process could be seen to assume malicious proportions. Canonizations are sometimes interpreted as purely political decisions on the part of the hierarchy. However, clearly, the politics ordinarily concerns the "when" more than the "whether." It is too prejudicial and reductionist to argue that canonizations "make" saints. I would want to argue that Balthasar assumes (perhaps even envisions) a practice of authority that complements the holiness of the saints, that is, which is a further step to their publicization, an official recognition of an authority that the saints would already have had attributed to them. What Stagaman says about practices of authority may be useful here. Stagaman claims that "[p]ractices of authority are distinguished from other human practices." According to Stagaman, what distinguishes the practices of authority is the fact that "the rules inherent in [them] are themselves the reasons for keeping the rules," and the reason why this is so is "because these rules are stipulated in laws, embedded in custom, or constitute the bedrock whereby the community has its life."[222]

---

214. Balthasar, *Seeing the Form (TA1)*, 590.

215. Balthasar, "Authority," 137; "Obedience in the Light of the Gospel," 238.

216. Balthasar, *The Office of Peter*, 147 and 244.

217. Brown, *The Churches the Apostles Left Behind*, 135–36, 145.

218. Balthasar, *The Christian State of Life*, 287.

219. Balthasar, "Our Shared Responsibility," 140–41.

220. The Congregation for the Causes of the Saints is responsible for the whole process.

221. Kilby has commented on the fact that Balthasar nowhere catalogues the factors contributing to the church's official recognition of the saints. See Kilby, *Balthasar*, 154.

222. The contribution that Stagaman has made through his work on authority is enormous, and its relevance to our own research will be evident throughout this book.

Where the saints are concerned, one may need to distinguish between the practices of authority of the saints themselves, and the practices of authority of the church concerning the saints. I have my doubts about whether it is reasonable to speak about the "practices" of authority of the saints. With the saints, it makes more sense to speak about actions that acquire authoritative proportions as a consequence of the holiness which others recognize in them.

A fourth point that one needs to take issue with is Balthasar's claim that juridical authority is actually the spiritual aspect of the church, rather than the mundane aspect of the church. As with Erich Przywara, Balthasar refuses to interpret juridical authority as the more concrete and worldly aspect of the church's mission. On the contrary he sees the "juridical formalism" of the church as her "spiritual aspect," as "the inmost form" of the church. Balthasar thus seems to invert the hylomorphic model of church. In doing so, the soul of the church is located in the power of the organization (which corresponds to the body), because of what he claims is its power to organize the "freely willed cooperation of superior and subject."[223] It is interesting that there are also passages where Balthasar attributes to the saints a power of jurisdiction. Although this may sound rather odd, in reality, it will not seem as outlandish if one bears in mind the original function of ecclesial authority. Initially, juridical authority would have been concerned more with the definition of dogma, the interpretation of the deposit of the faith, or the regulation of our language for expressing particular truths, and who better than the saints can provide such an interpretation and a language? This is reminiscent of George Lindbeck's rule-theory of truth. There are, quite naturally, several questions which arise from this. One of them is whether the ecclesiastical authoritative roles should be given to the saints, whether such roles inevitably transform into saints those who fulfill these roles, whether the physical absence or rarity of saints, at the level of the juridical in the church, damages or slows down the spiritual development of the church, and whether the church and theologians—Balthasar included— have really made serious attempts to resolve the issue of structural authority and transgression.

This is my fifth point. Balthasar acknowledges that structural authority may have been tinged with transgression, particularly because of the combination of "spiritual (and also truly juridical) evangelical authority" with the exercise of secular power, a practice that Balthasar finds unfortunate.[224]

Stagaman, *Authority within the Church.* xv.

223. Balthasar, *The Office of Peter,* 248.

224. Ibid., 28. See also Balthasar, *Cosmic Liturgy,* 31.

Balthasar out-rightly condemns the surrender of theology to "the fright-ening power of politics."[225] He is convinced that political integralism and emphasis on producing "politically correct dogmatic formulas" had nega-tive consequences on the church. Among the consequences, he mentions the extinction of a "living biblical theology," as well as the withdrawal of monastic spirituality into the cloister and the elimination of theological dialogue.[226] In his *Theo-Logic*, Balthasar mentions Augustine's appeal to the secular authorities against the Donatists, and the Inquisition's practice of handing over of heretics to the secular authorities for burning. He strongly condemns the use of "temporal power to extend the spiritual realm of Christ's authority."[227] He also condemns the use of "propaganda, advertising and marketing" to promote particular Catholic lines of thought. He con-demns those who promote "themselves with all means available," those who make "the attainment of positions of worldly power" their prime aim.[228] Balthasar candidly expresses disapproval of the "subtle spiritual kind of tri-umphalism," which in the past affected the hierarchy.[229] He laments that, in the Counter-Reformation, "the positive ecclesiastical structures and institu-tions were made into the definitive form of manifestation of divine glory."[230] Authentic authority, as Balthasar views it, has nothing to do with vanity, and Balthasar does not completely exonerate some saints from it. This does not mean that the saints never get to operate politically. In the absence of effective government within the church, the saints may be the authoritative figures that lead it back to stability. Balthasar expresses huge admiration for saints such as Maximus and Catherine of Siena, the former for having separated the Greek Christian tradition from the political integralism of the time,[231] the latter for her role in restoring the church after the Papal Avignon crisis. Such political activity is not at all, according to him, a "secular exer-cise of power," that is, one tinged with vanity.

The authority that Balthasar empathized with is best understood in the light of his doctrine of mission and of sacramentality, rather than of political triumphalism. In Balthasar, what really counts is the mission from above. Realities like martyrdom and mysticism almost become inconsequential,

225. Balthasar, *Cosmic Liturgy*, 34.

226. Ibid., 31.

227. Balthasar, *The Spirit of Truth (TL3)*, 402. See also 265–66.

228. Ibid., 405.

229. Balthasar, *Engagement with God*, 96.

230. Balthasar identifies Bellarmine and Baroque art as the main culprits. *The Realm of Metaphysics in the Modern Age (TA5)*, 110.

231. Balthasar, *Cosmic Liturgy*, 37, 42.

except as they reflect the mission that the individual is fulfilling. On the other hand, the doctrine of sacramentality, re-discovered by the movement of the *Ressourcement*[232] is clearly at the foundation of Balthasar's many claims concerning the authority of the saints. Balthasar maintains that authority is sacramental.[233] The question obviously arises as to whether authority is sacramental *always* and *everywhere*.

Perhaps the best way to understand Balthasar's position would be to use the seven sacraments and grace as an analogy for comprehending authority and its outcome. Catholics believe that the grace of the sacraments is a consequence of the action of the sacrament, not the merits of the priest or the participant (*ex opera operato*). With Balthasar, the sacramentality of authority always remains, irrespective of the merits of the Pope, or the co-operation, or lack of it, of the Christian. However, most theologians would agree that the *extent* of the outcome of sacrament, the *effect* that it will have, the response that will be generated, its fruitfulness, will depend, not only on the disposition of the recipients[234] but also on the authenticity of the individual exercising that sacramental authority (*ex opere operantis*, not just *ex opera operato*). In Catholic sacramental theology, the one doing the work does not directly determine the validity of a sacrament, but it does determine its fruitfulness. The same thing applies to authority in general. The holiness and reverence with which a minister exercises his authority will have a great effect on the potential fruitfulness. From the point of view of the person or persons exercising the authority, the authority may be valid, even when ineffective. But all of us would all agree that legal validity without spiritual effectiveness is inadequate. From the point of view of reception, the depth of the authoritativeness, the seriousness with which the authoritative demands are taken, the spiritual transformation which ensues as a consequence, will also depend on the one exercising that authority. In this respect, the distinction which Karl Jaspers (1883–1969) makes between the term "*Dasein*," which means existence in its most minimal sense, and "*Existenz*," which represents the realm of authentic being may also be useful. The minimal performance of the valid act could be compared to *Dasein* whereas the effective performance of the fruitful act could be compared to *Existenz*.

---

232. Boersma, *Nouvelle Théologie*, 31.

233. Balthasar, *Two Sisters,* 182.

234. *Catechism of the Catholic Church*, par. 1128.

CONCLUSION

Our intention for this chapter has been to establish the importance and the function of the saints in Balthasar's theology. We provided a hermeneutics of the saints as Balthasar would have it, deliberated on the significance of Balthasar's choice of saints, explored the different ways in which the saints function in Balthasar's theology, including (but not limited to) that of corroborating, validating, verifying, and supporting his claims. It was determined that, Balthasar emphasizes more than other theologians that the saints are authorities for theology and for the church. In this chapter, we determined that, in Balthasar, *exousia* is not detached from power, that there is an authority that complements the saints precisely because they are saints, that there is something specifically authoritative about the words and actions of the saints, and that the concept of authority has a plurality of meanings which can only be understood within the context of a theology of sacramentality and a theology of mission. We can conclude that, for Balthasar, authority is not restricted to the Magisterium and that, on the contrary, Balthasar ascribes to the saints an *auctoritas* which is both prior to, and analogical to, that of the Magisterium.

I am dealing here with a subject that has been left out of the frame, both by those who study the saints comprehensively—social and cultural historians, medievalists, literary specialists and feminists—and by Balthasarian scholars, namely, the "authority" of the saints. What I want to demonstrate is that there is something which we find alluring in the saints, and that Balthasar can help us to formulate this, since he presents the saints as a paradigm. There is something that fascinated and inspired him in their life and works, so much that he wanted, not just to divulge their wisdom, and to display their proficiency, but to provide a theology that would underscore their *phronesis* and their theological proficiency.[235] There is something that is so forceful and lucid about them that made him want to refer to them over and over again in his own theology and to set them down as a criteria for the assessment of the integrity of any theology, and of the ecclesiological reality itself. I would especially like to demonstrate that the "grounding" of this authority is especially significant for Balthasar. He could not have been attracted simply by the scholarly reputation of the saint. I want to demon-

235. Majdik and Keith have argued that phronesis, which is one of Aristotle's intellectual virtues, is neither science nor intuition. It is at the center of judgment in expertise, involving the recognition of norms that impinge on a situation. It is about an inventional capacity for apprehending good choices with respect to the "ultimate particulars" of each situation. The function of phronesis is to prepare us to be capable of such action, rather than itself being a function of action. See "Expertise as Argument," 376–77.

strate that there must have been something within, or beneath, their asceticism, their mortification, their martyrdom, their charisms, their reputation, which he himself thought was the one thing that mattered, and which he wanted to establish as that which distinguished the saints and made them authoritative. I would also want to demonstrate that the hermeneutic of the saint which Balthasar provides, and the focus on the grounding of the saints' authority, has the capacity to surmount the confusion ensuing from the injudicious postmodern application of the title "saint." It is important to note that I may sometimes need to freely interpret Balthasar's thought for him to be able to respond to the issues which I raise, but I hope that there will be no outright modification of his thought, and that readers of Balthasar can associate with what I am trying to claim.

After this introductory chapter, which acquainted the reader with Balthasar's writings on the saints, and the second chapter, which will deal with the state of the question in contemporary research, the book engages in dialogue with three dimensions in order to elucidate the different aspects of the "grounding" of the authority of the saints, i.e., why the saints acquire an authority for theology and for the church, and the different settings in which they seem to function authoritatively.

I would like to demonstrate that an exploration of the grounding of the saints' authority, requires a multi-dimensional approach, and will have multi-dimensional outcomes. The dimensions that I have identified are three: the existential (which will be dealt with in chapter 3), the epistemological (chapter 4), and the ecclesiological (chapter 5). I start with the most fundamental level and move on to the more concrete, the more structural, which is the ecclesial. Since Balthasar claimed that Christology should permeate all of theology, the Christological will be incorporated within all the dimensions, rather than be treated separately.

In the concluding chapter, I want to demonstrate that the concept of biblical equality and the issue of Chrisian egalitarianism creates problems where the authority of the saints is concerned.[236] Our emphasis on unity and on the equality of the saints within the *communio sanctorum* is often inconsistent with, and even counter-productive to our emphasis on the exceptional character of individual saints. This becomes evident in Balthasar. I also want to demonstrate that Balthasar's portrayal of the individual saints as outstanding individuals is weakened by his vision of the church as a community of equals, and that his portrayal of the church as a conversing community is debilitated by his emphasis on a governing authority that calls for obedience. It will be determined that, despite everything, no doubt can be

---

236. See Padgett, "What Is Biblical Equality?"

cast on the fact that, *de facto*, Balthasar gives to the saints an extraordinary prominence in his own theology and in his recommendations for theology, for the church and for humanity. I would also like to point out some of the consequences of having a theology concerning the authority of the saints.

Due to restrictions of time and resources, this book will only deal with a selection of texts. I have chosen what I considered most relevant to the subject, namely texts which would enable me to demonstrate and to interpret the authority of the saints in Balthasar's theology. Evidently, because of Balthasar's association both with the "retrieval of the Catholic Tradition,"[237] and with Karl Barth,[238] his work ought to be understood against the background of both Catholicism and Protestantism, even where the theology of the saints is concerned. However, because of Balthasar's own strong Catholic affiliation, and because of my own active involvement with the Catholic Church, the Catholic elements will be more evident.

---

237. Howsare, *Balthasar: A Guide for the Perplexed*, 147.
238. Balthasar, *The Theology of Karl Barth*, 383. See Wigley, *Balthasar's Trilogy*, 84.

CHAPTER 2

Theoretical Insights

INTRODUCTION

AT LEAST THREE THINGS were ascertained in the introductory chapter: first-ly, that Balthasar's work on the saints and on sanctity is integral to an under-standing of his work, secondly that, according to Balthasar, the saints can be used to respond to (and to resolve) the philosophical and the theological questions of his time, and thirdly, that, according to Balthasar, the saints' contribution is authoritative, and not merely informative, for theology and for the church. By now it is evident that the subject of this book is innovative for two reasons. Clearly, it examines a subject with reference to Balthasar's work which has not as yet been analyzed. But, more than that, this work deals with a subject that is relatively unexplored, namely the attribution of authority to the saints, or rather, the theology of the authority of the saints. Although scholars such as Victoria Harrison, Danielle Nussberger, and Patricia Sullivan have carried out research specifically on the theology of the saints in Balthasar, to the best of my knowledge, overall research about the theology of the authority of the saints within the church has not yet been carried out. As a consequence, it is not, properly speaking, possible for me to examine the contemporary state of the research. What I would like to do instead, is to indicate the more important theologians who have carried out research on the issues with which this book is concerned, and also to discuss some of the material which is being published. What I will want to demonstrate is that a lot of progress has been made in the scholarship dealing with Balthasar, with holiness, with the saints, and with authority within the church. Balthasar's theology of the saints is, to some extent, present in all of his works and, therefore, there is nothing in the literature about Balthasar that is not, at least minutely, relevant to our own focus area: the theology of the authority of the saints. What I have done here is select material which discusses the more pertinent issues involved.

BALTHASARIAN SCHOLARSHIP

In recent years, we have had theologians attempting to write more widely about Balthasar's thought, certainly no easy feat. Rodney Howsare has addressed what he calls, "perplexing aspects" of Balthasar's theology. He also discusses Balthasar's influences: Erich Przywara (1889–1972), Henri de Lubac, Adrienne von Speyr, and Karl Barth) and his method of doing theology. Among other things, Howsare works on Balthasar's theological style, and introduces the reader to central aspects of Balthasar's theology.[1] Howsare's work does not contribute directly to the subject of the grounding of the authority of the saints within the church. However, in discussing the central aspects of Balthasar's theology—the meaning of Scripture, freedom, the Trinity, and the Cross—he has contributed greatly to themes which are critical to this study, as will become evident in subsequent chapters. Howsare has also elaborated on Balthasar's method of doing theology by creating space for dialogue and debate between the saints. He describes how Balthasar brings Augustine and Aquinas "into dialogue with modern thinkers" such as G. W. F. Hegel (1770–1831), M. F. Scheler (1874–1928), and M. Heidegger (1889–1976).[2] Always, the assumption is "that thinkers across time can be brought into dialogue over the so-called big questions" which they would not "have foreseen." Howsare describes the outcome that ensues as "fresh," since "past thought" takes "on a new light in the context of current conversations."[3]

Where Balthasarian scholarship is concerned, Aidan Nichols' contribution to Balthasarian research cannot but be commended. Nichols is especially known for his introduction to Balthasar's Trilogy.[4] But he also has

1. In *Hans Urs von Balthasar and Protestantism* (2005), Howsare discusses the ecumenical implications of Balthasar's theological style and his contribution to ecumenical dialogue and in *Balthasar: A Guide for the Perplexed*, he comes up with suggestions concerning Balthasar's role in theology.

2. Howsare, *Balthasar: A Guide for the Perplexed*, 5.

3. Ibid.

4. Nichols, *The Word Has Been abroad*; Nichols, *No Bloodless Myth*; Nichols, *Say It Is Pentecost*.

several other works. The book that has proved most useful for this particular research is *Divine Fruitfulness*, published in 2007. Here, Nichols discusses the sources of Balthasar's theology, namely, the Fathers of the church, de Lubac, Barth, and Adrienne von Speyr, and discusses the main themes in Balthasar's theology.[5] Nichols has provided clarification of most of the concepts which are, in my opinion, at the root of the authority of the saints.[6]

Balthasar's theological integrity has been questioned by more than one scholar. Karen Kilby has radically criticized what seems to her to be Balthasar's omniscient position, or what she calls, his "presumption of a God's eye view," and his "extraordinary; and unwarranted, authority."[7] She argues that his standpoint is not always corroborated by appropriate criteria for judgment, yet that, at the same time, he expects his readers to consent.[8] Kilby adds that while expressing approval, or disapproval for a theology, including that of the saints, Balthasar does not develop the principles behind his positive or negative conclusions.[9] Although I can see why Kilby is so condemnatory, my interpretation is not as radical as hers. In my opinion, Balthasar's "God's eye view" is a reflection of his extensive knowledge of the saints. There is, I agree, what seems to be an authoritative tone to Balthasar's voice. Considering his erudition, I compare this authoritative voice to the impatient tone of a tutor who is tired of having to spoon-feed his students. There are various instances when Balthasar expects his readers to be familiar with the tradition, as well as with all the literary works which he himself knows well.[10] You could say that his authoritative voice comes from the fact that he can speak about God with the certainty he has acquired from the saints. It is the authority of the saints that furnishes him with this authoritative voice. Balthasar is not above, but within, and drawing the reader in, as it were. Balthasar's own vision of the saints themselves is that they were *within* tradition, *within* Scripture, and *within* history. Naturally, this should not excuse what sometimes sounds like arrogance, seems like obscurity, or acts as an avoidance tactic. In the meantime, I am convinced that, in using the saints so extensively, Balthasar is actually wanting to familiarize the reader with tradition, attempting to encompass his readers within it. Although Balthasar's own place or perspective within the tradition is not always made explicit, his position often becomes evident through his choice of schol-

5. Nichols, *Divine Fruitfulness*.
6. See Nichols, *A Key to Balthasar*.
7. Kilby, *Balthasar*, 162. See also 40 and 151.
8. Ibid., 55.
9. Ibid.,145.
10. See Nichols "Balthasar's Aims," 116.

ars, his choice of works, and the connections he makes, so that not only is Balthasar's erudition never doubted, but his insistence on speaking for the best specimens of the community (the saints) is—if not well-regarded by everybody—at least tolerated by most. It is Balthasar's erudite knowledge of the saints which gives him access to the "universal meaning" which comes from the form of Christ, which is reflected in the individual saints and in the wider *communio sanctorum*. According to Balthasar "[a]ll our destinies are interwoven" and it is possible to achieve clarity about the significance of the other.[11] In his *Convergences*, Balthasar envisions "the great I," which is formed by humanity as a whole, looking back "on the millions of little I's." He says that Christ is able to integrate these "little I's," this "formless and futile mass" into an organic whole.[12] Does this Ignatian vision of humanity gathered as one, and this hope in the universal meaningfulness of the totality of being, make of Balthasar an impertinent creature? Rowan Williams's essay on "Theological Integrity," could help us arbitrate. According to Williams, the test for a theology of integrity lies in its ties with the community. A theology of integrity—and I would certainly classify Balthasar's theology as such—"will not regard its conclusions as having authority independently of their relation to the critical, penitent community it seeks to help to be itself." The profound ecclesiological flavour found in Balthasar's theology is proof that he does not consider *himself* to be the measure of theology, and that he is therefore not playing God. Rowan Williams has argued that the "rigour" and "discipline" which characterizes theology, evokes a paradox, namely that of "keeping on the watch for our constant tendency to claim the total perspective."[13] This is done by "speaking to God," by "opening our speech to God's," and by "speaking *of* those who have spoken to God." Williams thus recognizes that speaking of the saints is actually the only kind of universal meaning possible without the tyranny of a "total perspective," rather than yet another means for one, in this case Balthasar, to express his self-inflated authority.[14]

Kilby has also claimed that Balthasar's work lacks a sense of "direction,"[15] that it consists of a combination of "collation, exposition, and commentary on the thoughts of others,"[16] that it denies the need to discuss

11. Balthasar, *A Theology of History*, 78.

12. Balthasar, *Convergences*, 132–33.

13. Williams, "Theological Integrity," 13.

14. Ibid., 8

15. Kilby, *Balthasar*, 21.

16. Ibid., 3.

concrete relationships,[17] that it refuses any concrete, reasoned account of how the things which differ are related,[18] that his method is purely an avoidance mechanism.[19] I find this criticism rather severe, simply because I can see no sign on Balthasar's part to relinquish the effort of struggling with the various individual perceptions. It is true that Balthasar sometimes "leaves it up to the reader to discover" these connections and dialogues, but to say that he *denies* the need to discuss these relationships does not do justice to his efforts. My interpretation is that what Balthasar is rejecting here is "the notion that he should narrate *a single* line of development of doctrine" [my emphasis]. Balthasar warns his readers that any connections which they discover "cannot all fit into any system,"[20] which is why he circles around the various theologies (biblical and extra-biblical), trying to approach each matter from various perspectives (what Kilby has fittingly called "radiating"). Here is the work, I would say, of someone who really does believe, not that he himself has the last word and the definitive overview, but that the one transcendent central point of theology needs expressing through a multiplicity of "rays,"[21] and that the saints themselves are this multiplicity of "rays."

For a description of the historical context, and consequently for an understanding of Balthasar, Hans Boersma's book *Nouvelle Théologie and Sacramental Ontology* proves very useful, since it discusses the influence of significant theologians and philosophers like Johann Adam Möhler (1796–1838), Maurice Blondel (1861–1949), Pierre Rousselot (1878–1915) and Joseph Maréchal (1878–1944). Boersma demonstrates how the *nouveaux théologiens* (including Balthasar) advocated a return to mystery by means of a sacramental ontology. In the process of his discussion, Boersma analyzes the most characteristic elements of the movement, namely the reintegration of nature and the supernatural, the reintroduction of the spiritual interpretation of Scripture, the approach to Tradition as organically developing in history, and the communion ecclesiology of the movement. All of these elements are relevant to Balthasar's theology of the authority of the saints, as will become clear in subsequent chapters. Among other things, Hans Boersma reflects on the emphasis which the *nouvelle théologie* makes on the vocation of the laity, the return to the Bible, the one source theory of

17. Ibid., 88.
18. Ibid., 89.
19. Ibid., 89–90.
20. Ibid., 88. See also Balthasar, *Studies in Theological Style: Clerical Styles (TA2)*, 22.
21. Kilby, *Balthasar*, 90.

authority, and the unity of nature and the supernatural.[22] In this study, I apply much of what Boersma has said about the *nouvelle Théologie* in general to Balthasar's theology of the saints, and, even more particularly to the theology of the authority of the saints within the church. This is not something Balthasar would necessarily disapprove. In his interview with Angelo Scola, Balthasar claims that the *nouvelle Théologie* is, strictly speaking, the theology of the saints, and consequently that it is not *nouvelle* at all, but rather "the oldest theology."[23]

My research would not be so productive if I did not make some attempts at unravelling what others have said about Balthasar's vision of the saint. In David L.Schindler's work, for example, it is claimed that Balthasar presents the saints as an antidote to Nietzsche's "God is dead." Schindler recognizes Balthasar's promotion of the saints as a means of "renewal of God in the cosmos."[24] This is a clear response to Nietzsche. In fact, Schindler creates a contrast between Balthasar and Nietzsche, arguing that Nietzsche calls for the formation of the Übermensch, that is for a *seizure* of heaven.[25] Schindler does not develop the contrast between the Übermensch and the saint, but it becomes clear from this essay, not only that the Nietzschean Übermensch and the saint are different, but also that any authority which is attributed to the saints is a consequence of their receptivity, rather than of their aggressive appropriation of authority. With Balthasar, heaven comes to earth as a free gift, and it is more a question of receptivity than of seizure.[26] Schindler's article contributes to the research question by provoking some very valid reflections on Nietzsche's Übermensch and the concept of archetype in Balthasar, on the heaven and earth motif, but especially by emphasising that it is the obedient attitude, rather than achievement, that is at the core of Balthasar's theology of the authority of the saints. On his part, Ben Quash provides a comparison between Balthasar's saints and Hegel's "great men of history," as well as between church and Christians (especially the saints) and Hegel's treatment of the State and the individuals within it. Both Schindler's and Quash's work are especially pertinent, even if their work may not be sufficiently adequate for analyzing a theology of the authority of the saints.

Balthasar's theological aesthetics, dramatics and logic, is yet to be applied to a theology concerning the authority of the saints. As a matter of fact, this book reflects some of my own efforts to do precisely that, namely to try

22. Boersma, *Nouvelle Théologie*, 14.

23. Scola, *Test Everything*, 14.

24. Schindler, "*The Significance of Hans Urs von Balthasar*," 34.

25. Ibid., 24–25.

26. Ibid., 25 and 27.

and unearth where it is that Balthasar grounds the authority of the saints. The contribution of Oliver Davies to the appreciation of *Theo-Aesthetics* and of Ed Block to the appreciation of *Theo-Drama* are especially important, the former because he provides what one could call an aesthetic epistemology, the latter because of his exploration of the dramatic nature of existence. Davies has focused on the intimate connection found in Balthasar between aesthetics and knowledge, on Balthasar's delineation of the dual structure of the beautiful (following Aquinas) in terms of the principle of form and splendor,[27] on Balthasar's supposition that form is always material and particular, on his inference that form is a sign and an appearance of the splendor and glory of being, on Balthasar's engagement with the beautiful,[28] on Balthasar's new analysis of faith as "aesthetic cognition,"[29] on Balthasar's reassertion of the transcendental value of Being, on the analogy between divine and worldly beauty, on the "theory of vision" and the "theory of rapture,"[30] and on the true "glory" of the act of existence.[31] All of these are very expedient for a theology of the authority of the saints. On the other hand, Ed Block focuses on Balthasar's explicit intention to emphasize the dramatic element found in Jesus' form of existence, in the ecclesial form of existence, and in "our mortal and transitory existence."[32] Ed Block interprets the issues raised in the *Theo-Drama* from the perspective of their relevance to drama. Indirectly, however, his arguments serve as a clarification for Balthasar's phenomenological description of the dramatic existence of the saints, both as individuals and as a body.[33] Most of what Block says about the tension between self and role, the suffering undergone in the accomplishment of one's mission, the authority of all those involved in the dramatic endeavour, the "answerability" of the audience, and other motifs, can shed light not only on the dramatic nature of the existence and mission of the saints, but also on the authority of the saints and the response to the authoritative nature of the dramatic holy life.

It is probably to Ben Quash that we owe the greatest debt where the dramatic is concerned. Ben Quash is known mostly for his work on "the dramatically social character of all our searching for truth" and on the

27. Davies, "The Theological Aesthetic," 133.

28. Ibid., 134.

29. Ibid., 135.

30. Ibid., 136.

31. Ibid., 139.

32. Balthasar, *The Spirit of Truth (TL3)*, 308.

33. On their part, Kilby and Quash have expressed reservations as to whether, in practice, Balthasar's theology is as dramatic as it makes itself out to be. Kilby, *Balthasar*, 63, 64, 166. Quash, *Theology and the Drama of History*, 161, 221.

"irreducibly social dimension to drama."[34] *Theology and the Drama of History* proves to be most relevant to us. Here, Quash examines the value and the potential of a theo-dramatic conception of history, claiming that this approach to history makes available insights which would remain hidden with other theological methodologies.[35] Theo-drama, he writes, "displays *human actions* and *temporal events* in *specific contexts*," and it explores actions, time and place "*in relation to God's purpose.*"[36] The three conclusions which Ben Quash reaches, where his investigation of Balthasar's drama of history is concerned, are especially helpful. Firstly, theo-dramatics always has an eschatological dimension. Secondly, theo-dramatics provides a better interpretation of freedom than other theological methods, and, thirdly, it provokes questions on ecclesiology and the saints.[37]

There are at least five other areas which are especially relevant where the authority of the saints is concerned. These are eschatology and the concept of universalism, the theology of nature and grace, the dialectic of the objective and the subjective, the theology of language, and the theology of the spiritual senses. Significant research has been done on each of these themes. I will only provide a quick overview of this research here.

The first of these is eschatology and the concept of universalism. In his book *The Eschatology of Hans Urs von Balthasar: Being as Communion*, Nicholas J.Healy is especially absorbed with the meaning of "the end" as Balthasar represents it, namely, Christ's return to the Father in the Spirit. He engages with Balthasar's writings on the *eschaton*, in order to demonstrate that Balthasar's understanding of "the end" includes, as he says, "a rigorous, and properly philosophical, reflection on being."[38] Because Nicholas J.Healy's work focuses on being, rather than on soteriology, it is Geoffrey Wainwright's exploration of Balthasar's eschatology[39] which I have found most helpful to my work. Wainwright refers to the lecture which Balthasar gave at the University of Trier in 1988 on *apokatastasis*, or universal restoration, which is one of the most controversial of his works. Universalism, or the belief that all will be saved, is doctrinally heretical, and was condemned by the Councils of Constantinople in 543 and 553 AD.[40] Wainright argues that Balthasar's fascination with *apokatastasis* "springs directly from his initial

---

34. Quash, "Drama and the Ends of Modernity," 140.

35. Quash, *Theology and the Drama of History*, 9.

36. Ibid., 3.

37. Ibid., 4.

38. Healy, *The Eschatology of Hans Urs von Balthasar*, 4.

39. Wainwright, "Eschatology," 113.

40. Ibid., 121–22.

intuitive and comprehensive perception of the 'shape' or 'pattern' (*Gestalt*) of the Christian faith, that is, from his vision of the Christ event."[41] The question of universal salvation in Balthasar's eschatology has been a debatable subject over the years. As with most postliberal theology, Balthasar merges a high Christology with an unlimited soteriology. This does not make Balthasar a universalist, but it does make it clear that he justified a universal *hope*.[42] The relevance of this work to my subject is evident. According to Balthasar, Christ has made saints out of all of us. God wishes everyone to be saved— and Balthasar himself dares to hope that all of us will be saved—even if he knows that *de facto* the possibility of some of us not being saved still exists. In this respect, Balthasar seems to be more sympathetic to the Protestant conception of justification which stands for absolute certainty than with the Catholic doctrine of sanctifying grace which is characterized by *incertitudo*. He also seems to alternate between wanting to avoid distinctions and equalizing everyone, while also emphasizing the special character of a few.

The questions for us become: firstly, why should anyone argue for the authority of the saints, and how can one do so, when everyone will be saved and the possibility of damnation has almost been completely undermined? Secondly, and this is even more fundamental: should we distinguish between justification and sanctification? If everyone has been justified, does it also mean everyone has been sanctified? Balthasar simply refuses to divide humanity into the elect and the damned.[43] He is outright in his rejection of double predestination.[44] He would rather be associated with *apokatastasis* than with Calvin's position or with that of the Jansenists who restricted the redemption to the "elect."[45] He does grant that some may be elected, but it is the Barthian doctrine of election, and not the salvation-damnation dialectic that rules his thought.[46] More precisely, it is "Barth's doctrine of the

41. Ibid., 115.

42. Ibid., 124. See also Ratzinger, "Christian Universalism."

43. Balthasar treats the position of Calvin and of classical Calvinism concerning the twofold division of mankind into the chosen (élus) and the damned (réprouvés) in *Dare We Hope*, 195–96.

44. Wainwright, "Eschatology," 124.

45. Balthasar, *The Theology of Karl Barth*, 36. See also Médaille, "The Daring Hope of Hans Urs Von Balthasar."

46. On the other hand, Balthasar accepts the doctrine of election of all people in Christ in the sense that Barth did. However, whereas, for Barth, the eternal predestination was *for* salvation and *for* sanctification, for Balthasar the election is *for* mission that incorporates both salvation and sanctification. Quoting Jeremiah, Paul, Jacob, John the Baptist, Samson, and Samuel as examples, Balthasar writes that "eternal predestination takes place in time as an election and separation (*segregatio*) from the world *even from the womb*." Balthasar, *The Christian State of Life*, 403.

election of all people in Christ, against any Calvinistic notion of a limited atonement"[47] that guides him. Although, as I have already stated, it would seem as if the issue of universalism is contrary to the concept of having authority attributed to the saints, this does not necessarily have to be the case: authority could be attributed to each one: there is no limit as to how many saints convey authority within the church and the world. Perhaps what we could say is that with some, there is no temporal limit. For instance, Austin argues that authority is something that transcends this world. He uses Dante to raise the issue of authority in the after-life, claiming that "the notion of authority is not antithetical to paradise," and that, when authority does not mean "authority over," it is possible for difference (which is entailed by authority) to be compatible with the equality expected in heaven. Balthasar claims that, within a context of close solidarity such differences convey no pain.[48]

The second important theme is Balthasar's theology of nature and grace. Howsare describes how Balthasar uses Henri the Lubac and Karl Barth who tried to reintegrate nature and grace.[49] Balthasar's theology of the saints cannot be understood except within the context of the theology of nature and grace, and a theology about the authority of the saints requires a sound reflection on the issue. David S. Yeago has provided us with the most stimulating approach to this aspect of Balthasar's theology. Yeago's focus is more specifically literature and culture, but, in the process, he discusses the relationship between nature and grace, claiming that Balthasar's *dramatic narrative configuration*—rather than a rule that could be described theoretically[50]—enables him to reconcile claims that may otherwise seem incompatible.[51] Thus, for example, it is possible to reconcile "[t]he certainty of the natural striving for the goal of our life and [the] *gratuity* of grace."[52] Furthermore, Yeago claims that "Balthasar's theological account of nature and grace . . . provides a distinctive paradigm for a reflective Christian engagement with the works and achievements of human culture."[53] As Yeago has said, with Balthasar, "culture does not have to be explicitly Christian to be intelligible and interesting to Christian thought—positively

---

47. Howsare, *Balthasar: A Guide for the Perplexed*, 10.

48. Austin, *Up with Authority*, 151–54, 158.

49. Howsare, *Hans Urs von Balthasar and Protestantism*, 98 and 123.

50. Yeago, "Literature in the Drama of Nature and Grace," 92.

51. Ibid., 93.

52. Balthasar, *The Theology of Karl Barth*, 296.

53. Yeago, "Literature in the Drama of Nature and Grace," 97.

or negatively,"[54] precisely "because all people in reality inhabit a creation that is ordered to Christ." On her part, Patricia Sullivan has noted a connection between Balthasar's theology of nature and grace and his theology of the saints. In this regard, I have tried to build on Sullivan's conclusions. Sullivan has also provided a comparison between Balthasar's theology of the saints and that of Rahner, claiming that the two theologies of the saints are grounded in "articulations of the relationship between nature and grace and, by association, the relationship between faith and revelation."[55] In terms of the authority, whether that which is inspired by the saints, or that which is attributed by others to the saints, nature and grace should be seen as integrated. To explain the authority of the saints in purely material terms is simply insufficient.

There is then the third theme: the objective-subjective dialectic, which is so significant in Balthasar. The familiar modern ontological disjunction between the subjective and the objective is inadequate for Balthasar. In this regard, Christophe Potworowski's work proves to be instructive. Potworowski explores Balthasar's notion of objectivity by examining three areas in which the ground of objectivity is laid out in complementary ways: in a phenomenology of the act of knowing, in the aesthetic experience, and in the dialogical situation. Potworowski maintains that, in Balthasar, "[o]bjectivity in knowing is based primarily on receptivity, service, and obedience."[56] According to Potworowski, in Balthasar, the aesthetic does several things. Firstly, it introduces "a new notion of objectivity into theology, transcending the pitfalls of subjectivism, yet avoiding the violence of extrinsicism."[57] Secondly, in Balthasar, objectivity takes the form of an attitude of "welcome" and an acceptance of mystery.[58] Thirdly, this original experience is usually intersubjective and dialogical.[59] Finally, in what he describes as "a reflection on the relation between scriptural interpretation and holiness," Potworowski claims that there are a number of implications which ensue from this notion of objectivity.[60] Potworowski's essay raises "[t]he question of credibility, which, for Balthasar, cannot be settled on the basis of anthropological reduction."[61] In this context, the saint is understood as the subject

54. Ibid., 101.
55. Sullivan, "Saints as the 'Living Gospel,'"2.
56. Potworowski, "An Exploration," 74.
57. Ibid., 78.
58. Ibid., 77.
59. Ibid., 78.
60. Ibid., 70.
61. Ibid., 77.

who "bring[s] the object to its objective truth."[62] This view of the saints sheds light on the issue of the authority of the saints. Moreover, in viewing knowledge as an act of obedience, Balthasar is able to argue that what the saints know is ultimately objective, without being either extrinsic (that is, without being hostile to their nature) or purely immanent (that is, without ruining the mystery). In this sense, there is a distinctive onto-epistemology that could be extracted from the saints.

Another important development in Balthasarian scholarship concerns the theology of language. Peter Casarella has done sterling work in this regard. Because my intention is to unearth the theology of the authority of the saints located in Balthasar's work, and because a very important aspect of the authority of the saints is that of expression and of proclamation, Casarella's explication of Balthasar's theological theory of language is highly expedient.[63] Casarella explains the relationship, in Balthasar, between the expression and the form of the Word. Form is the manner in which content is expressed, appearing "immediately in expression," but not reduced to expression.[64] According to Casarella the foundation for Balthasar's theory of language and the basis for his trinitarian hermeneutics is precisely this "polarity of expression and form." What is especially relevant for a theology of the authority of the saints is that, in this essay, Casarella examines Balthasar's "verbal anthropology," namely that "we are . . . God's own speech."[65] He maintains that, in Balthasar, the theology of the Word is linked with the human word, that each word spoken is measured by the testimony of a life, that the truth is measured by its correspondence to Christ, and that human speech can imitate divine speech, respond to God's speech, and is sacramental.[66] Furthermore, Casarella discusses the analogies which Balthasar develops between human speech and the liturgy. Finally, Casarella claims that this view of language can potentially contribute "to a renewal of Christian theology and the Christian state of life."[67] In Balthasar there is already an attempt to develop this in his representation of the saints as the mouthpiece of God, and in his emphasis on the fact that only the saints can renew and rejuvenate theology and the church.

Finally, there is the theological revival of the spiritual senses. Mark McInroy has produced a remarkable book about the recovery by Balthasar

62. Ibid., 75.

63. Casarella, "The Expression and Form of the Word," 40.

64. Ibid., 43–45.

65. Ibid., 56.

66. Ibid., 56, 58, 61.

67. Ibid., 64.

of the doctrine of the "spiritual senses," more precisely the faculties that can enable human beings to perceive the absolute beauty of the divine form through which God reveals himself. According to McInroy, in Balthasar, the spiritual senses help to resolve the high-profile debates in modern Catholic theology between Neo-Scholastic theologians and their opponents. McInroy investigates Balthasar's own exploration of the spiritual senses as provided by the Church Fathers, but also by Bonaventure (1221–1274), Ignatius of Loyola (1491–1556), Karl Barth (1886–1968), Paul Claudel (1868–1955), Romano Guardini (1885–1968), and Gustav Siewerth (1903–1963), all of whom influenced Balthasar's own doctrine. McInroy asserts that Balthasar breaks from previous articulations of the doctrine when he draws on the notion of the human being as a being-in-encounter,[68] concluding that Balthasar's model of spiritual perception provides a third option between Neo-Scholastic "extrinsicism"—which construes grace as simply added to a nature that is whole in itself—and "immanentism." McInroy's work serves as the ground for my own explorations on three issues: firstly, on whether, according to Balthasar, it is possible to deepen the capacity to perceive that which is non-corporeal and "spiritual," secondly, on whether, in Balthasar, the spiritual senses of the saints exhibit a perception and a vision that is out of the ordinary, and, thirdly, on whether, in Balthasar, holiness is the cause behind this enhancement of the ability to perceive God and to understand reality, and behind the authority that the saints elicit in others, or which is attributed to them by others.

Lamentably, Balthasar has been widely criticized for misrepresenting texts and quoting authors out of context. This is an accusation that must be taken seriously, since one cannot discuss the authority of the saints in Balthasar, or his implicit development of a theology of the authority of the saints if there are such serious doubts about the way Balthasar inter-prets texts. Alyssa Pitstick has even accused Balthasar of relying on posi-tions previously rejected by the Magisterium. Published in 2007, Alyssa Pitstick's book deliberates on the doctrine of Christ's descent into hell, an aspect of theology which Balthasar believed had been "overlooked and misinterpreted,"[69] and which he sought to rehabilitate. Pitstick sets this theology within a dogmatic context, comparing Balthasar's doctrine with the traditional doctrine of the church, and claiming that Balthasar's is at odds with the teaching of the Fathers and of the Doctors of the church. According to Pitstick, although Balthasar attempts to present the doctrine as a rereading of historical sources, his own interpretation of it was not only

68. McInroy, *Balthasar on the Spiritual Senses,* 120.
69. Pitstick, *Light in Darkness,* 5.

different but even entailed a rejection of Catholic tradition. Significantly, Pitstick does not think it necessary to examine Balthasar's work along with Adrienne's, even though Balthasar's theology of the *descensus* is generally attributed to Adrienne's influence.

Pitstick is not the only one who has criticized Balthasar for providing one-dimensional readings of texts. Ben Quash has criticized Balthasar for providing a simplistic reading of Euripides and of Shakespeare, and for overdetermining them theologically.[70] On his part, Martin Simon has argued that Balthasar provides a reading of Hölderlin that is much more Christian than it ought to be.[71] Philip Endean accuses Balthasar of misrepresenting Rahner.[72] Karen Kilby also sheds doubts on Balthasar's interpretation of texts. She accuses Balthasar of misusing the many "figures" whom he refers to, or whom he quotes directly.[73] She says that the exploration of Balthasar's work "should be combined with a certain wariness, a readiness to question him, to wonder how he knows what he seems to know, to ask where he stands so that he can tell us what he wants to tell us."[74] Kilby claims that Balthasar does not provide an impartial reading of tradition. He only uses the elements of tradition which "fit with and illustrate an already established [concept]." She says that sometimes he even modifies these elements to suit his purposes. Indeed, while agreeing with Kilby that Balthasar can sometimes come out as an "idiosyncratic. . .reader,"[75] and while agreeing with Brian E.Daley that Balthasar has his own "theological enterprise,"[76] we certainly cannot condone the impression that Balthasar is *always* prejudiced in his readings, or that he *deliberately* misrepresents the thought of others. In all honesty, as a hagiographer in his own right, Balthasar has a distinctive way of interpreting the words, visions, and writings of the saints. His reading of the saints may sometimes be "idiosyncratic" but that does not make it necessarily erroneous, or bigoted. Peter Henrici's assessment of Balthasar's philosophy and literary theory can easily be applied to Balthasar's theological method, namely, "to allow himself to be taught by the great writers and

---

70. See Quash, *Theology and the Drama of History*, 138–44. See also O'Regan, "Review of *Theology and the Drama of History* by Ben Quash," 294.

71. On Balthasar's reading of Hölderlin, see Simon, "Identity and Analogy." On Balthasar's interpretations of texts, see Block, "Balthasar's literary Criticism," 208.

72. Endean, "Von Balthasar, Rahner, and the Commissar," 33–34.

73. Kilby, *Balthasar*, 35.

74. Ibid., 167.

75. Ibid., 8.

76. Balthasar, *Cosmic Liturgy*, 16–17.

by their spiritual adventures, but at the same time . . . to preserve the free-dom to think differently, or even to think the opposite."[77]

Kilby has also expressed misgivings concerning how Balthasar treats the saints in particular. This is a much more serious allegation in our regard. Kilby suggests that Balthasar treats the saints in too romantic and nostalgic a manner.[78] On his part, Steffen Lösel has described the saints of the Chris-tological Constellation as "un-fleshly."[79] While accepting that Balthasar may have misunderstood or misinterpreted some things, I would contend that there is no evidence of dishonesty, obstinate intention to deceive, or pathological chronic distortion on Balthasar's part. If we were to agree that Balthasar's reading of tradition, and his interpretation of the saints, were persistently jaundiced, the whole issue with which this study deals, namely, the saints' authority and the grounding of the authority of the saints ac-cording to Balthasar, would become a hopeless endeavor. On the contrary, I will argue that Balthasar's use of the saints is quite appropriate, choosing those whom he considers—as the professional theologian that he is—to be most knowledgeable on the issue being debated. Just to give one example, in developing his theology of history, using Augustine, Irenaeus, and Bo-naventure is a mature choice, and not a biased one in the negative sense. Naturally, Balthasar is not always predictable. Brian E. Daley has pointed out that he fails to include saints whom one would have expected him to include because of their compatibility with his work.[80] In my opinion, Balthasar's work lends itself more to criticism for its lack of clarity than for misrepresentation. It is a lack of clarity that, most would agree, probably comes from having published in his own publishing house without an edi-tor to point out his inadequacies.

SAINTS AND HOLINESS

My main argument for this book is that, ultimately, there is an authority that is associated with holiness. Although, as I said earlier, the theological investigation of this subject is still relatively unexplored, the same cannot be said about the various aspects with which this book is involved. For example, a lot of work has been published on the subject of holiness. For

77. Henrici, "The Philosophy of Hans Urs von Balthasar," 155.

78. Kilby, *Balthasar*, 154.

79. Lösel, "Conciliar, Not Conciliatory," 40.

80. Among these, Daley mentions Clement of Alexandria, Athanasius, Gregory Nazianzen, and Cyril of Alexandria. See Daley, "Balthasar's reading of the Church Fa-thers," 202.

his publication, Stephen Barton commissioned international experts from a wide range of theological and related disciplines (social scientists, philosophers of religion, feminists, biblical scholars, historians, moral theologians and systematic theologians) to reflect on the topic.[81] Evidently, the subject of holiness and the saints is not exactly a current subject, nor is it the sole property of the theologian. My research has taken me back at least 50 years, to books like Paul Molinari's *Saints: Their Place in the Church*,[82] Peter Brown's *The Cult of the Saints: Its Rise and Function in Latin Christianity*,[83] Donald Weinstein and Rudolph M.Bell's *Saints and Society: The Two Worlds of Western Christendom, 1000–1700*,[84] Thomas J.Heffernan's *Sacred Biography: Saints and Their Biographers in the Middle Ages*,[85] Kenneth L.Woodward's *Making Saints: Inside the Vatican: Who Become Saints, Who Do Not, and Why*,[86] Edith Wyschogrod's *Saints and Postmodernism: Revisioning Moral Philosophy*,[87] Lawrence Cunningham's *A Brief History of Saints*.[88]

Where Balthasar is concerned, holiness is ultimately a theological subject. In his essay on theology and holiness, Antonio Sicari maintains that "the holiness demanded by Balthasar of theology and of theologians is an objective rather than a subjective matter, or even a 'methodological' rather than an ascetical and moral one."[89] Sicari claims that what Balthasar is saying is not that theologians should be saints, but that theologians ought to be saints in order to be theologians. Sicari argues that Balthasar is questioning what it is to be a theologian.[90] Karen Kilby's reading of Balthasar is also, as I understand it, methodological. According to Kilby, Balthasar's "suggestions cluster around the notion" that saints and theologians need "to pay more attention to [each] other."[91]

In this regard, Danielle Nussberger's perspective is, in my opinion, more radical. Nussberger claims that, rather than simply trying to encourage theologians to pay more attention to the saints, what Balthasar is doing

---

81. Barton, ed. *Holiness Past and Present.*

82. Molinari, *Saints: Their Place in the Church.*

83. Brown, *The Cult of the Saints.*

84. Weinstein and Bell, *Saints and Society.*

85. Heffernan, *Sacred Biography.*

86. Woodward, *Making Saints.*

87. Wyschogrod, *Saints and Postmodernism.*

88. Cunningham, *A Brief History of Saints.*

89. Sicari, "Hans Urs von Balthasar: Theology and Holiness," 121.

90. Ibid., 122.

91. Kilby, *Balthasar*, 154–55.

is trying to encourage other theologians to be resources for the saints.[92] In practice, this would mean that theologians are meant to seek out the present-day saints, and to be at their service in every sense: to supply them with their own knowledge and to provide them with whatever assistance they may require. In fact, this is what Balthasar seems to have done with Adrienne. Whether he is recommending his own lifestyle (and not just methodology) to all other theologians is less certain. In Nussberger's case, the authority of the saint for the theologian is made more obvious, since the degree of captivation by the saint of the theologian takes the form of a ministering to the saint. This interpretation certainly exacerbates the already problematic nature of the relationship between Balthasar and Adrienne. I have no objection to the use of Balthasar as a resource for understanding the inextricable unity between theologian and saint, which is what Nussberger does,[93] but such exemplars remain forever controversial.

The developments which have taken place within the field of hagiography have much to say in this regard. New directions in hagiography have raised fundamental issues of interpretation and method, particularly feminist ones. For example, writing about medieval saints in particular, Catherine M. Mooney claims that the voice of the hagiographer must be distinguished from that of the saint because there are differences between "the way the women . . . speak of themselves from the ways their male associates speak about them." Her co-authors provide various instances where portrayals of sanctity are influenced by gender. They find that "[w]hether authored by women or men, most texts regarding women bear the indisputable signs of men's controlling influence." They also deduce that "[m]ost clerical writers . . . were much more than scribes and simple translators, even when they claimed to be only that."[94] Women's stories were transformed, or rather manipulated by men. Moreover, Mooney and her colleagues identify several themes about which one finds differences between men and women, and between saints and their hagiographers.[95] Although dealing with medieval saints, these findings are very relevant to our subject, for various reasons. They put Balthasar's own interpretation of the female medieval saints (Hildegard, Clare of Assisi, Catherine of Siena etc.) into question. These findings also raise the issue concerning Balthasar's role as spiritual director and *amanuensis* (transcriber, editor, and publisher) of Adrienne. Finally, they raise the issue concerning the actual authority that can be attributed to

---

92. See Nussberger, "Saint as Theological Wellspring," Abstract.

93. Nussberger, "Theologians and Saints," 155.

94. Mooney, "Voice, Gender and the Portrayal of Sanctity," 7.

95. Ibid., 9–15.

saints whom we know only indirectly. Perhaps the only feasible argument would have to be similar to that concerning biblical inspiration. Here, we have learnt to accept that only the bible in its original languages, and not in its translations, can claim to be inspired. If ever the authority of a saint is officially established, perhaps we would have to say that this authority is to be attributed only to the original life, action and words, and never to the repetition, or the restatement, which is possibly always indirect and biased in the case of female saints with a male editor. Within the context of postmodern paranoia and suspicion, it could become even more difficult to establish the authority of a saint. We should not forget, however, the emphasis which biblical theologians have made on the fact that tradition also serves as a corrective. The community which appropriates the saints' life and teaching also ensures that the reality is not misrepresented. Although the basic unity of doctrinal reasoning is the individual, the arbiter of doctrinal reasoning is always the *communio sanctorum* (the community), and in particular the *Communio Sanctorum* (the holy ones within the community). The value of tradition, both oral and written should not be minimized, even where hagiography is concerned.

On another note, some research has focused on the discourse about the saints as a counter discourse for existent frameworks. One example is the work carried out by Edith Wyschogrod. In *Saints and Postmodernism: Revisioning Moral Philosophy,* Wyschogrod claims that hagiographic texts could act as an intratextual counter-discourse to existent theological or institutional frameworks.[96] Her argument is based on her conviction that narrative conceptions of ethics may respond better to the impasses created by the confrontation of various moral theories. She claims that the move to the life story is an important step, but agrees with Jean-François Lyotard that the idea of narrative as the encompassing framework for moral philosophy is at the risk of the same *naïveté* as using moral theory as a master narrative. Wyschogrod argues that both the metaphysical presuppositions of theoretical thought, and the philosophical biases in which narrative has been grounded must be brought into critical perspective. According to her, altruism is at the basis of her postmodern analysis.[97] Altruism does not

---

96. The work Steck has done is also significant. Besides his book on *The Ethical Thought in Hans Urs von Balthasar,* Steck also studied the saints more specifically. In his essay "Studying Holy Lives," he elicits six reasons why the saint is very valuable for the ethicist.

97. This altruism is not equivalent to the altruism of a sentimental and parochial hagiography, nor is it the liberal altruism endorsed by John Stuart Mill or some recent analytic ethicists—but it is still altruism. Wyschogrod, *Saints and Postmodernism,* xx. See also Matzko, "Postmodernism, Saints and Scoundrels," 27.

feature as strongly in Balthasar's theology of the saints. In fact, the concept of altruism hardly features at all. This means that Balthasar does not ground the authority of the saints in morality and altruism but elsewhere. Secondly, whereas with Wyschogrod's postmodern moral philosophy there is an emphasis on the narrative conception of ethics, with Balthasar, the emphasis is on other things. For Balthasar, the aesthetic and dramatic conceptions of holiness respond better than the theoretical, or even the narrative conceptions. Balthasar prefers a phenomenological description of life on the premise—I believe—that it handles the aesthetic and the dramatic aspects of reality better. Moreover, such a description responds better to the impasses created by the confrontation of various doctrinal theories than would either doctrinal polemics (detached from life) or pure narrative hagiography.

Wyschogrod is not the only one who has done work on the connections which exist between theology and narrative. John Navone's book, *Seeking God in Story*,[98] is, as he describes it, "part of an expanding theological discourse on the narrative quality of religious experience" and "an introduction to a theology of story." The book includes, among other things, a survey of what scholars have been saying about the relationship of faith and theology to story. These include scholars like James Wm. McClendon, Stanley Hauerwas, David Tracy, and Andrew Greeley. As we have already hinted, rather than "a theology of story," Balthasar's work is better described as a theological aesthetics, dramatics, and logic of the life of the saints, or a theological phenomenology of the mission of the saints. His choice for a phenomenological descriptive framework has the added advantage of incorporating the aesthetic and the dramatic as well as the logical. Moreover, in being a phenomenological description, rather than a narrative one, it reduces the risks of misinterpretation.

On his part, D. M. Matzko has contributed to the body of research by comparing modernity with postmodernity where the saints are concerned. Matzko argues that whereas the predominant framework of modern moral deliberation resists the naming of saints, because of its subversion of rationality and its individualized subjectivity,[99] postmodernism is "not a framework from which a new idea of sainthood can emerge," but it is a framework and a time in which saints can "re-emerge" and "can have a renewed force in creating human community."[100] Where the saints are concerned, it would be difficult to situate Balthasar either in a modern or in a postmodern context, just as it is difficult to situate him within the medieval context, in spite of the

98. Navone, *Seeking God in Story*. See also Goldberg, *Theology and Narrative*.

99. Matzko, "Postmodernism, Saints and Scoundrels," 22.

100. Ibid., 19, 22.

fact that that context is the golden era of hagiography. Matzko's claim that a narrative framework cannot be sustained when the basic unity of moral reasoning is the individual, is especially relevant. In his emphasis on the social context of holiness, Balthasar has a lot to contribute in this regard.

It will have become clear by now that saintliness bears within itself the traces of various distortions brought about by postmodern analysis.[101] Often, contemporary works contest the traditional notion of sainthood, deconstruct the meaning of the term "saint," and claim that the saints' lives are to be found across a broad spectrum of belief systems and institutional practices, and do not just emanate from one specific religious community. For example, in the book *The Making of Saints: Contesting Sacred Ground*, the anthropologist James F. Hopgood uses the term "saint" to include folk saints, "near-saints," and icons or secular saints,[102] besides the "true" saints. All "saints" have one thing in common: Like the "true" saints, the former receive expressions of love, grief, and adoration, and the places significant to their lives become places for pilgrimages. According to Hopgood "[t]he difference . . . between an icon, secular saint, or church-canonized saint is not resolved."[103]

Although Michael P.Murphy has claimed that Balthasar "shares an affinity with the philosophical position of most postmodern theory,"[104] my opinion is that Balthasar's analysis of the saint differs radically from the conclusions reached by many modern and postmodern scholars. It is true that Balthasar's concept of the *communio sanctorum* as a "conversational community," and of tradition as a participation in an ongoing debate, is reminiscent of the multiplicity of voices (including that of the addressee) which characterize the postmodern narratives. However, the difference between Balthasar's and any postmodern reading of the saints is significant. My conviction is that Balthasar's work has potential to resolve certain issues, not least because he focuses on the grounding of the saints, rather than purely on the context which "canonizes" that saint, or the response of those who encounter the saint, whether that takes the form of love, adulation or the desire for pilgrimage.

The theologian David Moss acknowledges the crisis in the very concept of sanctity. His claim is that "the very idea of sanctity is being threatened

---

101. Dickinson, *The Postmodern Saints of France.*

102. The latter include people like Che Guevara, Elvis Presley, Evita Peron, and James Dean.

103. Hopgood, *The Making of Saints*, xvii.

104. Murphy, *A Theology of Criticism*, 57. Two central themes of postmodernism—its critique of modern rationality and its critique of modernist politics—are very evident in Balthasar.

today by psychology's 'hermeneutics of suspicion,' which would demolish the ideal of sanctity as a disguised psychopathology or as a play for power."[105] In his work, Moss has emphasized four things. Firstly, he has emphasized the central place of the saints and of the struggle for holiness in Balthasar's theology,[106] just as I did in the introduction to this work. Secondly, he has argued that the saint's life, which is the "*intelligibile in sensibili*,"[107] is the *form* through which the truth of Christian doctrine is grasped and becomes "followable."[108] Thirdly, Moss has emphasized that the effect of the saints is universal,[109] and, finally, he has insisted that the central task of the theologian is that of providing an exegesis of the saints' objective mission. These arguments are extremely relevant to our task. Furthermore, Moss identifies three dimensions of saintly existence—the theological, the christological, and the mariological—which, he says, are always "present and embedded" in Balthasar's treatment of the saints. He claims that these three dimensions reveal to the eyes of faith another three dimensions, namely, unity, obedience, and fruitfulness.[110] Finally, Moss mentions Balthasar's regard of the lives of the saints as the key to the understanding of the history of the gospel, and as "the prolongation of revelation."[111] In this book, I engage with various claims that Moss makes, and rework some of his conclusions to suit my own project. Among other things, I focus on different dimensions to those identified by Moss. The ones I develop here are the existential, the epistemological, and the ecclesiological, claiming, not only that these are the three dimensions where the saints function authoritatively, but also that this is where the grounding of the authority of the saints is to be situated.

In its tendency to deconstruct the concept of saints and sanctity, postmodernity has simultaneously been characterized by a more ecumenical, or even inter-faith interpretation of the saints. This is a key issue. To speak about the authority of the saints requires a clear understanding of who these saints are to whom this authority is to be attributed. Prompted by the Roman Catholic theologian Elizabeth Stuart's persistence that "canonization be extended to include Hindus and Protestants," Gavin D'Costa claims that one cannot call non-Catholics "saints in the technical liturgical sense." D'Costa claims that, despite what Rudolf Otto, William James, and John Hick have

105. Moss, "The Saints," 80.
106. Ibid.
107. Ibid., 85.
108. Ibid., 83.
109. Ibid., 81
110. Ibid., 86–91.
111. Ibid., 92.

said, saintliness and holiness are not properly speaking "trans-religious" or "cross-religious" concepts.[112] He does concede, however, that a person who is seen as a saintly example of holiness within his or her tradition may also be seen as a saint-*type* in another,[113] a notion that is similar to Matzko's "saints-by-analogy" concept.[114] It is in the intratextual way that we ought to understand Balthasar's notion of the saints and sainthood. Speaking from below, if any "saints"—including those from outside the Catholic community—are to be reckoned as holy, their holiness is to be compatible with that of the community, and if they are to be recognized as authoritative, the authority must originate from within the community and be regulated by it.

Štrukelj's book *Teologia e Santita' a Partire da Hans Urs von Balthasar*,[115] engages with many of the issues with which this book does. Štrukelj discusses Balthasar's designation of holy theologians as "pillars of the Church,"[116] the saints as a lived theology, holiness as the essence of theology, and the force present in the witness of the theology of the saints. Pope John Paul II had said that modern man listens more willingly to witnesses than to tachers, and if he does listen to teachers, it is because they are witnesses.[117] What Balthasar seems to have wanted to do was to explain why the witness given by the saints was of a different nature to that given by a non-saint. There is, in Štrukelj, a strong inclination to interpret Balthasar's claims concerning the holy life as itself theological, to associate, not unlike Balthasar, authentic theology with holiness, and to interpret the strong apologetic capacity of the saints as an authority. Unfortunately, like most others, Štrukelj only scratches the surface of such claims.

The role of the saints in Balthasar's theology has itself been the subject of some controversy. M.A.McIntosh has argued that Balthasar explores the participation of the saints and mystics in the life of Christ in order to understand Jesus' divine-human reality "from within."[118] His argument is that, when Balthasar delves into "what the saints experienced," "it is Christology that stands to gain most."[119] According to McIntosh, it is in his eagerness to learn "from the saints about Christ" that Balthasar fuses and reinterprets

112. D'Costa, "The Communion of Saints and Other Religions," 423.

113. Ibid., 424–25.

114. Matzko, "Postmodernism, Saints and Scoundrels," 22.

115. Štrukelj, *Teologia e Santita'*.

116. Balthasar, "The Gospel as Norm," 294.

117. See *Evangelii Nuntiandi*, 41. Quoting Pope Paul VI, Address to the Members of the *Consilium de Laicis*.

118. McIntosh, *Christology from within*, 21.

119. Ibid., 25. See also 2 and 26.

"the Maximian hypostatic structure with an Ignatian structure of mission and election."[120] Although I would agree with McIntosh's argument for the primacy of the Christological, I believe that this argument has a tendency of diminishing the importance of the *Mitspieler*, the secondary roles played by the saints in the entire drama, and in a way it may show that Balthasar is limited in his account. It would mean that Balthasar wanted the saints to interpret Christology when there is evidence that the opposite is also true, that is, that Balthasar wants Christ to interpret the saints. McIntosh could be interpreted as saying that the saints have a role of little significance, and therefore that their authority is inconsequential. We could perhaps interpret this in the light of the Pelagian controversy. In Pelagius, the doctrine of "*imago Dei*" is grounded in humanity striving for self-realization, and the human capacity for becoming God is fundamentally anthropocentric. In Augustine, the doctrine of "*imago Dei*" is grounded in God in Christ as our origin and goal, and the human capacity for becoming God is construed as fundamentally Christocentric.[121] My opinion is that Balthasar follows Augustine and Barth, but that he does not thereby ignore the anthropological. Had Balthasar's *only* aim been Jesus Christ, he would not have chosen to use the phenomenological method to study the saints, since, as a method, it is more properly suited to accommodate a discussion of the interpreter, than of the object to be interpreted. This is not to say that the importance of Christ is diminished. Balthasar sees the human "*deificatio*" as integral to his Christocentric picture. As Fergus Kerr points out, despite what Karl Barth says, "it is surely outrageous to claim that the figure of Christ is occluded in Balthasar's biographical studies of some saints."[122] Rather, even if this may not have involved a conscious decision on his part, the authority of the figure of Christ becomes more evident the more he attributes authority to the saints.

On a very different note, the issue of the recognition of sainthood by the institution is integral to my insistence on a theology of the authority of the saints. Even here, there are some pertinent publications. Perhaps best known in this regard is the work of Kenneth Woodward. His book on the making of saints deals specifically with the politics and bureaucracy of contemporary saint-making.[123] The accentuation on the politics of canonizations continues with the historian Janine Larmon Peterson, this time

120. Ibid., 42.

121. Robinson, *Understanding the "Imago Dei,"* 96.

122. Kerr, "Forward: Assessing this 'Giddy Synthesis,'" 9. Cf. Barth, *Church Dogmatics,* 4/1:767.

123. Woodward, *Making Saints.*

not the politics of the Magisterium, but the politics of the clergy and the laity at the grassroots. In her book *Contested Sanctity*, Peterson describes the process through which the disputed saint was created, and argues that, in disputed sainthood, a community's religious devotion towards disputed saints (individuals whom the populace venerated in the face of papal and inquisitorial opposition) was used as a means of challenging the papacy's authority and expressing desires for political and spiritual independence.[124] Since the authority of the saints is closely associated with both the official, and the popular recognition of an individual life, canonization takes on a particular importance. It would seem as if the canonization of the saints is irrelevant for Balthasar, since he uses various saints who never went through the canonization process. This means that in Balthasar, canonization is not the only thing that grounds the authority of the saint. What is it, then, that gives canonicity to the saints? In "The Gospel as Norm," Balthasar widens the concept of canonization, claiming that a "synthetic" individual whose "Yes" is indivisible "is a canonical Christian," that is, one whose speech and example is to be considered normative, irrespective of whether that Christian has been "canonized by the Church or not."[125] It would also seem as if Balthasar gives little importance to the ecclesial canonization *per se*. In his view, the saints who are worthy of esteem are those saints whom the Spirit himself canonizes, rather than those which the church does.

ADRIENNE VON SPEYR

How we interpret Adrienne von Speyr is integral to our understanding of the authority of the saints, because it will dictate who is included among the saints, as well as the criteria for deciding not just how reliable the theology of the saints is, but how reliable others consider it to be. Kilby suggests that whenever Balthasar does not indicate another source in the tradition, and whenever what he says cannot be accounted for elsewhere, then he may be relying on Adrienne.[126] Although I understand Kilby's concern, it would be risky to conclude that Adrienne is the source of all that may seem inexplicable in Balthasar. The exact relationship that existed between Balthasar and Adrienne has been hotly debated among scholars in the past decade. It should be said that this is not the first relationship where the spiritual director assumes the responsibility of publicising a visionary's experience. For instance, writing about the medieval mystic Mechtild of Magdeburg,

124. Peterson, *Contested Sanctity*.
125. Balthasar, "The Gospel as Norm," 292–93.
126. Kilby, *Balthasar*, 159.

Voaden writes that Heinrich of Halle, her spiritual director, had encouraged her writing, as well as arranged and edited her visions.[127] If Adrienne's authority was simply restricted to being a theological resource, Kilby would find no objection. She has herself pointed out, that "it is not unheard of for theologians in the Catholic tradition to look to the writings of the mystics as a theological source."[128] What Kilby has objected to is the *proximity to [the] theological source.*" Catholics do not usually have problems with *chronological* proximity. If they did, they would not be venerating and citing holy individuals before any official recognition has been announced. Our contemporaries Mother Theresa of Calcutta and Pope John Paul II are a case in point. If it is Adrienne's authoritative tone that Kilby objects to, then we would just have to respond that many now dead canonized saints wrote theology in an authoritative voice even during their own lifetimes, as Mongrain has said.[129] My question is, are we perhaps uncomfortable with a priest who confesses his debt to a woman? Or with a woman who inspires a priest? Or with an enigmatic woman inspiring a theologian? Are we objecting to the interference of a holder of office in a mystic's life? Do we object to the obedience on the part of the mystic to her confessor?[130] Whatever our opinion may be in this regard, if we were to apply the phenomenological descriptive approach which Balthasar himself applied to the saints, we would have to accept Adrienne's authority in Balthasar's regard, just as much as his authority in her regard.[131] Even so, the level of authority may need to be measured. Kilby claims that Balthasar does not "appeal to von Speyr's experience to ground the credibility of what he maintained," although he does sometimes rely on her visions and her writings.[132] These reflections by Kilby contribute to our own research question in that they reflect on the different levels of authority one could attribute to the saints, whether authority just denotes influence and inspiration or whether it denotes "justification." My claim is that Adrienne is integral to Balthasar's theological enterprise, and that there are instances when she goes beyond being a mere "influence and inspiration." Peter Henrici has even suggested that some of Balthasar's work on

127. Voaden, "All Girls Together," 83. See also Coakley, *Women, Men and Spiritual Power*, 1–15.

128. Kilby, *Balthasar*, 30.

129. Mongrain, *"Review Symposium,"* 99.

130. See Kilby's discussion of the expression "under obedience," which gives some hint as to Balthasar's involvement in von Speyr's experience. *Balthasar*, 29–30.

131. Beattie has argued that, in the confessional, Adrienne von Speyr is the *casta meretrix*, whereas Balthasar is in *loco Christi*, being sexually tempted. Beattie, "Sex, Death and Melodrama," 158.

132. Kilby, *Balthasar*, 9.

other saints or figures is not just tinged by Adrienne's visions and writings, but actually revolves around them. More specifically, Henrici claims that Balthasar's work on Thérèse of Lisieux, on Elizabeth of Dijon, on Reinhold Schneider (1903–1958), and on Georges Bernanos (1888–1948) actually revolve "around Adrienne's mission."[133]

Matthew Lewis Sutton has provided an overview of Balthasar's statements regarding the relationship between himself and Adrienne von Speyr, and of the three main interpretations of this relationship.[134] The first interpretation is represented by Edward Oakes and by Alyssa Lyra Pitstick. Their position is that Balthasar's work stands on its own and does not necessitate a joint examination with Adrienne's works. In this case, there is a respect and appreciation for Adrienne's works, but the scholarly engagement of her works is believed to be unnecessary for an understanding of Balthasar's theology.[135] A second group of interpreters, represented by Kevin Mongrain, deny that this relationship had any theological impact on Balthasar. Rather than a positive theological influence on Balthasar, Adrienne is seen as "a negative psychological presence that should be extricated from any theological reading of von Balthasar." Scholars like Kevin Mongrain and Alissa Pitstick argue that her influence on Balthasar was a negative one.[136] The third group, among whom Sutton situates himself, claim that Adrienne's relationship with Balthasar is essential to understanding him and deserves serious scholarly engagement. This group includes Raymond Gawronski, Aidan Nichols, Angelo Scola, Michelle Schumacher, Jacques Servais, Justin Matro, and Blaise Berg. These scholars place an emphasis on the changes that happen in Balthasar's theology after his first meeting with Adrienne. They also emphasize the co-founding of the *Johannesgemeinschaft*, Balthasar's setting up of the Johannes Verlag in Einsiedeln, and Balthasar's use of Adrienne's works in his own, especially her theology of the descent of Christ into the Hell.[137] Sutton offers his own interpretation of this relationship by using Paul's theology of charism, and particularly by expounding Balthasar's doctrine of the double charism. He claims that the outcomes of this double charism will be a reinterpretation of central aspects of Balthasar's theology which include his theology of Holy Saturday, trinitarian theology, and the theology of the communion of saints.

133. Henrici, "Hans Urs von Balthasar: A Sketch of His Life," 7–44. See also, Kilby, *Balthasar*, 32.

134. Sutton, "Hans Urs von Balthasar and Adrienne von Speyr's ecclesial relationship," 50–63.

135. Ibid., 56–57.

136. Ibid., 57–58.

137. Ibid., 58–59.

THE COMMUNION OF SAINTS

David Stagaman has identified a shift, evident since after the second world war, from hierarchy to dialogue, so that "the will of God is not communicated simply and directly to Church officials, but through a Spirit whose activity in the Church is . . . pluralistic."[138] The *communion* ecclesiology that has developed in the past decades focuses on dialogue, communication, and listening within the church. It is based on an appreciation on the part of the bishop for all that the Spirit is doing within the church. As it happens, ecclesiologies of communion are diverse, and they are embraced by all kinds of theologians: *ressourcement*, liberation, feminist, and so on, as Nicholas M.Healy's work has made clear. Jean-Marie Tillard, John Zizoulas, Leonardo Boff, and Elizabeth Schüssler Fiorenza, are only some of the theologians who have embraced some form of an ecclesiology of communion.[139]

In 1992 the CDF issued a "Letter to the Bishops of the Catholic Church on Some Aspects of the Church Understood as Communion." *Communionis Notio* espouses an ecclesiology of the church as the sacrament of salvation for humanity and asserts the priority of the authority of the universal church. For this reason, it has been criticized because its emphasis is on unity and the *immediate* . . . communion,[140] rather than on dialogue, communication, and listening, within the church. Thus, whereas *communio* ecclesiology is normally contrasted to a more universalist ecclesiology, the official *communio* ecclesiology puts more emphasis on the priority of the universal church. Richard Gaillardetz has compared the official *communio* ecclesiology to earlier institutional ecclesiologies, criticizing the former particularly because of the priority which it gives to the universal church over the local churches.[141]

In this context, Elizabeth A.Johnson's book, providing what she calls in her subtitle, *A Feminist Theological Reading of the Communion of Saints*,[142] is one of the rare books which deals directly with the communion of saints. Johnson's is an "inclusive companionship paradigm."[143] Guided by the metaphor of "friends of God and prophets," Johnson attempts to salvage this symbol, so that it may function "in a befriending and prophetic way." Her hope is that this symbol might nourish women, and nourish the church,

---

138. Stagaman, *Authority within the Church*, 4.

139. Mannion, *Ecclesiology and Postmodernity*, 70.

140. Ibid., 64.

141. Ibid., 68.

142. Johnson, *Friends of God and Prophets*.

143. Ibid., 2.

and consequently assist the church to really become a communion of saints and prophets.[144] Her exposition is very interesting and valid, her use of the *communio sanctorum* is laudable, but there is not much in her feminist reading that bears a resemblance to Balthasar's own theology of the *communio sanctorum* with its emphasis on dialogue, rather than memory.

Although J.-M. R. Tillard published his book *Eglise d'Églises* in 1987,[145] David McLoughlin claims that it was Cardinal Martini of Milan who first recommended to the church that it work through a theology of *koinonia/communio*. This was in 1999, during the European Synod.[146] Clearly, therefore, whatever Balthasar wrote about the *communio sanctorum* was written prior to any intimation of such an ecclesiology. I believe that Balthasar's *communio* ecclesiology is distinctive not only because it was developed before all other known communion ecclesiologies, but also for other reasons, namely, because it is based on the traditional doctrine of the *communio sanctorum*, because it provides a vision of the church as both *communio* and hierarchy,[147] because Balthasar manages to preserve the eschatological nature of the *communio sanctorum*, without dismissing the importance of the *communio sanctorum* for practical ecclesiology, and because the concept of *communio* enables Balthasar to stretch much further than the limits of the church. Balthasar's theology of the saints is based on a communion ecclesiology that is quite distinguishable from other such ecclesiologies, and any reference to the saints as an authority should take these features into consideration.

THE AUTHORITY OF INTERPRETATION

Needless to say, Balthasar's exegetical method has been the subject of some debate in more recent research. One of those who has written extensively on the issue of Balthasar's reading of the Scriptures is W.T.Dickens.[148] Among other things, Dickens evaluates Balthasar's views of scriptural authority in the church and the ways in which scripture functions authoritatively in his *Aesthetics*. Dickens acknowledges the criticisms against Balthasar's exegesis posited by Joseph Fitzmyer, John O'Donnell, Stephen Happel, and Louis Dupré. He then responds by arguing that, although Balthasar's approach in

144. Ibid., 3.

145. Tillard, *Church of Churches*.

146. McLoughlin, "Communio Models of Church," 181.

147. About the post-Vatican II rival ecclesiologies, see Lösel "Conciliar, Not Conciliatory," 23–24.

148. Dickens, *Hans Urs von Balthasar's Theological Aesthetics*.

the *Aesthetics* is informed by historical criticism, yet it is compatible with pre-modern approaches. He also argues that Balthasar's *Theological Aesthetics* are in fact a worthy model for Post-Critical Biblical Interpretation.[149] What Dickens says about Balthasar's vision of the church as the location for scriptural interpretation, about Balthasar's conviction that the proper purpose of scriptural interpretation is the development of lives conformed to Christ,[150] about Balthasar's "literal-figural" mode of interpretation and about the benefits that ensue from such a mode of interpretation,[151] are all useful arguments, leading to an appreciation of the saints' role in interpreting the scriptures, and of the authority with which the saints do that. For the most part, Balthasar recommends the saints and their teachings both because of their originality and because of their propensity for clarity.[152]

Also, of particular interest, is what Dickens says about Balthasar's accent (as also de Lubac's) on the multivocity of the bible as text,[153] a multivocity which Balthasar applies to the saints and to the principles which they represent. There is also, in Dickens, a reference to the pre-modern conviction that capturing Jesus Christ through static definitions is impossible. Balthasar would have agreed that the life-form, is more efficacious than propositions. According to Balthasar, "the very effort to put as much as possible into thoughts and formulations can imperceptibly lead us away from the source of prayer."[154] Finally, there is Balthasar's insistence on biblical interpretation as a continuing task for the church. On this issue, I will want to emphasize the authority of the eyewitness and the eligibility of subsequent saints to interpret the Scriptures. As Howsare has said, Balthasar "has shown that theology can proceed according to a strong revelocentric stance without thereby placing a straitjacket on theological development."[155]

Dickens uses Roger Aubert, Robert Murray S.J., and Sandra Schneiders to argue that "among Catholics the Bible simply no longer functions in the lives of the faithful as it once did to provide the interpretive lenses through which they view and understand reality."[156] Dickens is claiming that the postliberal approach is weakening. What Dickens has failed to note

---

149. Ibid., 1–3

150. Ibid., 237.

151. Ibid., 6. See also 237.

152. Ibid., 65. Dickens notes that it was Paul himself who asserted that the *beati* were granted a clearer vision.

153. Ibid., 7, 10.

154. Balthasar, *Prayer*, 256–57.

155. Howsare, *Hans Urs von Balthasar and Protestantism*, 163.

156. Dickens, *Hans Urs von Balthasar's Theological Aesthetics*, 19.

is that Balthasar views *the saints* as a corrective, that is, as a means whereby "to revive both biblical literacy and a biblically informed imagination,"[157] and consequently, cultivate the *sensus fidelium*. In the meantime, what Dickens has said about the advantages of the "literal-figurative readings" of the Bible is easily discernible in Balthasar's work. Such readings are said to enable "fruitful dialogue among theologians," assist agreement over "what is essential to Christian proclamation and action," and nurture the *sensus fidelium*,[158] since ecclesiastical leaders, ordinary Christians as well as professional theologians and exegetes would share a sense of what lies at the heart of the Gospel.[159]

I have my doubts as to whether anybody would deny the authority of the saints on the practical level, that is, whether anyone can deny either the authority which is evident in the actions, deeds, exploits and writings of the saints or the authority which is attributed by others to their actions, deeds, exploits and writings. For example, if one were to read Werner Löser's essay on "The Ignatian Exercises in the Work of Hans Urs von Balthasar," one would realize what an essential role Ignatius plays in Balthasar's theology. Löser gives a number of examples, one of these being the original version of *The Christian State of Life*, written in 1945, which Löser claims was meant to focus on the theology of the *Exercises*.[160] Other examples include: what Balthasar says about the three forms of abandonment, the thinking with the church, the two modes of faith (represented by Martin Luther—by grace we are saved—and Ignatius—good works are means for salvation),[161] the discernment of the Spirits, the image of humanity before God, and the emphasis on indifference. As Löser says, "[n]ot only did Balthasar frequently take up texts and motifs of the Ignatian Exercises to interpret them in terms of larger theological contexts; he shaped his own theological conception out of the spirit of the Exercises."[162]

AUTHORITY WITHIN THE CHURCH

Kenneth Wilson has said that the question "what is to be taught and believed and on whose authority?" is "both profoundly stimulating and difficult."[163]

---

157. Ibid.

158. Ibid., 20.

159. Ibid.

160. Löser, "The Ignatian Exercises," 106.

161. Balthasar, "Two Modes of Faith," 85–102.

162. Löser, "The Ignatian Exercises in the Work of Hans Urs von Balthasar," 119.

163. Mannion, *Readings in Church Authority*, 91.

Even deeper than this question are four more fundamental questions, namely, the nature of authority, the grounds upon which authority is established, the manner in which such authority comes to be attributed, and the way in which such authority is upheld. Clearly, neither faith nor knowledge are possible without authority. And yet the criteria for the acquisition of authority or the assigning of authority are not easy to outline. Gerard Mannion asserts that "something can be authoritative because general agreement and support is reached concerning its truth, validity, or desirability" but also because it represents what is "true," "good" and so on.[164] This book is meant to serve as evidence that the authoritativeness of the saints, of their life, their actions and words (including the texts attributed to them), is not a straightforward matter, and yet that it underlies much of what Balthasar wrote not just about the saints, but about most things. Austin maintains that "neither documents nor dead persons nor bureaucratic institutions nor even reason can be, in the true sense, an authority." He says that "[w]ithout the living authority of a scholar actively engaged in the work that scholars do, which includes the study of "authoritative" texts, authority is at best latent or potential; it is not actual authority."[165] I tend to disagree with Austin, and I tend to believe that Balthasar would do so too. If Austin were right, we would only be able to claim the authority of a *living* saint, and a dead saint's authority would depend purely on the scholar who revived him or her. However, authority could also lie in a saint long-departed, irrespective of whether we appeal to his wisdom or not. This is because authority is not just something we attribute to someone, but also something that is aroused in others by the authoritative figure, whether we respond to it or not. Moreover, to use a phrase borrowed from Alisdair MacIntyre, it also lies in "privileged texts," that "function as the authoritative point of departure" for inquiry.[166] The reason why Balthasar can maintain the authority of a saint who has passed on is precisely because of his model of theology as a "collaborative enterprise" and his image of the church as a "colloquium" or "conversational community." In Balthasar, the saints (what I have been calling the *Communio Sanctorum*, with capital letters) are very much alive in the *communio sanctorum*, and they remain an authority even when they are long deceased, even when they are still unknown![167] On his part, Stagaman

164. Mannion, *Readings in Church Authority*, 4.

165. Austin, *Up with Authority*, 37.

166. Healy, *Church, World and the Christian Life*, 117. Referring to MacIntyre, *Whose Justice? Which Rationality?*, 383.

167. In *Up with Authority*, Austen uses Yves Simon, Michael Polanyi, Oliver O'Donovan, and Richard Hooker to discuss social, epistemic authority and political and ecclesial authority.

maintains that authority is not an attribute of a person. It is not a subjective reality. Neither is it the attribute of a thing, i.e., an objective reality.[168] Authority is rather "the bond experienced by all members of a community as they interact in certain relationships."[169] And it is a practice.[170] Among other things, Stagaman claims that we are to understand the authoritative as "that set of norms and values the community holds or desires to hold," and to understand authority as a quality of human interaction which is "grounded in the authoritative."[171] It seems to me that Stagaman plays with the words "authority" and "authoritative." The authoritative is seen as "the standard by which authority is evaluated." Perhaps this is the chicken and the egg problem. What is it that comes first: authority or the authoritative? I believe that the relationship between biblical tradition and the Scriptures can help us understand the issue. Tradition came before the Scriptures, but it also endures to maintain it. Authority would have come before the "authoritative" and is always required to support the "authoritative." Stagaman also contrasts authority with authoritarianism, insisting that only the former is legitimate, and he maintains that there are three distinctive features of Christian and Roman Catholic authority, these being its mystical character, its eschatological character and its sacramental character.[172] In his statements Stagaman seems to make deductions about authority without sufficiently clarifying what the authoritative is. My tendency in is to invert this process. In my view, thoughts, words and actions become authoritative because they arise from a recognized authority, or rather, the process would have started with authority first.

One of the more relevant distinctions which Stagaman makes is that between authority as understood synchronically—in which case the tension or the balance may be between equals or between unequals living at one time—and authority understood diachronically. Here, the tension or balance is between equals or unequals living in different times. This distinction is important, since the authority of the saints as explored in this book is meant to refer to both its synchronic and diachronic aspects. As Stagaman says, "[w]hen authority is analyzed diachronically, it is found embedded in traditions which bear the past into the present, but also critically assess that

---

168. Stagaman, *Authority within the Church*, xv.

169. Ibid., xiv.

170. Ibid., xv.

171. Ibid., xv and 31. Stagaman's comparison of authority to freedom, and of the authoritative to the character of an individual person is quite helpful.

172. Ibid., 122–23.

heritage in light of the demands that the future makes on the community."[173] The temptation is to state that, with Balthasar, the saints only have diachronic authority. But this would be too simplistic a statement, and would not be able to embrace the contemporary saint or saints.

Where church authority is concerned, Francis A.Sullivan's work on authority and the Magisterium is still paradigmatic. In the 1980s, Sullivan was writing about the nature, function, and limits of the teaching authority of the church, as well as on the relationship between the Magisterium and Catholic theologians. Using Aquinas's distinction between the *magisterium cathedrae pastoralis* and the *magisterium cathedrae magistralis*, Sullivan suggested that theologians should share in the pastoral magisterium of the bishops, along with catechists, teachers of religion in schools and those involved in the formation of the seminarians.[174] It seems to me that Balthasar would attribute to the saints both roles: the *magistralis* and the *pastoralis*, not necessarily everywhere and not all the time, but certainly in some places, in particular circumstances, and at certain moments in history.

CONCLUSION

My intention for this chapter has been to situate my research topic within the wider context, identifying some of the more important work that has been done on Balthasar, holiness, the saints, and on ecclesial authority. The questions concerning the authority of the saints are yet to be tackled, namely, whether, even among the saints, it is possible to conceive and to concede different levels of sanctity, on a kind of continuum of holiness, whether authority correlates positively with the degree of holiness,[175] whether it is a question of the saints already having more authority than the non-saints, or a question of what they ought to be assigned, and whether a saint who is considered authoritative ought to be considered authoritative on material as well as spiritual issues.

Having established Balthasar's confidence in the extraordinary proficiency and "authoritativeness" of at least some saints (including Adrienne), and Balthasar's association of authority with holiness, the next thing is to determine the different dimensions in which holiness—which we associate with the saints—acquires an authority for theology and for the church. These dimensions also correspond to the different settings in which the

173. Ibid., xv.

174. Sullivan, *Magisterium*, 204.

175. Deane-Drummond has described this idea of hierarchy "in degrees of glorification" as "rather troubling." See "The Breadth of Glory," 54.

saints function authoritatively. The three dimensions which I came up with, after some consultation, were the existential, the epistemological, and the ecclesiological. I want to focus on two questions in particular: firstly, what do I mean when I claim that Balthasar associates authority with holiness? And secondly, what is the ground of the authority of the saints? This is not the same as asking "what make a saint holy?". It is rather a question of asking about what it is about holiness that makes the individual so authoritative, so influential. I will be seeking to determine—and I will attempt this in each of the next chapters—where the saints' authority is grounded, that is, what it is that Balthasar attributes their authority to in each of these dimensions, and what are some of the arguments which Balthasar brings forward to substantiate his claim that the saints have existential, epistemological, and ecclesiological authority precisely because they are saints. My hope is that some of what I state here would serve as the groundwork for further reflection on the issue.

CHAPTER 3

The Existential Dimension

INTRODUCTION

CONSISTENT WITH THE TRADITIONAL belief in the existence of the saints as a motive of credibility,[1] Balthasar argues that that which expresses "with plausibility for the world the truth of Christ's Gospel . . . is the existence of the saints who have been grasped by Christ's Holy Spirit."[2] There is nothing extraordinary in this claim, except that sometimes Balthasar seems to reduce the *motiva credibilitatis* to just this one: the authentic Christian life. The "perfect proof of the truth of Christianity" is to be found in the "perfect" Christian.[3] It is the Christian who embodies for the world the evidence of the "rightness (*Richtigkeit*) of Christ's truth."[4] In Balthasar, the other *motiva credibilitatis*: the miracles of Christ, the prophecies, and even the church's own growth and holiness, and the church's fruitfulness and stability,[5] seem to take second place in comparison with the emphasis on the individual Christian.

In this chapter, I will want to interpret what I think Balthasar means when he says that the saints are the "most sublime figures of human

---

1. Balthasar, "Does Jesus Shine Through?," 18.
2. Balthasar, *Seeing the Form (TA1)*, 494.
3. Ibid., 229.
4. Ibid., 214.
5. *Catechism of the Catholic Church*, par. 156.

existence,"[6] and I would like to demonstrate that, in Balthasar's theology, the saints have existential authority precisely because they are these "sublime figures of human existence." I would also like to determine what it is about a life of holiness, which, according to Balthasar, makes the saints so authoritative (that is, arouses authoritativeness in them, or drives others to attribute authority to them), in the existential domain. I would also like to show that it is from within their genuine human existence that the saints function authoritatively. Finally, I would like to establish that the authority which Balthasar attributes to the saints, in the existential domain, is analogous to that attributed to the Magisterium for two reasons: firstly, because the saints are presented as those individuals whom one consults on existential issues, and, secondly, because the saints are those individuals whose existential stance one would want to emulate. This is precisely the kind of authority which the Magisterium demands and which the individual Christian is expected to attribute to it, that is, that it be consulted, and that it be emulated.

EXISTENCE AS THEOLOGICAL

The connection which Balthasar establishes between theology and existence, between Christian thought and life,[7] is central to my argument. Like the *nouveaux théologiens,* Balthasar believes that "theology had the duty to connect with the experiences of people's actual day-to-day lives,"[8] and that dogmatics should never be "far removed from life."[9] Balthasar is not just saying that theology should use the experience of existence as one of its sources, nor is he merely suggesting a method of correlation.[10] Balthasar is not just saying that we need to attend to existence in order to make theology *relevant.*[11] I interpret Balthasar as saying that it is attention to existence that makes theology *possible,*[12] and it is attention to existence that validates the

6. Balthasar, *Seeing the Form (TA1),* 28–29.

7. Balthasar, *Convergences,* 15.

8. Boersma, *Nouvelle Théologie,* 4.

9. Balthasar, *Convergences,* 68.

10. The method of correlation, which is generally associated with Paul Tillich, correlates insights from Christian revelation with the issues raised by existential, psychological, and philosophical analysis.

11. Whereas for Heidegger, truth lies hidden beyond particular things, for Balthasar, the mystery of being is revealed, that is, made immediately apparent, in and through the encounter of particular beings. See Schindler *Hans Urs von Balthasar and the Dramatic Structure of Truth,* 6.

12. As Scola states in his essay "Christian Experience and Theology," "[t]he priority of experience over theology is ontological." Balthasar is saying that the reflection on existence is already theology.

truth or falsity of theology.[13] There is some similarity here with Bonaventure's theology of holiness. Bonaventure believed that spiritual transformation is achieved when theological study is subordinated to and integrated into the spiritual life. On his part, Balthasar is saying that the existence of the saints both generates and adjudicates theology (to use a legal term), that is, the existence of the saints provides us with a measure. It stipulates which theology is authentic, and therefore, which theology is worth keeping and which is not. It is a question of validity rather than relevance. Within the context of George Lindbeck's Postliberal analysis, the saints would be "those who have effectively interiorized [the] religion." For this reason, it is they who are best able to judge "which of the changing forms is faithful to the putatively abiding substance."[14] According to Balthasar, this judgment of theology by the saints is possible "[e]ven when the saints have not been theologians, nor themselves very learned."[15] And they may "radiate the most tremendous theological truths," even if they are not "aware of their sanctity."[16]

The saints seek to existentialize dogma.[17] What Balthasar says about Thérèse and Paul is very helpful in this regard. Balthasar claims that Thérèse sees her life as a realization of her doctrine, and even proposes her life as an example for the church.[18] Paul also demonstrates "the nature of Christian sanctity by pointing to himself." Using Paul, Balthasar argues that, in a "faith lived in one's existence," one finds the "proof" of dogma, the "coherence" of dogmas, the "objective intelligibility" of dogma and the "subjective comprehensibility" of dogma.[19] What I think Balthasar is doing is transferring—and attempting to correct—the dualism of Tyrrell's theology of revelation (dogma, or scholastic rationalism vs. the lived experience of the saints), into the realm of theology in general.[20] Tyrrell was certain that the true teachers and theologians in the church are the saints. According to Tyrrell, theology sometimes contradicts the facts of the spiritual life, and, when it does this, it loses its reality and its authority. For Balthasar, the saints are the *loci* where dogma complements existence. Not only is life seen as the realization of

13. Balthasar, *A Theology of History*, 26. Balthasar considers the term existential theology as a "tautology."

14. Lindbeck, *The Nature of Doctrine*, 79

15. Balthasar, *Two Sisters,* 25.

16. Ibid., 60–61. See also Balthasar, *Seeing the Form (TA1),* 229.

17. Balthasar claims that one of Adrienne's aspired goals was "the existentialization of dogma." Balthasar, *First Glance,* 68.

18. Balthasar, *Two Sisters,* 30.

19. Balthasar, *Seeing the Form (TA1),* 229.

20. Loome, "Revelation as Experience," 117–49.

doctrine, but doctrine is seen as the realization of life. It is in this context that Balthasar's concept of a "theological existence" is to be understood. Thérèse and Elizabeth are among those who "devote their lives entirely to the reality of faith to live 'theological existences.'"[21] Balthasar wants to show that any authority which the existence of the saints gains is a direct consequence of it being intrinsically theological: their existence generates theology, serves as a measure against which to appraise theology, and existentializes the dogma generated by theology.

It is because Balthasar wants to explore how it is that the saints have such a huge bearing upon the task of theology, that he conceives of a phenomenological approach to hagiography. He claims that what he wants to do through this innovative method (because it had not been used in hagiography before) is to understand the "movement from the biographic and the personal to the dogmatic."[22] He wants to understand what is entailed in the process of "dogma developing out of experience."[23] He wants to comprehend how doctrinal comprehension and articulation follow from one's encounter with God in real life. To do this, he finds no better way than that of observation and description, hoping that the phenomenological method will enable him to capture, and to portray to others, the movement from existence to dogma, which, according to him, is not extrinsic; at least with the saints it is not. With the saints, theology is not something extrinsic to existence. They are theological beings, and theological thought follows, ensues, so to speak, automatically, from life.

Balthasar would have been aware that the term "theological existence" cannot be understood in a univocal sense when applied to different individuals. I am sure that he would have been willing to grant that there are different intensities, so to speak. There is a difference in the *quality* and the *quantity* of holiness which is, in turn, reflected in the *quality* and the *quantity* of the theology that materializes from such existents and vice versa. What is certain is that Balthasar is willing to grant that there is always a correlation between the saintly existence, and the theology that emerges from it. What he says is that: more theology, a better theology, a more authentic one, emerges from a life that is more holy, that is, more in correspondence with Christ, than from a life that is less holy, and less in correspondence with Christ. In his sight, the more beautiful, good and

21. Balthasar, *Two Sisters*, 11, 300. Balthasar provides a concept of a lived life as being a "theological existence," contrasting it with "existential theology," which he defines as a theology based on experience.

22. Balthasar, *Two Sisters*, 31.

23. Balthasar recognizes that modern hagiography has focused too strongly on the historical and the psychological point of view. Balthasar, *Seeing the Form (TA1)*, 231.

true that existent is, the more beautiful, good and true is the theology that arises from that existence, sometimes even when no speech is involved. According to Balthasar, strictly speaking, only the theology produced by the saints deserves the proper title of "theology," since, according to him, authentic theology is constituted primarily by a holy existence, and only in the case of the saints does existence truly constitute theology. Naturally, this is a deduction that others make in the saints' regard, not one which the saints would presume for themselves. According to Balthasar, ecclesial recognition is ultimately more reliable than any claim made by the pneumatic person him or herself.[24] The theology which saints produce is—sometimes quite inexplicably, in human terms—esteemed by others, in the sense that others recognize its worth. Thus, others within their community will apprehend that the theology which the saints supply, is more beautiful, good and true than that of others, whose existence lacks holiness. Speaking from below, the endurance over time of that theology is guaranteed. Speaking from above (as Balthasar often does), the Spirit espouses such theology and warrants its survival. Writing of Maximus, Balthasar says that as "a humble monk, he seems almost deliberately to have avoided or concealed any claim to authority in the intellectual realm—there is never the slightest gesture of pretension."[25] And yet, Balthasar emphasizes, over and over again, the authority of Maximus on the theology of both East and West.[26] For both Erigena and Cyparissiotes, Maximus was an essential, indeed sometimes, the unique authority for interpreting the often obscure passages of Dionysius, particularly "in questions important to mystical theology—the nature of God, attributes of the Divine, and even the procession of the Holy Spirit."[27] He is "the most daring systematician of his time." He is "an incontestable pillar of the Church." His is an authority that comes from the fact that he was a good theologian, but also from the fact that he was a monk, a spiritual advisor, a writer, and above all, a saint and a martyr.[28] Maximus was also "Catholic"—although he belonged to an ecumenical tradition when East and West were still undivided—which also contributed to his authority.[29] Does Maximus's authority then originate from his lack of pretention, his daring, his aptitudes, his religious connections, his martyrdom, his ecu-

24. Balthasar, "Obedience in the Light of the Gospel," 252.

25. Balthasar, *Cosmic Liturgy*, 30.

26. Sherwood, "Survey of Recent Work on St Maximus the Confessor," 431.

27. Geanakoplos, "Some Aspects of the Influence of the Byzantine Maximos the Confessor on the Theology of East and West," 159–60.

28. Balthasar, *Cosmic Liturgy*, 29.

29. Sherwood, "Survey of Recent Work on St Maximus the Confessor," 433.

menical relation? Or does his holiness bring this authority about, that is, is his authority specifically grounded in his holiness?

In Balthasar's theology, while the theological transparency clearly belongs to all the saints, there are some saints whose mission is more specifically doctrinal. Writing about the "content" of the "great missions," Balthasar says that it "has been something primarily objective: some task, some foundation, the formulation of a doctrine or the objective exposition of certain aspects of revelation."[30] He quotes M.M.Philipon to state that, "with some saints, not with all, the mission is not only that of a holy life but also of a doctrine, as with John of the Cross (1542–1591), Francis de Sales (1567–1622) and many of the founders of Orders."[31] According to Balthasar, Thérèse of Lisieux also had an explicitly doctrinal mission.[32] Balthasar claims that her "little way" can be regarded as "the Catholic answer to the demands and questions raised by Luther."[33]

For Balthasar, to be holy is to surrender to the Father's will, but, in conjunction with this—so to speak, concurrently—to be holy is to think, or even to speak, correctly about God. Thus, in Balthasar, the light which the saints shed on various doctrinal matters to do with human existence—the "doctrine of man," the "transcendental locus of human freedom," the suffering of God[34] and others—has value by the very fact that the light is shed by men and women who freely surrendered themselves, and thus became soil for a proper theological existence. The theology which arises from theological existences is, so to speak, truly existential, in at least three senses. First of all, it arises from their existence. Secondly, it is corroborated by their existence. And thirdly, it is, so to speak, effortless. For Balthasar, the saints are "dogmatic" from the outset.[35] They can express theology just by being who they are, and their actions (drama), their thoughts and their words (logic) become valid for others just because these actions, thoughts and words belong to, and arise from a saintly existence. The "sheer existence [of the saints] proves to be a theological manifestation."[36] Naturally, problems will arise when one reflects on so called "heretics" who are considered, at one and the same time, holy, such as Savonarola, Wesley, and Kierkegaard.

30. Balthasar, *Two Sisters,* 9.

31. Ibid., 37.

32. Ibid., 233 and 413.

33. Ibid., 95–96.

34. Balthasar, *The Realm of Metaphysics in the Modern Age (TA5),* 50.

35. Balthasar, *Seeing the Form (TA1),* 231. Balthasar goes on to say that for such an experience, dialogue is necessary: "[T]he Spirit speaks to us in our interior."

36. Balthasar, *Two Sisters,* 25.

One would have to explain how and why it is possible to have a theology which is judged as heretical and incorrect, while arising from such theological existences.

What Balthasar says in this regards becomes almost predictable when set within the wider context of the theology of the late nineteenth and mid-twentieth centuries. In his book *Action*, Maurice Blondel had emphasized the significance of lived human lives rather than of rational apologetics, and he had given an account of faith that was related to the whole realm of human experience.[37] In the 1930s, Yves Congar identifies a "hiatus between faith and life" in his essay *"Une conclusion theologiques à l'enquête sur les raisons actuelles de l'incroyance."*[38] A decade later, Jean Daniélou publishes his *"Les Orientations présentes de la pensée religieuse,"* in which Daniélou writes about the "rupture between theology and life,"[39] a rupture which he attributes to the "strictly extrinsic character of the supernatural in neo-Thomism."[40] Also, around this time, Romano Guardini (1885–1968) and Karl Adam (1876–1966) developed "a distinctive style of theological thought" more generally known as "a theology of life."[41] Whereas in the extrinsicist model, represented by the neo-scholastics, the object of faith remains external to the believer—it is simply "something to be assented to on the divine authority that is vouchsafed to the Catholic Church"[42]—with Balthasar we have an attempt at internalizing the object of faith, without falling into immanentism.

Balthasar seems to be saying something similar to what Thomas Aquinas did, namely that body and speech work together: "the body demands language," and that, alternatively, language demands the body to speak the truth.[43] But Balthasar is saying more than that. Not only is he saying that the two (body and language) *need* each other. He is also saying that the two, body and language, *corroborate* each other, that is, that body (aesthetics) and language (logic) do not contradict each other,[44] but rather validate each other. Orthopraxy and orthodoxy authenticate each other. In Balthasar, "to begin with orthopraxy without first opening [one]self to the sight of the

37. Blondel, *Action* (1893). See Boersma, *Nouvelle Théologie*, 31.

38. Boersma, *Nouvelle Théologie*, 23.

39. Ibid., 2.

40. Ibid., 4.

41. Cf. McClendon, *Biography as Theology*, 155.

42. Dickens, *Hans Urs von Balthasar's Theological Aesthetics*, 35.

43. Rogers, "Bodies Demand Language," 181.

44. Casarella has put it very succinctly: "[J]ust as the Christian expression of the truth is measured by its correspondence to Christ," so "[e]ach word spoken is measured by the testimony of a life." See Casarella, "The Expression and Form of the Word," 56.

truth, [one's] praxis could never be right (*orthos*) in God's sense."[45] Likewise, an orthodoxy that is not upheld by a life of holiness could never be right. Balthasar does not just say that a holy existence improves the quality of one's theology, but that it is only the actual living of a holy life which gives rise to correct speech about God.

Ultimately, according to Balthasar, this ability to produce correct speech about God would be one of the factors that makes the saints authoritative and influential in the existential domain. It is the ability to theologize that comes as a direct consequence—or rather as a complement—of a life lived in holiness. Balthasar writes that "the best authority for [a] statement of *theoria*" is the one who both sees (*theoria*) the witness of the Spirit for Christ, and walks (*praxis*) with Jesus.[46] Balthasar is able to say this because, for him, theology, or speech about God, is part and parcel of praxis. It "involves man's entire bodily constitution and has man's 'total existence' for its content."[47] Balthasar maintains that

> It is immaterial whether the Gospel is preached by word or by example, for the two are inseparable; the testimony to Jesus is always a testimony of both word and works . . . the testimony of the word has no value without works, while the testimony of one's life can speak louder that the testimony of words.[48]

We have here an actualistic ontology which is very similar to Karl Barth's. Both conceive God and man as beings-in-action. The conception of ethical agency is based on a unity between being, knowing, doing and achieving.

The first question that arises is: what difference is there between the nature of a holy existent (a saint) and that of someone whose existence is not holy? In answer to this, we could say that the difference, with Balthasar, is that the saints exist more. They exist more because they are more of what they should be. Their beauty, truth, and goodness—even in the eyes of others—lies primarily in their unspoilt humanity, that is, in the stance taken by them as finite creatures, vis-à-vis God and vis-à-vis the world. There is something about the being of the saints that goes further than others, that is more accepting of their creaturely finitude. This is why Balthasar chooses to

45. Balthasar, *The Spirit of Truth (TL3)*, 191.

46. Ibid., 192.

47. Ibid., 361. For Balthasar, discourse is ontological. It is rooted in the physical.

48. Balthasar, *The Christian State of Life*, 341. Balthasar's focus on word and life has huge significance. The apostolic constitution *Dei Filius* emphasizes the neo-Thomist belief in "miracles and prophesies" as being "the most certain signs of revelation." *Dei Filius* 2.1 (DS 3009).

THE EXISTENTIAL DIMENSION 93

explore the metaphysics of "saints," and not the metaphysics of non-saints—even if most of the saints he chooses are not canonized, or mainstream saints.[49] The saints' own existence (even without the speech) can tell us more about metaphysics than the non-saints can (even if they may attempt to speak). The saints are the ones who come closest to an amalgamation of existence and essence, of their being human and their mission. In addition, this quality in the saints is perceptible, so that others can often tell that these holy individuals have become what they were meant to become.

Clearly, for Balthasar, to be a Christian is not simply to have as "ultimate goal the civilizing and humanizing of the world," as it is with theologians involved with politics. The French philosophers Maurice Blondel (1861–1949), Emmanuel Mounier (1905–1950) and Pierre Teilhard de Chardin (1881–1955) would all agree with Balthasar that the task of the Christian is not political involvement.[50] According to Balthasar, the task of the Christian is more specifically existential—and this is the Pauline and the Johannine view—to be with Christ, to be like Christ and to live for Christ. In order to describe the nature of the saint, Balthasar uses the philosophical category of *Entsprechung* (correspondence), which is found in the Neoplatonic-Areopagite and in the Thomistic tradition[51]. Correspondence does not mean identification. On the contrary, Balthasar claims that "[t]he authentic saint is always the one who confuses himself the least with Christ."[52] Correspondence means taking up Christ's form. According to Balthasar, existence *can* take up the *forma Christi*,[53] and *ought to* take up this *forma Christi*.[54] More importantly, existence becomes comprehensible only "as a function of [this] Christ-form."[55] Thus Balthasar joins the Gospels and the Pauline corpus to argue that "Christian sanctity is 'Christ-bearing,' 'Christophorous' in essence and actualisation."[56] In the existential domain, an existent can become authoritative, and can function authoritatively, when his or her "Christophorous" form becomes visible to others. According to Balthasar, there are at least three existential stances which would

49. We should remember that Balthasar's is, as Schindler describes it, a "metaphysics with a theological point of departure." Schindler, "Hans Urs Balthasar, Metaphysics, and the Problem of Onto-Theology," 103–4.

50. Balthasar, *Engagement with God*, 69.

51. Babini, "Jesus Christ: Form and Norm of Man," 222–23 and 227.

52. Balthasar, *Seeing the Form (TA1)*, 215.

53. Ibid., 464. See also Balthasar, *The Christian State of Life*, 212.

54. Balthasar, "Experience God?," 29. See also Balthasar, *The Christian State of Life*, 67; and Balthasar, *Cosmic Liturgy*, 125.

55. Balthasar, *Seeing the Form (TA1)*, 515. See also 28.

56. Ibid., 562.

explain why some individuals function more authoritatively. Firstly, there is the access to the original form that is Christ. Here it is the saint reflecting the Christ form. Secondly, there is the access which the individual Christian has to his own image as it is contained in Christ. Here it is the saint reflecting on the "ideal" form of him or herself which is in Christ. Thirdly, there is the assumption by the Christian of the form of Christ.[57] And, finally, there is the assumption by the Christian of the image of him or herself which is contained in Christ. The authority ensues from the fact that something of the mystery of Christ is made visible in concrete form to the world through each Christian who con-forms to the form which Christ gives to his or her existence.[58] Balthasar thus speaks the language of Plato, claiming that there exists a faultless ideal for every man and every woman. Unlike a typical neo-Platonic idealist, Balthasar would acknowledge that this ideal form is always to be found in Christ, that it is possible for individuals to draw quite close to that form (which is in Christ), and even that it is possible to embody such a form.

THE CREATED VS. THE UNCREATED ORDER

Clearly, Balthasar's hagiography is inspired by his "meta-anthropology" which focuses on the being (the existence) and the essence of man (what essentially defines him). As opposed to John Scottus Eriugena, Balthasar emphasizes the ontological distinction between God and creation.[59] "[D]ialectically: the stronger the union between God and man becomes, which the Word of God effects, the more clearly we see the difference between them."[60]

In Balthasar's work, the real saints would be more aware than anybody else, of the difference between God and themselves.[61] Whereas medieval hagiography would have emphasized the supernatural qualities of the saints, and approximated the saint toward the divine, Balthasar emphasizes the disparity, even if—as with any analogy—he also acknowledges the likeness. In Balthasar, likeness to God and differentiation from Him co-exist in the

57. Williams defines "authoritative" as "transparent to its origin." Williams, "Theological Integrity," 15.

58. Howsare, *Balthasar: A Guide for the Perplexed*, 130, 136. Unlike Barth, whose Christocentrism tends to reduce all activity to the activity of Christ, Balthasar also emphasizes the secondary roles.

59. Nichols, "Balthasar's Aims," 121.

60. Balthasar, *The Theology of Karl Barth*, 292.

61. Balthasar, *First Glance*, 138. Writing about this difference, Adrienne says that "somewhere there is an elementary non-correspondence."

saints more than in anyone else. More than anybody, the saint would be that creature who "accepts [his or her creaturely] state of image and likeness and renders to God the reverence and service that are his due from one who is at a remove from him."[62] Saints would know that they are finite creatures, rooted in humanity.[63] And they would live in a way that shows it. Balthasar totally rejects the pantheism associated with Eriugena and with Hegel.[64] In Balthasar, this *maior dissimilitudo* between God and creature is even grounded in the dissimilarity within God himself, who could even abandon himself.[65] David L.Schindler has described how liberalism "entails a superficial ('*super-facies*') existence," and how the picture portrayed by Nietzsche—that of *forcing* the infinite within the finite—is very different to that portrayed by Balthasar, which is one of "*the breaking open* of the infinite within the finite." I would agree with Schindler that it is Balthasar's stance—and not Nietzsche's—that "enables the human-earthly to achieve . . . genuine depth or profundity: that is, truly to go beyond the surface boundaries that constitute its reality as finite."[66] The saints' authority arises from this bursting of the infinite within the finite, and from the recognition by others of this actuality.

A second point concerns the "*potentia oboedientialis.*" Whereas Karl Rahner emphasizes the "*potentia oboedientialis*" (our openness to God, our desire for the beatific vision), and the "supernatural existential" (that is, the gift of the capacity to accept grace), Balthasar focuses on the nature of this *potentia* (and, in a sense, corrects Aquinas), emphasizing that "the transnatural powerfulness denoted in the word '*potentia*' in the phrase '*potentia oboedientialis*' is not in the least a powerfulness of the creature." He claims that, if this were the case, it would be a form of the *potentia naturalis*, when, in fact, this is a case of the "powerfulness of the Creator." At the same time, Balthasar insists that the *potentia oboedientialis* presupposes the *potentia naturalis*—since the created intellectual being must exist in order that God can display his grace in it—but it is not the same as the *potentia naturalis*.[67] In this regard, although Balthasar concedes that Rahner is justified in preserving *natura pura* as a "residual concept,"[68] in agreement with De Lubac,

62. Balthasar, *The Christian State of Life*, 68–69. See also 75.

63. Balthasar, *The Realm of Metaphysics in Antiquity (TA4)*, 404.

64. Kerr, "Balthasar and Metaphysics," 233.

65. Balthasar, *The Theology of Karl Barth*, 286.

66. Schindler, "The Significance of Hans Urs von Balthasar," 30.

67. Balthasar, "Movement toward God," 40. See also *Love Alone Is Credible*, 384. Quoted in Howsare, *Balthasar: A Guide for the Perplexed*, 38–39.

68. Balthasar, *The Theology of Karl Barth*, 298–302.

Balthasar maintains that a *natura pura* does not exist in reality.[69] Nature is *intrinsically* open to grace,[70] and the purpose of nature was, from its origin, to be an instrument of grace.[71] The authority of the saints is thus to be attributed above all to the *potentia oboedientialis* (that is, the powerfulness of the Creator), but the *potentia naturalis* remains essential.

Thirdly, it should be said that, contrary to Eckhart, Balthasar emphasizes the concreteness of being.[72] In Balthasar, as in Gregory of Nyssa, finitude is a positive characteristic of finite being, rather than a deficiency.[73] The *maior dissimilitudo*, this "relationship of difference" with God is not shameful. Difference is no "degradation."[74] Being a creature "outside God . . . is not something suspect but something excellent."[75] With Balthasar "[i]t is in the humanity that we find God, in the world of sense that we find the Spirit."[76] The creature is "saved only in the express preservation and perfection of his nature,"[77] so that man (or woman) does not have to become supernatural. In Balthasar's theology, existence becomes, for the experienced person, "a luminous space which he has embraced,"[78] and the way of perfection lies in the acceptance of human existence.[79]

In Balthasar's view, withdrawal from the world, both of the individual and of the church,[80] is, therefore, erroneous. It "leads only to betrayal of the original analogy between God and creature" and, Balthasar adds in his typical overstated manner, "to the destruction of mankind."[81] Not only is the

---

69. De Lubac had stressed the impossibility of defining what would remain of nature had it not been ordered to grace. See Sullivan, "Saints as the 'Living Gospel,'" 3. De Lubac had stressed the impossibility of defining what would remain of nature had it not been ordered to grace.

70. Balthasar, *The Theology of Henri de Lubac*, 69. See Howsare, *Balthasar: A Guide for the Perplexed*, 18.

71. Balthasar, *The Christian State of Life*, 216.

72. Nichols, "Balthasar's Aims," 121.

73. Balthasar, *Presence and Thought*, 29.

74. Ibid.

75. Balthasar, *The Spirit of Truth (TL3)*, 418.

76. Balthasar, *Prayer*, 9. See also *Seeing the Form (TA1)*, 230–31.

77. See Balthasar, *Cosmic Liturgy*, 208, 289–90, and 256–57, for Maximus's idea of human perfection. Yeago describes Balthasar's "nature" as "human historical existence, the reality of free and finite creatures groping splendidly and horribly and always unpredictably after the sense of their lives." See Yeago, "Literature in the Drama of Nature and Grace," 98.

78. Balthasar, *Seeing the Form (TA1)*, 239.

79. Ibid., 438.

80. See Balthasar, *Razing the Bastions: On the Church in this Age*.

81. Balthasar, *The Christian State of Life*, 183.

Christian to accept the reality of human nature as it is—the "fundamental option" toward his or her existential situation, as in Rahner—he or she is also to take "the finite, ontologically dependent concrete reality of individual material things, seriously" and to value concrete reality "reverently." He or she is called to "the task of performing the act of affirming Being,"[82] "to be the guardian of metaphysics in our time."[83] What is significant is that, in Balthasar, this would apply to the saints in particular. As a true Christian, the saint is the one who works towards logically establishing the objectivity of being,[84] the one who works towards establishing the world as "a sacred theophany."[85]

We have already indicated in our first point that, through his emphasis on the *analogia entis*, Balthasar not only preserves the *in tanta similitudine maior dissimilitudo* with the Creator, which was enunciated at the Fourth Lateran Council, but also pays tribute to it. Balthasar's position is that being "needs to be held distinct from God, neither confused with him, nor detached from him, but reconciled with him through the proportionalism (or analogy) of divine creation."[86] This leads us to our fourth point. With Balthasar, the creature is never neutral toward God, whether in its being, its action or its thought.[87] As Schindler has pointed out, even the postmoderns, like Nietzsche and Derrida, insist that "the reality of God is such that his presence or absence changes everything."[88] This is, ultimately, an understanding of the creature that is regulated by its relationship with its Creator. To be with God, or to be without Him, is simply not the same thing. Balthasar articulates this concept of the analogy between "concrete created nature and the concrete nature of God" most radically in his *Présence et Pensée*.[89] Having emphasized that the creature can never "have" God, he adds that one could contemplate the possibility of having—naturally, within the terms of the analogy itself—the path of the creature "in a certain fashion 'be' God."[90]

82. Balthasar, *The Realm of Metaphysics in the Modern Age (TA5)*, 648.

83. Ibid., 656. See also 646.

84. Daley, "Translator's Foreword," 18.

85. Balthasar, *Seeing the Form (TA1)*, 679.

86. Davies, "Von Balthasar and the problem of Being," 12. See Balthasar, *Seeing the Form (TA1)*, 244–45; and *Prayer*, 156–57.

87. Schindler, "The Significance of Hans Urs von Balthasar," 21.

88. Ibid., 19.

89. Balthasar, *Presence and Thought*, 81. Balthasar maintains that it was Gregory of Nyssa who established this analogy that was to define his agenda for doing theology in subsequent decades.

90. Ibid., 111.

This brings us to the fifth and final point. The involvement with God as Balthasar understands it, and as he develops it, presents a way of *being* God, in a significantly different way from the *theosis* of the east. In Balthasar, the model for every authentic relationship with God (historical, personal and universal) is precisely this: "the absolute abandonment of Christ to the will of the Father."[91] *Theosis* as Balthasar understands it involves being one with the intra-trinitarian dynamics, attitudes and relationships, rather than with God's essence. Christian existence takes on the meaning of a process (the movement) whereby one yields him or herself to be modelled by Jesus' attitude in relation to the Father.[92] This is, as Ben Quash has said, an "actualist" rather than an "essentialist handling."[93] What is significant is that Balthasar articulates the hope that every Christian may experience, and manifest, not only the attitude of Jesus towards the Father's authority, but also the Father's authority for Christ on the Cross, an authority that Balthasar describes as "concrete, intimate and inevitable," "demanding and unrelenting." In this regard, Balthasar claims that "if Christians are actually to achieve the radical and extreme obedience" of Christ all the way to the Cross, they must be given an authority that is analogical to the Father's authority vis-à-vis Christ.[94] Therefore, with Balthasar, the Christian becomes authoritative when he or she participates in the obedience of Christ, when he or she participates in the authority of Christ, and thirdly, when he or she participates in the Father's authority in relation to Christ. Thus, the Christian comes to be *with* authority.[95]

THE LIFE OF THE SAINTS AS EXPRESSIVE OF GOD'S FORM

Having determined what we believe are the main characteristics of Balthasar's meta-anthropology—which are, evidently, reflected in his hagiography—and before I proceed to provide arguments that are even more focused on the saints' authority, I would like to spell out some of the features

91. Balthasar, *The Realm of Metaphysics in the Modern Age (TA5)*, 51.

92. Balthasar, *Prayer*, 88–89.

93. Quash, *The Modern Theologians*, 114.

94. Balthasar, *The Christian State of Life*, 257.

95. The accusation that Quash brings against Balthasar, concerning the frailty of the dramatic because of the emphasis on obedience, may need to be rethought. See Quash, *Theology and the Drama of History*, 161, 221. The authority that is attributed to the Christian is not the same as Christ's. In Christ, divine authority "speaks in the I-form." Balthasar, *Seeing the Form (TA1)*, 185.

of the life of the saints that makes them expressive of God's form, according to Balthasar. These are, first and foremost, the transcendentals themselves. The beauty, truth, and goodness present in the saints themselves makes them expressive of God's form. However, one can identify, in Balthasar, other existential features which make *auctoritates* out of the saints. These other features can be grouped under three subtitles, namely, the aptitude of the saints to reclaim human existence, the entrenchment of the saints in the world, and the saints' attitude of surrender. Let me begin with the transcendentals, which are the most straightforward among the existential features which contribute to the authority of the saints.

The Transcendentals

As with Denys the Areopagite, and the *nouvelle théologiens*, Balthasar maintains that mystery has permeated the created order.[96] Consequently, the created spirit has a way through nature to the Creator. In all the transcendentals of being: beauty, goodness, and truth, it is possible to see that it is the glory of God that is being manifested.[97] The saints' form, which expresses such beauty, goodness, and truth, is a manifestation of God's own glory.[98] Christologically speaking, anyone who participates in Christ's form—as the saints do—himself or herself becomes a manifestation of the beautiful, the good, and the true which is in God, since the Christ-form is the archetype of such beauty, goodness, or truth. The christocentrism of Barth thus becomes, in Balthasar, a christocentric anthropocentrism.

Significantly, Balthasar is associated with his statement that being beautiful does not necessarily mean being agreeable to the person with a creative aesthetic sensibility, so much so that, in Balthasar, beauty embraces the crucifixion. I think one could safely say that Balthasar similarly refashions the meaning of the other transcendentals as well, so that being beautiful, good, or true is not necessarily to do with pleasure, graciousness, or accuracy. This is very important, since the goodness, the beauty, and the true which we associate with the saints may likewise not always be attractive and appealing.

Typical of Balthasar is the view from above. In Balthasar, drama is a *theo*-drama, just as aesthetics and logic are a *theo*-aesthetics, and a *theo*-logic. It is therefore not separate from that of the Trinity. It is a "*theo*-drama" *within* the Trinity. This drama between God and man within the Trinity

96. Boersma, *Nouvelle Théologie*, 32.
97. See Henrici, "The Philosophy of Hans Urs von Balthasar," 165.
98. Balthasar, *Two Sisters*, 92–93.

could be understood both as extension of the exchange that creates the divine drama and as an immersion within that exchange. Steffen Lösel has said that the "conflict of infinite and finite wills," which we find in the *Dramatics*, is an extension of an inner-divine *theo*-drama between the infinite wills of Father and Son in the Holy Spirit.[99] On his part, Nicholas M.Healy sees the human and the divine drama more as an immersion, or a merging, than as an extension. Healy maintains that Balthasar has set one within the other, rather than one alongside the other. The dramatic "here" is "grounded in the primary drama 'beyond,' in the life of the immanent Trinity,"[100] so that our existence is interpreted as "a play that we play within the overarching divine play," and we should situate our own roles within the "primary drama" in order to understand them, both as individuals and as church.[101] This is probably not a question of either or. Both images are implied. What is certain is that Balthasar situates this integration of dramas within the ontological and the existential order, making it an interesting form of the Eastern notion of *theosis*.

In addition to it being a *theo*-drama, in Balthasar, this drama is characterized by a "tensiveness" that is "inherent in all aspects of Christian existence."[102] Kilby has noted how, in Balthasar, Christ himself causes, and intensifies the drama. Conflict, tension, polarization, commitment, and suffering ensue as a consequence of Christ.[103] On their part, the saints are illustrations, but also acute secondary examples—the primary being Christ—of this tension, of this state of being stretched tight. The saints know what it means to be tempted and distraught, in trying to preserve the equilibrium between heaven and earth. Particularly in his works on Thérèse and Elizabeth, Balthasar explores the saint in the contextuality of her very existence, and attempts to learn from outside what the "inscape" is, that is, what goes on within the saint, what the mental processes of the saint are, what the inner drama is like,[104] how the individual saint grapples with her own demons, and so on. It is this dramatic struggle—which merges with the intra-trinitarian struggle, or is an extension of it—which makes the saints expressive of God's form.[105] David L.Schindler has claimed that, in Balthasar, the saints

99. Lösel, "Unapocalyptic Theology," 221.

100. Healy, *Church, World and the Christian Life*, 61.

101. See Balthasar, *The Dramatis Personae: Man in God (TD2)*, 53.

102. Healy, *Church, World and the Christian Life*, 72. See Balthasar, *The Christian State of Life*, 218–19.

103. Kilby, *Balthasar*, 60–61.

104. This is a notion attributed to Gerald Manley Hopkins. See Balthasar, *The Spirit of Truth (TL3)*, 336

105. Ibid., 153.

labor to *receive* heaven, rather than to *seize* it, as with Nietzsche.[106] Schindler is right, but "to *receive* heaven" does not mean to relinquish all elements of intensity and force. Paradoxically, it is this responsive conduct that enables the saints to become authoritative. In Balthasar, being holy is being able to actively receive the beauty, goodness, and truth which is in the Triune God. It is here—between heaven and earth—as David Moss has said, that the lives of the saints serve as "a kind of pulpit" and "a sermon."[107]

The Reclamation of Existence

In Balthasar's theology, as in Ignatius of Loyola, man and woman are "called into existence for the historical actuality of meeting with [God]."[108] The *telos* of each and every individual is to be conformed to Christ, or rather to the Idea of him/herself which is contained in Christ.[109] In Balthasar, the saint is someone who has received insight into the mystery of existence and who exemplifies the essence of his or her existence. Subsequently, the authority of the individual saint is grounded in the cognizance of his or her *telos*,[110] and in the recognition of others that the *telos* features very powerfully in that individual's existence. This is not merely "Aristotle's *causa-et-finis* metaphysical realism."[111] It is, specifically, Balthasar's Christian ontology. With Balthasar, the more we are conformed to the "Idea," that is, to the individual truth of ourselves in Christ, discovered in prayer, the more intrinsically human we become, and consequently, the more able we are to provide a credible image of humanity to others. We acquire authority when, rather than evading our existence, we claim it for ourselves. Subsequently, we not only grasp that we are, and what we are, but we also appreciate who we ought to be. We acquire authority because, in becoming a form through which the glory of God may manifest itself, we are transported into an existence that is

---

106. Schindler "The Significance of Hans Urs von Balthasar," 25, 27.

107. Moss, "The Saints," 89.

108. Balthasar, *The Christian State of Life*, 463.

109. Balthasar, *Prayer*, 186. Whereas the neoscholastic notion was that human beings have two separate ends, the natural and the supernatural, *Ressourcement* theologians maintained that human beings have one single end, namely, to see God. Howsare, *Balthasar: A Guide for the Perplexed*, 11, 15. See also Boersma, *Nouvelle Théologie*, 53.

110. The Judeo-Christian portrayal of the human being stresses that there is more to one's *telos* and the fulfilment of one's nature than simply coming into existence. See Harrison, *Homo Orans*, 283.

111. Kerr, "Forward: Assessing This 'Giddy Synthesis,'" 10.

characterized by fruitfulness, by solidarity, and by nuptiality,[112] all of which enable us to function authoritatively.

To re-claim one's existence suggests that our existence had at some point been lost. Within a world where sin is a reality, to reclaim one's existence is to accept one's finiteness, one's pure ordinariness, one's inconspicuousness, one's hiddenness. This is the essence of holiness. The saints have done precisely that. They may represent "the universal" but "they are thoroughly ordinary men with that ordinary *eidos* or meaning to their humanity which is immanent in this world: Simon, son of Jonah, John, son of Zebedee."[113] There is something here that reminds us of Heidegger's *Dasein* in the sense of a being-there. In Heidegger, the fundamental constitution of *Dasein* is a being-in-the-world.[114] In Balthasar, the kind of involvement that being-there signifies is made possible by his understanding of both eternity and bodiliness. The authority of the saints is grounded in their very normality, and it is within this very commonplaceness that the saints function as an authority.[115] Balthasar asserts that in the saints—in Abraham, Isaac, Jacob, Joseph, Moses, the charismatic Judges, the Prophets and the Martyrs of faith, and Mary—"we confront life in the Holy Spirit, hidden life which is inconspicuous, and yet *so* conspicuous that its situations, scenes, and encounters receive a sharp, unmistakable profile and exert an archetypal power over the whole history of faith."[116]

Another feature of the life of the saints that grounds their authority and enables them to function as an authority is the unity of their existence. Especially in his early, post-war works, Balthasar often presents the individual as a microcosm of the world which is fragmented and broken. According to Balthasar, how is it possible for the saints to defeat this fragmentariness, how is it that this unity of the saints' existence provides them with authority, or enables others to attribute authority to them? First, we must remember that, in Balthasar, it is only Christ who can draw the separate experiences into a whole.[117] Only he can bestow form and unity upon our life.[118] Only he can act as "the center of the gravity of life."[119] So the implication is that there

---

112. Balthasar, *Theology: The New Covenant (TA7)*.

113. Balthasar, *A Theology of History*, 117.

114. Heidegger, *Being and Time* (1927).

115. See Balthasar, *Seeing the Form (TA1)*, 565.

116. Balthasar, *Seeing the Form (TA1)*, 36. It is with Blaise Pascal that Balthasar associates this revelation-hiddenness dialectic.

117. Balthasar, *Convergences*, 120–21, 124.

118. Ibid., 132.

119. Balthasar, *Seeing the Form (TA1)*, 515.

is a direct correlation between one's relationship with Christ and a certain harmony in one's life. According to Balthasar, complete unity will never be achieved in this world, but, as Christians, "our existence will one day be given to us as unity . . . precisely as our form, in which we really encounter ourselves for the first time and are finally that which we had always wanted to be."[120] In Balthasar, the mission which we are assigned by Christ often acts as the unifier of our existence. Mission unifies the history, the psychology, and the "little anecdotes and details that characterize saintly lives."[121] The saint's very existence is characterized by a heightened sense of purpose and of meaning which, so to speak, fuses his or her separate parts together.

In the introduction to his *L'Action*, Blondel had established that the most fundamental philosophical question is whether human life has a meaning (*un sens*), and whether man has a destiny. He had claimed that the solution offered to this question cannot be negative. It is from the fact that there is meaning that Blondel establishes that *il y a quelque chose*.[122] Balthasar's theology strongly grounds the authority of the saints in this: in the meaning that God has given to their existence, sometimes even before their birth. In Balthasar, the creature cannot be, and cannot find meaning except in relation with God.[123] What Balthasar says about the "ultimate meaning" of the Christian's existence is very Ignatian. Meaning emanates from one's "life before God,"[124] one's divine calling,[125] "the service of God."[126] In this, Balthasar challenges the modern existentialists who would insist that the most important consideration for individuals is their individuality, and who would maintain that it is the individual—not society or religion, and its labels, roles, stereotypes, definitions, or other preconceived categories— who is responsible for giving meaning to life and living it authentically. In Balthasar, the saints' existence responds to the claims of the existentialist philosopher. As opposed to the existentialists, the saints derive the meaning of their existence, of their life, of their history not from within themselves but from God (who often communicates through the church).[127] The basic presupposition of the theology of the saints is that existence has no meaning unless God reveals its purpose when he "imparts a distinctive and divinely

120. Balthasar, *Convergences*, 127. Also 125.

121. Balthasar, *Two Sisters*, 27. See also *The Christian State of Life*, 460–61.

122. Blondel, *Action* (1893). See Conway, "A Positive Phenomenology," 588.

123. Schindler, "The Significance of Hans Urs von Balthasar," 22.

124. Balthasar, "Martyrdom and Mission," 287.

125. Balthasar, *The Christian State of Life*, 83. See also 191.

126. Balthasar, *Two Sisters*, 299.

127. Balthasar, *Prayer*, 94.

authorized mission."[128] Balthasar states that "For each Christian, God has an idea that fixes his place within the membership of the Church; this idea is unique and personal, embodying for each his appropriate sanctity."[129]

Therefore, with Balthasar, every existent "possesses a certain degree of powerfulness of being . . . in such a way that he poses a demand to the world around him."[130] Balthasar associates this "powerfulness of being" especially with the saints. True sanctity, he says, "can become so dazzling in the testimony of Christians that its beauty and rightness will be visible and evident."[131] One could say that, firstly, the authority of the saints arises from the clarity which the saints enjoy with respect to the meaning of their existence. Secondly, that the saints start functioning as an authority, when the meaning of their existence also becomes evident to the community, when the mission and the manner of being holy is endorsed by others, even if this may only happen many generations into the future. And thirdly, that the saints function as an authority by supporting and building the community.[132]

Balthasar emphasizes the "absolute uniqueness of every person (the *Je-Einmaligkeit*),"[133] and he attributes a particular authority to this uniqueness. The "incomparability" of the individual person is not "predicated of him as a quality of his being," but as a consequence of his personhood.[134] Whereas existentialism would have emphasized the uniqueness and isolation of the individual experience in a hostile or indifferent universe, in Balthasar, the individual participates in Christ's own uniqueness, and there is no isolation. Uniqueness stands for the incomparability between Christian subjects, that has a theological source, since it is God alone who can define the Christian subject and designate him or her in his qualitative uniqueness.[135] The authority of the saints is grounded in the uniqueness of the relationship with God that each of them has—since "it is to this particular, irreplace-

128. Balthasar, *The Dramatis Personae: The Person in Christ (TD3)*, 207.

129. Balthasar, *Two Sisters*, 20.

130. See Balthasar's discussion of *Seinsmächtigkeit* in his essay on "Authority," 128–9.

131. Balthasar, *Seeing the Form (TA1)*, 603.

132. Balthasar, *The Dramatis Personae: The Person in Christ (TD3)*, 271.

133. "*Einmaligkeit*" is generally translated as "singularity" or "unicity," but I prefer the term "uniqueness." See Balthasar, *Romano Guardini*, 39.

134. Balthasar, *Man in History*, 45. Mark Ouellet has pointed out that the advantage of Balthasar's "theological conception of the person," is that "it establishes at once both uniqueness and ecclesiality." Ouellet, "Foundations of Christian Ethics," 238.

135. Writing about Adrienne, Balthasar maintains that the supernatural dimension did not efface Adrienne's natural individuality: "rather it underlined it." See Balthasar, *First Glance*, 47.

able human being that God speaks"—as well as in the unique portion of the truth which God has revealed to each one, and which each one is meant to convey. Balthasar emphasizes this in his book on *Prayer*. Every man is unique in that he or she "has his own particular truth, expressing the special, historical relationship which God has with him," and which "has its place within the universal covenant-truth."[136] Nonetheless, there are some saints where uniqueness takes on a deeper significance. Here, uniqueness becomes a deeper participation in the uniqueness that is attributed to God. Balthasar describes this process in his *Theology of History*. He writes that

> One or a few are chosen to capture something of the aura of uniqueness which is of the essence of royal grace, and as individuals to some extent to share in it: naturally, in the name of all, and as mediators between the uniqueness of the King and the ordinariness of the people. . .The fact that the radiance of uniqueness has fallen on them, giving them an *eidos* of a new value, raising it to the level of all-fulfilling uniqueness, is due solely to their having been freely chosen.[137]

The recognition by others of such uniqueness in each of the saints is often accountable for the authority which is attributed to such figures.

Entrenchment in the World

In Balthasar's theology, the saints are also assigned authority because of their entrenchment in the world, which, in turn, enables the saints to function as an authority. One called by God is "not of the world" (John17:14). And yet, the individual whose self is open to God "receives authentic power to penetrate the world."[138] Balthasar sees the saints as individuals who struggle dramatically within the world rather than evade it. In Balthasar, "openness to the world" is "to live the real."[139] It is to overcome the "huge" and "seductive" temptation to flee this "everyday existence." It is only the person who overcomes such a temptation to flee that acquires the wisdom that others find so attractive.

In his *Catholicism*, published in 1938, De Lubac had said that "if Christians continue to proclaim louder than all others the need to flee from

136. Balthasar, *Prayer*, 37.

137. Balthasar, *A Theology of History*, 116–17.

138. Balthasar, *Prayer*, 265.

139. According to Balthasar, openness to the world is not to be understood as "dialogue" and directly experienced "sociability." Neither is the value of a life to be calculated in terms of tangible productivity. See Balthasar, *Two Sisters*, 9.

the world, *fugiendum a saeculo*, it is with quite a different meaning and with another emphasis,"[140] than that associated with certain philosophies or religions. In Balthasar, to die to the world in Christ should not take the form of an alienation.[141] On the contrary, it means "to give oneself, along with Christ, for the world and for its benefit."[142] In his *Aesthetics*, Balthasar presents Christianity as the religion which offers the best answer concerning the rapport with the world, claiming that Christianity has replaced the *despicere mundum*, which also includes "the passive endurance of contempt of the world, with the *despici a mundo*."[143] Using the saints, Balthasar challenges the widely-held misconception of the *despicere mundum*, claiming, in contrast, that it is possible to both make one's stand exclusively in God and to be open to the world. Mary, he claims, has existentially shown that the two are "complementary concepts."[144] In the saints, Balthasar sees evidence of this stance before God and of a concurrent entrenchment in the world, and endorses it. The saints acquire authority and assume an authoritative function precisely because of their embeddedness within the world.

Since there is nothing that says embeddedness as much as our body, corporeality is to be considered one of the main features of the life of the saints that entrenches them in the world, and, at the same time, makes them expressive of God's form. Balthasar's emphasis on corporeality creates some opportunity for dialogue with Postmodernism, for which the significance of the body is undeniable. As Wyschogrod has argued, in postmodernism, rather than proclamation or argument, it is the saint's body, the flesh, that is to be taken as the unit of significance in saintly life. Balthasar claims that the role of man's corporeality is central,[145] and that "man can only finally

---

140. De Lubac, *Catholicism*, 67.

141. Block has called our attention to Balthasar's "careful" historical outline where he traced the notion of alienation, starting from Neoplatonism through Eckhart and Nicholas of Cusa, to Fichte, Schelling, and Hegel. See Block, "Hans Urs von Balthasar's Theo-Drama," 191.

142. Balthasar maintains that this is another point which was pushed too far into the background in official monastic theology. See Balthasar, "Are There Lay People in the Church?," 178.

143. Balthasar, *The Realm of Metaphysics in the Modern Age (TA5)*, 50–51. Balthasar considers this latter principle (*despici a mundo*) to be itself "an elevation and fulfilment of metaphysics," because, he says, it explains "ontologically the ontic (historical) event of salvation."

144. Balthasar, *The Christian State of Life*, 206. On ibid., 478, Balthasar condemns psychology for often ascribing "to those called by God: lack of concern about the world and society; uncontrolled emotional complexes; even fear of life itself."

145. Balthasar, *Seeing the Form (TA1)*, 313–14.

attain salvation in and through his corporeal existence."[146] John O'Donnell has pointed out that "bodiliness" is one of Balthasar's favourite words.[147] Despite his emphasis on bodiliness, some have suggested that Balthasar's theology is profoundly hostile to the body, and that this is most apparent in his treatment of sexuality.[148] Although his treatment of sexuality may leave a lot to be desired, and although his work may show "lack of true understanding of earthly, created and biological reality,"[149] Balthasar's emphasis on the incarnation, on faith as grounded in life, and on the visibility of forms of beauty, goodness, and truth, are more than enough to prove his genuine appreciation for the physicality of our presence in the world. Naturally, one could argue that some saints never did integrate their sexuality, and that they never really accepted their corporeality. In reply to this objection, Balthasar would probably emphasize that the saints assumed the form of Christ, or the form of themselves contained in Christ, and he would mention instances where saints manifested physical evidence of their oneness with him,[150] and that this would surmount any discourse about sexuality.

Balthasar emphasizes that our bodies implant us within the world, empowering us to leave an indelible imprint upon it. Naturally, in his view, it is always "in" Jesus Christ and "oriented toward" Jesus Christ "that man has been set in existence as a being of spirit and body."[151] In Balthasar's theology, there is no space for Manicheism. Earthly life is not a prison, the body is not a punishment, and all flight from the body is anti-Christian.[152] In fact, "all philosophy, theology and mysticism that is hostile to the body. . .is anti-Christian."[153] To become whole does not mean to dissolve mystically.[154] "God," he writes, "did not descend to the level of flesh simply so that

146. Balthasar, *Engagement with God*, 80.

147. O'Donnell, *Hans Urs von Balthasar*, 57.

148. Beattie, "Sex, Death and Melodrama," 168. See also Beattie, *New Catholic Feminism*.

149. Deane-Drummond, "The Breadth of Glory," 54.

150. Wyschogrod, *Saints and Postmodernism*, xxiii.

151. Balthasar, *Prayer*, 264.

152. See Weinstein & Bell, *Saints and Society*, 248.

153. Balthasar, *The Spirit of Truth (TL3)*, 247. According to some, Catholicism reaffirmed the unbridgeable gulf between the world and the spirit. For centuries, the Roman church taught "that the life of penance and humility could be achieved fully only by withdrawal from the world." Weinstein & Bell, "Saints and Society," 119. Quoting Weber, *The Protestant Ethic and the Spirit of Capitalism*, which emphasizes the "asceticism" and "otherworldliness" of Catholicism.

154. Balthasar, *Seeing the Form (TA1)*, 586. The principle is incarnational. Balthasar admired Maximus for bringing "into Chalcedonian Christology the whole Asian mystique of divinization on the higher level of the biblical mystery, and of the personal

we should 'ascend' from flesh to spirit."[155] Our flesh must remain, even if somehow altered. Origen's eschatological ideal of a "city of souls" is not what Balthasar anticipates. In Balthasar, the human body is itself a gift, offering "the human spirit an inconceivably sensitive and versatile set of instruments to make itself thoroughly comprehensive."[156] According to Balthasar, "the patristic notion of divinization" may not have been "sensitive" enough "to the proper ontological and cognition distinction between the creature and God," but this should not bring about a dissolution or a hostility to the body.[157]

The issue of corporeality is closely related to another of Balthasar's more important contributions to contemporary theology and exegesis, namely, his recovery of the spiritual senses (*sensus spiritualis*),[158] a doctrine first elaborated by Origen and later reformulated by Bonaventure and Ignatius of Loyola. The spiritual senses presuppose bodily senses, but, whereas Platonism understood the world of the senses as an obstacle, as "the prison and the veiling of the spirit,"[159] Balthasar considers the senses more as a gift which enables us to respond to God's revelatory form. In this regard, the contribution of Maurice Merleau-Ponty (1908–1961) cannot be overlooked. Merleau-Ponty brings back the body as a way of being in the world, and he interprets perception as an embodied activity.[160] Especially in his doctrine of the spiritual senses, Balthasar does not fail to emphasize that our whole being is involved when we perceive an object. Balthasar also claims that the natural, bodily senses may become "Christian;" "in so far as they have been formed according to the form of Christ."[161] The spiritual "senses and faculties" are our senses which, having been liberated through the cross,

> can fix upon God . . . acquire something of the pneumatic quality of the Lord's glorified senses even prior to our own resurrection, so that, in him and together with him, we can grasp the Father and the Spirit and the entire world beyond.[162]

---

synthesis of an incarnate God, rather than on the lower level of natural dissolution and fusion." Balthasar, *Cosmic Liturgy*, 48.

155. Balthasar, *Prayer*, 263.

156. Balthasar, *Truth of God (TL2)*, 252.

157. Howsare, *Hans Urs von Balthasar and Protestantism*, 158.

158. Schindler, writing about Peter Casarella's contribution on "Experience as a Theological Category: Hans urs von Balthasar," 109.

159. Balthasar, *Prayer*, 269.

160. Merleau-Ponty, *Phenomenology of Perception*.

161. Balthasar, *Seeing the Form (TA1)*, 424. See also *Cosmic Liturgy*, 285; and *The Spirit of Truth (TL3)*, 195.

162. Balthasar, *Prayer*, 270.

Thus, it is safe to say—although Balthasar does not specifically state this with reference to the saints—that, according to Balthasar, the authority of a saint would be grounded in his or her spiritual senses, which are awakened through the grace of the Incarnation, and through the believer's initiation into Christ's suffering, death and resurrection.[163] In this sense, the saint could be recognized as authoritative, and may function as an authority, because his or her corporeal senses have been aroused, more precisely, christianized, and this has an effect on others who then attribute authority to them.

The other central feature which one associates with bodiliness is time.[164] Bernhard Blankenhorn has said that Balthasar appeals to the Johannine interpretation of theological time to back up his language about God.[165] In fact, Balthasar also appeals to the Johannine interpretation of theological time in order to back up his language about man. In Balthasar, time is neither a substance in its own right (an independent ontological being), nor a property of a contingent being in the sense of being dependent on that being. Neither is it a property of God's being. Eunsoo Kim has pointed out that Balthasar does not simply repeat the traditional concept "of divine timelessness, immutability, or impassability." In fact, he "explicitly rejects any univocal attribution of temporality, mutability or passibility, any process notions of the creature becoming of God."[166] Time originates through the generation of the Son from the Father in eternity, and the nature of time is the "receptivity" of the Son for his existence from the Father. Thus, God is the "primal origin" of time (as of space). Balthasar then conceives of God's eternity as "supra-time" in an analogical way, so that there is, in Balthasar, a big difference, but also a real and positive relation, between God's eternity and human time.[167] We have here what Blankenhorn has called "the negation of purely creaturely time."[168] But this is not a negation of time—the finite remains finite—but rather a seizure of time, in the sense of Horace's *Carpe Diem*, while, paradoxically, being also an obedient "waiting" for God's will. In speculative terms, Balthasar grounds the authority of the saints in their

163. Ibid., 269–70. Balthasar claims that this "actually fulfills and over-fulfills Platonism's ultimate goal (which it could not attain) in a totally unpredictable way."

164. Eunsoo Kim claims that Balthasar's is "one of the most significant contributions to the contemporary debates on the understanding of God's eternity and its relation to time." See Kim, "Time, Eternity, and the Trinity," 349. See also Dalzell, *The Dramatic Encounter of Divine and Human Freedom*, 253–85.

165. Blankenhorn, "Balthasar's Method of Divine Naming," 253.

166. Kim, "Time, Eternity, and the Trinity," 348.

167. Ibid., 351.

168. Blankenhorn, "Balthasar's Method of Divine Naming," 254.

involvement with real time. As with Maximus, in Balthasar, the immediate experience of the divine presence and consolation takes place within the total movement of temporal existence.[169] And it is here that the saint must find it. Balthasar follows Augustine in describing sin as a desire to avoid the claim of others and of time. In his *Theology of History*, Balthasar claims that man will try to escape "real time," the time in which he encounters God, "by withdrawing into some timeless philosophical or mystical 'eternity'; but this is not, for him, existential time." This unreal time, will, according to Balthasar, throw man "back again into the experience of empty, annihilating time," which is self-centred time.[170] Since "Christ's act of existence as man" was a historical event within time, the follower of Christ can only participate in Christ by accepting time, and by evaluating time in the light of the archetype and the prototype, who is Christ.[171]

One feature of the being of the saints that makes their life and teaching authoritative, and enables them to function authoritatively, is what I would call their diachronic extension. Christ's "pattern of life . . . embraces a compass infinitely and incomprehensibly vaster than that normally reckoned to be the scope of an ordinary human existence," since it spans over "the timelessness of the underworld," and that of eternity.[172] Through their participation in Christ, the "life-forms" of the "chosen" ones—those who have con-formed to Christ—will endure.[173] Here Balthasar is evidently influenced by Sergei Bulgakov and Rudolf Pannenberg, whose attention to the proleptical character of revelation is quite renowned. But there surely is some influence from Heidegger as well in this regard. Heidegger claimed that *Dasein* is always oriented towards the future. The existence of the saints reaches back into the past and extends forward into the future, through its participation in the *Christus prolungatus* in history. The Old Testament "saints" receive their retroactive fulfilment in Christ,[174] whereas the Christ-event already contains within itself all the "figurations" which could appear in the future.[175] It is a future that is built on an understanding of the world that is rooted in trinitarian relationships. Here, the saints' participation in the trinitarian relationships becomes the feature that makes their life and teaching diachronically extensive, and enables them to function authoritatively even beyond their life-time.

169. Balthasar, *Seeing the Form (TA1)*, 282.

170. Balthasar, *A Theology of History*, 41.

171. Ibid., 40–41.

172. Balthasar, *Engagement with God*, 36–37.

173. Balthasar, *Seeing the Form (TA1)*, 36.

174. See Oakes, "Balthasar's Critique of the Historical-Critical Method," 164, 166.

175. Balthasar, *Convergences*, 93–94.

Surrender

Perhaps the feature of the life of the saints that makes their life and teaching especially authoritative existentially, and enables them to function authoritatively not only within the church, but also within being over-all, is, paradoxically, their surrender.[176] Balthasar grounds the authority of the saints in a dogmatic expertise that comes from an attitude of surrender. In Balthasar, the saints mediate divine authority, not necessarily in the sense that divine power is visible in them, although this is also possible, but certainly in the sense that one can see in them the surrender to God's absolute power. According to Balthasar, grace "claims and expropriates us." It "compels us" and "bestows absolute authority on God in us."[177]

Balthasar's emphasis on this theology of surrender has been the cause of some criticism, because it has been said that it diminishes the drama. Such criticism may or may not be deserved. What is certain is that there is, in Balthasar, a correlation, not only between existential surrender and holiness—the Christian saint is the one "who has made the deep-rooted act of faith and obedience to God's inner light the norm of his whole existence"[178]—but also between existential surrender and the theological enterprise. In Balthasar, knowledge of God, theology and dogma are simply inconceivable without surrender. In Balthasar, one "knows" God, and "possesses" Him, only when one is oneself "expropriated and handed over."[179] More will need to be said about surrender and the theological enterprise in the next chapter. With regards to the first of these however, that is, the correlation between surrender and holiness, it would be appropriate to provide a few examples. In *Cosmic Liturgy*, Balthasar attributes the almost effortless victory of dyothelite Christology at the Third Council of Constantinople and the prestige of the synod to "the martyrdom of the pope, [of] Maximus, and [of] Maximus's companions."[180] Writing about Elizabeth of the Trinity, we are told that she

---

176. Balthasar uses various terms to describe this theology: obedience and availability, abandonment, readiness for service (*Bereitschaft*), inner dedication, yielding, expropriation (*Enteignung*), unselfing (*Entselbstung*), handing-over, being led, death, consent, dispossession, renunciation, self-emptying, kenosis, *exinanitio*, selflessness, self-emptying, sacrifice, abandonment, serious penance, renunciation, and so forth.

177. Balthasar, *Seeing the Form (TA1)*, 162.

178. Ibid., 165.

179. Balthasar, *The New Covenant (TA7)*, 400. Quoted in Vogel, "The Unselfing Activity of the Holy Spirit," 24.

180. Balthasar, *Cosmic Liturgy*, 44.

is able to develop an explicitly trinitarian doctrine because her mind goes out toward its object so completely, leaving only the very slightest scope for her own personality and history—just sufficient to remain a subject for the operations of the Trinity.[181]

In Thérèse, there is renunciation on all levels.[182] Even the yearning for God, so powerful in the Psalms, the *desiderium visionis Dei*, is to be given up. Balthasar follows the trend the theological doctrine of surrender has taken throughout the history of Western metaphysics when he discusses the metaphysics of the saints.[183] Not only does Balthasar use the saints to sum up the theological aesthetics of the "postmedieval Western tradition,"[184] Balthasar also offers the saints as a corrective to it. Two examples should suffice. The first involves Nietzsche. Balthasar uses the saint as an antidote to Nietzsche's concept of the "master-morality," which emphasizes power, strength, egoism, and freedom.[185] The second example involves Transcendental Thomism. Here, Balthasar uses the saints to condemn spiritual utilitarianism.[186] He wishes to avoid the risks associated with Transcendental Thomism, namely that of "measuring and appreciating objective revelation and the means of grace by the degree to which they satisfy the individual's spiritual longings."[187] The saint becomes an authority, not—as with Nietzsche—because of his or her drive toward domination and exploitation of the inferior, nor—as with spiritual utilitarianism—because of an endless pursuit for spiritual merits,[188] but because he or she relies completely on God, because, as Nichols describes it, he or she becomes

a kind of personalized version of *esse* in its outpouring, a personalized version of the way that for Thomas Aquinas being in its dependence on God only consolidates itself in giving itself away to beings. The saint, not the cosmos, in other words, now becomes the epiphany of glory.[189]

---

181. Balthasar, *Two Sisters*, 300–301.

182. Ibid., 43–44, 272, 274, 276, and 278.

183. Balthasar, *The Realm of Metaphysics in the Modern Age* (TA5), 48–140.

184. Nichols, "Balthasar's Aims," 123–24.

185. Nietzsche, *Beyond Good and Evil*, 223–32.

186. See Balthasar, *Two Sisters*, 150. This is a strong element in De Lubac, *Catholicism*, 191.

187. Dickens, *Hans Urs von Balthasar's Theological Aesthetics*, 32.

188. Balthasar claims that "we are forbidden to prescribe any anthropologically normative mode of access." See Balthasar, *The Spirit of Truth (TL3)*, 31.

189. Nichols, "Balthasar's Aims," 123.

D. M. Matzko has justifiably stated that sainthood (and the saint) is a scandal to modern morality "because it counters the modern moral standards of autonomy, freedom, and choice."[190] In contrast with the modern approach, in Balthasar, the human-divine relationship requires a "double, reciprocal dispossession: of God into the human form and of man into the divine form." The life of man "attains its form by letting itself be shattered to become the form of God," whereas the life of God "gains man for itself by renouncing its own form and [by] pouring itself into the form of existence unto death."[191] As was said before with regards to *theo*-drama, in Balthasar, these two dispossessions do not remain parallel and disconnected. They actually merge. The saint's expropriation, his *sich-geben*, is conceived only "in light of the dogma of God's own expropriation,"[192] and is possible only because the Divine Persons make it possible.[193]

Surrender is, as Blankenhorn has said, among the human characteristics which Balthasar interprets as attributes of perfection in God.[194] With Balthasar, the process of expropriation that goes on within the Trinity seems to be identical to the process which makes the individual authoritative. Balthasar states that "the Spirit's introduction into this milieu of love" between Father and Son—opened up by the Son's self-surrender to the world—is *"also the Spirit's self-surrender to the person who receives his testimony"* (my emphasis).[195] Indeed, there is nothing that screams authority more than having the Spirit surrendering himself to an individual, and turning that individual into a proper *imago Trinitatis*. Balthasar is thus claiming that God's "allowing us to participate in his Godhead . . . occurs not in a second process, but in the one and only process. This is the *admirabile commercium et conubium*. In God's condescendence lies man's exaltation."[196]

Where authority is concerned, the next question would concern visibility. What is it in the saints that makes their surrender visible to us? How does that surrender come through? In Balthasar's theology, surrender often takes the form of a readiness. It is a readiness to be, do and say what God wills, not just on the individual level, but also on the communal. Even "the

190. Matzko, "Postmodernism, Saints and Scoundrels," 20.

191. Balthasar, *Seeing the Form (TA1)*, 673.

192. In Balthasar, the Son's incarnation includes Christ's "pro-existent living, suffering and dying." See Balthasar, *The Spirit of Truth (TL3)*, 197.

193. Ibid., 300; and Balthasar, *The Christian State of Life*, 157–58. See also Bulgakov's intratrinitarian kenosis. Howsare, *Balthasar: A Guide for the Perplexed*, 142.

194. Blankenhorn bases his argument on Balthasar, *The Last Act (TD5)*. "Balthasar's Method of Divine Naming."

195. Balthasar, *The Spirit of Truth (TL3)*, 74, 300.

196. Balthasar, *Seeing the Form (TA1)*, 302. See also 126, 164, and 604.

goal of the communion of saints" is "to hold oneself ready," "the abandonment of all aims of one's own, in order that God's aims may be fulfilled
through his own people."[197] "Readiness" is everything, whether it takes the
form of a "readiness for engagement" or a readiness for "an endurance."[198]
The authority arises from the fact that it is the form of Christ which "brings
out in man . . . the readiness to go to the very limit in obeying the Father's
commands."[199] From the perspective of historical theology, the saints
procure an authoritative place within Tradition, because they exhibit to
perfection the Thomistic view of being as "being-for-one-another," while
at the same time exhibiting the Ignatian view of *indifferentia*.[200] However,
unlike in Christian Platonism, where indifference and continence "carried
strong overtones of flight from the world,"[201] for Balthasar, "[i]ndifference
is the highest possible degree of openness to the world." By emphasizing
it, Balthasar makes classical *apatheia* an instrument for the Pauline idea of
overcoming the world by becoming "all things to all creatures."[202] My interpretation is that, in Balthasar, the authority of the saints is also grounded in
their extraordinary freedom, which is a direct result of their preoccupation
with the will of God, rather than their own. This is a freedom that enables
them to express themselves both theologically and in other ways, without
amor proprio. According to Balthasar "no violence is done to human nature
in making such an act of submission" to the divine will.[203] Thus, whereas
Marx, Freud, Marcuse, and others had attempted to remove "the legal structures of existence" in order that "from there may result a free human disposition," Balthasar inverts the sequence, proposing "a change of disposition"
rather than of structures, arguing that "by itself [this will alter] the whole
status and character of the structures (which in fact cannot be removed)."[204]
The official Magisterium made a statement on similar lines in 1964,

197. Balthasar, "The Communion of Saints," 97

198. Balthasar, "Martyrdom and Mission," 296–97.

199. Balthasar, *The Spirit of Truth (TL3)*, 204.

200. Balthasar often uses the term *apatheia* to mean "passionlessness," "indifference" or "inner freedom." See Balthasar, *Cosmic Liturgy*, 281–83, 331.

201. Balthasar describes Origen, Evagrius, and Dionysius as the three Alexandrian
Platonic theologians, who met and mingled "[o]n the bedrock of a philosophy of created being that was valid in its own right." Balthasar, *Cosmic Liturgy*, 37.

202. Ibid., 282.

203. See Balthasar, *Two Sisters*, 21, 320; Balthasar, *Engagement with God*, 29, 38;
The Christian State of Life, 60. Balthasar cannot be accused of Quietism, since, in his
theology, the person does not "drown his will in the will of God."

204. Balthasar, *Engagement with God*, 79. See also Balthasar, *Seeing the Form (TA1)*,
111.

[T]he Church will rediscover its youthful vitality not so much by changing its external legislation, as by submitting to the obedience of Christ and observing the laws which the Church lays upon itself with the intention of following in Christ's footsteps.[205]

With such a depiction of reality, we would then have to say that Balthasar attributes the authority of the saints, both as individuals and as a community, to the fact that they are freer than most, and that this freedom enables them, not only to be more, but also to do more, to know more and to understand more.[206] The saints would function authoritatively because they are unhindered and unconstrained by fear and by ulterior motives. Everybody knows, however, that to establish the *status quo* on the grounds of individual disposition, regardless of social structures, has its risks. The theological concept of *kenosis*, which Balthasar uses to describe both Christology and the nature of the life of the Trinity, can easily become problematic if it leads to the subjugation of a race or of a gender. The spiritualization of a disfunctioning society has radical consequences which Balthasar himself would certainly not have wanted to maintain. In claiming that the authority of the saints is a direct consequence of their surrender, and that it is one's surrender to God's will that makes a saint transparent to the divine authority, Balthasar does not intend to encourage fideism or pietism. There is an active and a rational aspect to this surrender, based on the understanding that God himself will not abandon the poor, but neither will he defend the unjust.

THE AUTHORITY THAT COMES FROM PARTICIPATION

In *The Christian State of Life* Balthasar continues to impress upon us that holiness will not ensue simply from an *imitation* of Christ, or from serving as a *reflection* of the drama and self-effacement that takes place within the Trinity. It ensues from a *participation* in this very drama.[207] All sorts of things are possible if there is "direct participation in the divine essence": it is possible to behold God, to be purified, to be justified, and to be sanctified.[208] Balthasar emphasizes that "no one becomes a saint without appropriate participation in the Cross."[209] In Balthasar's theology, the authority of the saints,

205. *Ecclesiam Suam*, 51.

206. The latter is what Simon argued concerning freedom in general. See Austin, *Up with Authority*, 25.

207. Balthasar, *The Christian State of Life*, 257.

208. Balthasar, *The Spirit of Truth (TL3)*, 448.

209. Balthasar, "Fragments on Suffering and Healing," 260.

in the existential dimension is grounded in their participation in Christ's way of being in the world. Balthasar claims that

> the Christian's life and state do not simply run parallel to the earthly existence of Christ as though he had to live until his earthly death in imitation of the state in which Jesus lived until the crucifixion. Christian life is not a mere imitation of the Lord's hidden and public life. On the contrary, it is from the beginning and *at every moment a participation not only in the Cross but also in the Resurrection of the Lord.*[210]

In his *Theo-Drama*, Balthasar examines three ways in which the issue of participation has been addressed in the history of theology: that of the Fathers, that of Eckhart and the Rhineland mystics, and that of St John of the Cross.[211] As Ellero Babini has pointed out, the philosophical category of participation acquires a particular significance in Balthasar's work, precisely because it is situated within a dramatic context.[212] Balthasar excludes "any suggestion that believers, who are, after all, created spiritual subjects, [a *Geistessubjekt*] are brought into the hypostatic union of the God-man. He also excludes any form of Eucharistic union that would be understood as an incorporation into Christ's physical body."[213] We have already insisted that, in Balthasar, "the otherness of God and the creature . . . is not destroyed."[214] In *Engagement with God*, participation takes the form of a "partnership," an "involvement" an "abiding in the source."[215] In his study of Barth, Balthasar states that participation is "both something conscious and ontically real," but there is "an unconditioned priority to the ontological over the cognitive."[216] Balthasar contends that the concept which he is portraying is based on that portrayed by Paul, where the "metamorphosis . . . is above all an assumption of form, the receiving of Christ's form in us."[217] The transformation spoken of by Paul "is no 'moral' transformation accomplished by making the copy similar to its exemplar, rather it is virtually a 'physical' change in which the sovereign power of the exemplar is expressed in the copy . . .

---

210. Balthasar, *The Christian State of Life*, 220.

211. Balthasar, *The Last Act (TD5)*.

212. Babini, "Jesus Christ: Form and Norm of Man," 222–23, 227.

213. Balthasar, *The Spirit of Truth (TL3)*, 292. See also what Pius XII, *Mystici Corporis Christi*.

214. Ibid., 234.

215. Balthasar, *Engagement with God*, 46–47.

216. Balthasar, *The Theology of Karl Barth*, 365. See Sullivan, "Saints as the 'Living Gospel,'" 5.

217. Balthasar, *Seeing the Form (TA1)*, 529.

causing the exemplar to shine forth from the copy."[218] Balthasar's concept is clearly indebted to that of Maximus in the *Ambigua*, which emphasizes the reciprocal relationship between divine incarnation and human deification dealing, among other things, with the transformational, theophanous effect upon the human body when the saints become united wholly to God.[219] In Maximus, the unity of God and the creature "will go as far as the point of 'indivisible identity' and will stop just short of the irreducible difference of natures."[220] Other approaches to participation which inspire Balthasar are those of Pierre de Bérulle,[221] and of George Bernanos.

In Balthasar's theology, any authority granted to the saints, in the existential dimension, is grounded in the participation in inner-Trinitarian relationship and extra-Trinitarian operation.[222] Balthasar considers especially authoritative those saintly theologians who have achieved an "equilibrium" within theology between "the personal effort to acquire the *intellectus fidei* and the participation . . . in the object of faith within one's life-experience."[223] Moreover, Balthasar is especially enthusiastic about those saints who can express the depths of their participation in Christ. Balthasar maintains that "the more a person participates (*teilnehmen*), in the original Christ-experience the more must he (and can he), in turn, communicate (*teilgeben*)" this Christ experience. Balthasar claims that this communication is precisely the reason for such an experience. The "intrinsic teleology of [one's] experience" lies in the communication of it.[224]

CONCLUSION

In this chapter, I explored Balthasar's notion of existence as expressive of God's form, identified some of the existential features of the saints' life that make the saints expressive of God's form, and focused on surrender and participation in the mystery of God as the reality which makes the saints authoritative. However implicitly, Balthasar wanted to develop a theology

218. Balthasar, *Two Sisters*, 464.

219. Sherwood recommends further study on the concept of "participation," which is, according to him, perhaps "the acutest problem in Byzantine theology." See Sherwood, "Survey of Recent Work on St Maximus the Confessor," 435.

220. Balthasar, *Cosmic Liturgy*, 353.

221. In Bérulle, "[t]o partake of the divine life means to participate in the fundamental state and attitude of Jesus." See Balthasar, *The Realm of Metaphysics in the Modern Age (TA5)*, 123.

222. Balthasar, *The Spirit of Truth (TL3)*, 234–35.

223. Balthasar, *Seeing the Form (TA1)*, 602.

224. Ibid., 306.

of the saints that reflected his agreement with theologians like Daniélou, Guardini, de Chardin, and Adam and his responses to philosophers such as Aristotle, Mounier, Blondel, Husserl, Merleau-Ponty, and Heidegger. He sought to provide a sacramental ontology, which enables us to view the whole of existence as theological, but particularly that of the saints. He also wanted to establish that there is a correlation between a life of holiness and the ability to speak correctly about God, as well as to claim that, with some saints, the mission is specifically doctrinal, and the experience of existence has dogmatic import. Balthasar is trying to prove that it is from within their genuine existence that the saints function authoritatively. My interpretation is that, in Balthasar's view, a holy existence stimulates in the saints qualities that make them authoritative. The existential features which characterize the saints in their holiness drives others to attribute authority to them. Finally, in presenting the saint as someone whom one consults on existential issues, and as someone whose existential stance one observes and emulates, intentionally or unintentionally, Balthasar attributes to the saints an authority that could analogously be compared to that of the official Magisterium of the church. Needless to say, in Balthasar, these existential features would also have served to challenge, not just traditional hagiography, but also philosophical, theological and ecclesial trends, not just contemporary to him, but also long-standing.

If I am correct in my own interpretation of Balthasar, that is, if this is really what he was trying to do, then I seriously think that Balthasar did a good job of it, even if this depiction may seem rather vague. Probably because of our prejudice towards the epistemic, to speak of existential authority is not really sufficient. This is why, in the next chapter I will discuss the epistemological dimension, and determine how it is that, in Balthasar, the saints acquire authority in the epistemological domain. I will also be arguing that the epistemological dimension is probably the principal dimension where the saints function authoritatively.

CHAPTER 4

The Epistemological Dimension

INTRODUCTION

Where the epistemological dimension is concerned, Balthasar is indebted to various contemporary philosophers, like Maréchal (d.1944), Przywara (d.1972), Maritain (d.1973), and to contemporary theologians like Mouroux (d.1973), Bultmann (d.1976), Rahner (d.1984), Frei (d.1988), and de Lubac (d.1991). In this Chapter it will be determined that, in Balthasar, the saints are acknowledged to be epistemologically proficient. I will want to demonstrate that, in Balthasar, there are aspects of holiness that furnish the saints with epistemological authority (both for theology and for the church), as well as that the saints function authoritatively epistemologically. It will become evident that whereas in the existential dimension, an authority is someone who exemplifies the essence of existence, in the epistemological dimension, an authority is someone whom one invokes when there has been a failure to know and to whom one must submit in the process of learning.[1] This makes the authority of the saints analogous to that of the Magisterium. For is this not the authority that the Magisterium normally demands (namely, that it be invoked when there has been a failure to know)? And is this not the authority which the individual Christian is expected to attribute to the Magisterium (namely, to submit to it in the process of learning)?

Before I proceed, I would first like to say something about the important role which authority plays in the apprehension of truth. Victor Lee

1. Austin, *Up with Authority*, 46.

Austin maintains that "authority is necessary if we are to flourish as beings who have knowledge," that "authority is . . . positively related to knowledge of the truth," and that "it is epistemic authority that accounts for how our knowledge is greater than what reason can deliver."[2] In this chapter, I will continue to delve into the questions already outlined, namely: why is it that the saints are considered to be *auctoritates* in Balthasar's eyes? What is at the basis of this authority? What is the grounding of this appreciation of the saints and of their theological contribution? Whereas in the third chapter, I dealt with the question of the authority of the saints from an existential perspective, this chapter will deal with the epistemological grounding of the authority of the saints. It will be determined that, in Balthasar, the epistemological domain is both an essential source of the authority of the saints, that is, that which drives us to their side, but also the place where they function authoritatively. It will be argued that the saints exercise epistemic authority when they share with us what they know and understand about God and his economy, and that we attribute to them epistemic authority both when we acknowledge their proficiency and when we submit to them in the process of learning. It will also be determined that, in the epistemological domain, Balthasar thinks that the epistemic authority of the saints is grounded in their faith and in their love. That is where their deep knowledge, their extraordinary understanding, their grasp of the truth comes from. It is also grounded in their participation in the archetypal experience, and in the quality of their mysticism and their contemplation. Their epistemic authority is also grounded in their very lack of attachment to this very knowledge which they have acquired. Finally, I will demonstrate that, in Balthasar, because all knowledge is interconnected, because there is no theology that is independent of the rest of theology, the epistemic authority of the individual saints is also dependent on the epistemic authority of the whole *communio sanctorum*.[3]

THE AUTHORITY THAT COMES FROM FAITH

Possibly the best way to understand Balthasar on faith is to compare him with Barth and Przywara.[4] In Balthasar, the *analogia entis* does not contradict the

2. Ibid., 2, 42.

3. In this respect, for Balthasar, the saints are similar to "the community of authorities" described by Austin, whose members "challenge, test, validate, qualify, and incorporate one another's assertions of truth." Ibid., 65.

4. See Henrici, "The Philosophy of Hans Urs von Balthasar," 151.

analogia fidei, as with the early Barth.[5] With Balthasar, being itself already contains a likeness of God (*analogia entis*). But there is a godlikeness that derives from faith as well. What makes Balthasar's understanding of faith so particular is that he sees it as a partaking in the dynamics of the immanent Trinity. In Balthasar, the synthetic power of the active "faculty" of believing (as *habitus* and *virtus fidei*) resides in God "in whose light and act the believer participates."[6] Christian faith is "more than a psychological fact, more than something belonging to human nature." It is something "specifically supernatural, something effected by God"[7] and residing in him.[8] Described in aesthetic terms, the light of faith is said to stem "from the object which, revealing itself to the subject, draws it out beyond itself (otherwise it would not be faith) into the sphere of the object."[9] In the epistemological dimension, the saints become most authoritative in their co-operation with God in the act of faith, in their readiness to be drawn into the form of God.[10]

In accord with Catholic tradition, Balthasar maintains that "this faith must not be taken in isolation to be an infallible criterion but has to prove itself in the various expressions of a lived life of faith; that is, it must show itself to be genuine through signs."[11] It is not just that Balthasar sees life as an expression of faith. It is that faith arises from the person's life. In Balthasar, "living by faith" is "an experience that arises from the totality of the person's life."[12] Here, Balthasar would be in agreement with Augustine, but also with Jean Mouroux, whose work on Christian experience was so influential in the 1950s. Subsequently, with Balthasar, any authority which the saints

5 See Ratzinger, "Christian Universalism," 131.

6. Balthasar, *Seeing the Form (TA1)*, 179.

7. Ibid., 222–23. In his *Convergences*, Balthasar states that "it is not the subjective impression which releases" the Christ event in my psyche. Nor is it the "the power of my faith which connects me to my unity in Christ." This would be "a psychologizing of faith." Balthasar, *Convergences*, 129–30.

8. Balthasar, *Seeing the Form (TA1)*, 179. Balthasar claims that, in faith, "what is involved is not at all a projection of the mythopoetic religious imagination," but God's "fantasy." Ibid., 172.

9. Ibid., 181. See also 465–66; Balthasar, *The Realm of Metaphysics in Antiquity (TA4)*, 394; Balthasar, *The Spirit of Truth (TL3)*, 203; and Howsare, *Balthasar: A Guide for the Perplexed*, 81.

10. On its part, the subject ought not to grasp or attempt to control the object, but to receive it actively, so that the object is allowed to unfold for the subject. See Howsare, *Balthasar: A Guide for the Perplexed*, 11–12, 79. See also Balthasar, "Does Jesus Shine Through?," 17–18.

11. See Stuart, "Sacramental Flesh in Qeer Theology," 65–75.

12. Balthasar, *The Spirit of Truth (TL3)*, 282.

express would have to be grounded both in a life that is steered by faith and in a faith that arises from life.[13]

Because faith is understood as an encounter of the person with God, experience becomes an "indispensable" concept.[14] In Balthasar, experience is an "*event*," and that which alone can become an experience (*Erfahrung*) is man's "act of entering into the Son of God."[15] On the other hand, faith is not "a purely emotional occurrence." It is not "a single content or state, a sensual or spiritual perception, a feeling or a particular experience."[16] Faith is an *attitude* with which the "*genuine* believer" identifies himself. The believer will not emphasize "the elements of experience to the detriment of the central element of faith."[17] This is in total contrast with Medieval hagiography, where it was, customarily, the extraordinary experiences which attributed reliability and credibility to those "saints" who claimed them. Using Ignatius of Loyola (consolation or desolation), Bernard of Clairvaux (*sapor*), and Aquinas (*cognitio per connaturalitatem*), Balthasar delineates what it is that a "truly living Christian experience of faith includes." His view is that the above are part of the Christian experience of faith. They could even be "breakthroughs to new depths of experience," but, on their own they are not faith, because they could also very well be mere psychological effects.[18] As Ben Quash has pointed out, Balthasar also criticizes Bultmann for his anthropological reduction of faith to "the sightless decision whereby 'my' existence is transformed." In this case, the Christ of faith is grasped only in the "pro me" of the process of transformation of my existence.[19] Consequently, in Balthasar, any authority emerging from faith can only be grounded in experience if experience is understood as man's "act of entering into the Son of God," and not as a feeling or a taste alone. Such experience always involves the transformative power of grace, so that authoritativeness would have to be a consequence of one's transformation in Christ.[20]

We have already established that, in the existential dimension, it is only the actual living of a holy life which gives rise to correct speech about God. In the epistemological dimension, Balthasar underscores the necessity of

13. There is an emphasis on faith being "an 'embodied' response." See Balthasar, *Prayer*, 36.

14. Balthasar, *Seeing the Form (TA1)*, 219.

15. Ibid., 222.

16. Ibid., 238–39, 169. The reference could be to William James, to Schleiermacher, or even to George Tyrrell.

17. Ibid., 412.

18. Balthasar, *Seeing the Form (TA1)*, 412.

19. Quash, "Hans Urs von Balthasar," 118.

20. Balthasar, *Two Sisters*, 20, 467.

a committed faith which alone makes theology possible. There is evidence of this in his exegesis, but also in his fundamental theology and in his dogmatics. As Howsare has said, Balthasar "is deeply suspicious of any attempt to bracket faith in order to get to the simple facts."[21] Balthasar refuses the phenomenological reduction which follows from *epoché*. In its philosophical usage, popularized by Edmund Husserl, *epoché* describes the theoretical moment when all judgments and assumptions about the existence of the external world are suspended. The bracketing out of unexamined assumptions about the world is considered to be necessary in order to allow the phenomena to speak for themselves and to more easily allow the examination of the phenomena as they are originally given to consciousness. For Balthasar, the object cannot simply be cut away. According to him, for example, the socio-historical criticism of the Gospels, and Rudolph Bultmann (1884–1976)'s anthropological reduction of faith cannot provide a credible account. Faith in Christ and commitment to him is indispensable for the theologian. For Balthasar, the representation of theological truth cannot be impartial, and commitment is necessary.[22] Against modern theological apologetics,[23] Balthasar maintains that the scientific objectivity of theology "rests on the decision to believe," and "there can be, therefore (theologically considered), no neutral objectivity, no consideration of the object of belief without belief, or apart from belief and unbelief."[24] In Balthasar's theology, it is not the saints' capacity to use reason in order to prove faith's content that gives them credibility.[25] Balthasar claims that those believers whose faith is what it should be "are *right*."[26] The credibility of their theology is grounded in the fact that their theology is stimulated and sustained by their faith in Christ, and in the fact that their faith participates in that of Christ. It is the quality of the Christian's faith—which is much more than a mere cognitive assent to propositions—that enables him or her to speak correctly about God. In Balthasar, one's faith is a participation in the very faith which is in God (since faith is, above all, a divine attribute).

21. Howsare, *Balthasar: A Guide for the Perplexed*, 150. Howsare also points out that Balthasar criticises certain Enlightenment style approaches to the biblical text which demand pure theological neutrality (78).

22. Balthasar, *Seeing the Form (TA1)*, 223–24.

23. Modern theological apologetics linked faith and reason together, whereas Balthasar breaks this link. See Davies, "The Theological Aesthetic," 134.

24. Balthasar, *Convergences*, 51.

25. Balthasar, *Engagement with God*, 102.

26. Balthasar, "Our Shared Responsibility," 147.

THE AUTHORITY THAT COMES FROM KNOWLEDGE

There is then the authority that comes from knowledge. The *Aesthetics* is full of deliberations on knowledge. Balthasar discusses human knowledge (in the context of his discourse on Plato),[27] knowing and not knowing (in his deliberation on the dialectic of sensory manifestation),[28] the distinction between conjecture and absolute knowledge (in the context of his conversation with Nicholas of Cusa).[29] Probably the more relevant consideration of theological knowledge is that provided in his discussion of the relationship between *pistis* and *gnosis* (in his discussion on faith),[30] and of aesthetic reason (in the context of his dialogue with Anselm).[31] Knowledge is also at the forefront in Balthasar's discussion about the knowledge of the saints, more precisely on folly and glory, in his sections on "Holy Fools" and "The Christian as Idiot."[32]

In Balthasar, knowledge is not independent of the commitment, the passion, of the knower. As with Michael Polanyi, in Balthasar, the character of knowledge is personal, but "personal" is not equivalent to relativism or subjectivism.[33] Balthasar is able to avoid both "the false objectivism and naïve realism which mark so much modern rationalism/ empiricism," as well as avoid the false subjectivism and skepticism which marks the various forms of modern idealism and postmodernism. He finds support in the Church Fathers, in High Scholasticism,[34] as well as in later theologians and philosophers like Möhler, von Drey (1777–1853), Newman (1801–1890),[35] Blondel, and Maréchal who had also taken this stance.

Balthasar's theory of knowledge is significantly different from that of various other philosophers or theologians we know. As Anthony Cirelli has pointed out, in order to counter the dominance of subjectivity in modern German (and Western) philosophy since Kant, Balthasar appealed to the theocentric epistemology of Gregory of Nyssa. Here, finite thought is utterly dependent on God and not on finite subjectivity, and the creative powers (the *logoi*) of God enable us to come to know God.[36] If we take the saints

---

27. Balthasar, *The Realm of Metaphysics in Antiquity. (TA4)*, 171–201

28. Balthasar, *Theology: The Old Covenant (TA6)*, 37–38.

29. Balthasar, *The Realm of Metaphysics in the Modern Age (TA5)*, 238–47.

30. Balthasar, *Seeing the Form (TA1)*, 131–41.

31. Balthasar, *Studies in Theological Style: Clerical Styles (TA2)*, 213–37.

32. Balthasar, *The Realm of Metaphysics in the Modern Age (TA5)*, 141–204.

33. Polanyi, *Personal Knowledge* (1962).

34. Howsare, *Balthasar: A Guide for the Perplexed*, 72.

35. Ibid., 13.

36. Cirelli, "Re-Assessing The Meaning Of Thought," 416–24.

THE EPISTEMOLOGICAL DIMENSION 125

to be personifications of the *logoi* of God, the conclusion becomes clear: we are able to know God through the saints. On his part, Peter Henrici argues that, from a methodological point of view, Balthasar is closest to Anselm, whose philosophical doctrine of knowledge "explains the truth of revelation and the process of knowledge as disclosure/concealment."[37] Victoria Harrison has claimed that Balthasar's religious epistemology converges with Hilary Putnam's "internal realism."[38] On my part, I believe that the theological epistemology which is most helpful is that of Jacques Maritain (1892–1973), who was in turn influenced by Augustine and John of the Cross. David C.Schindler has already linked Bal,thasar to Maritain in his philosophical investigation of Balthasar's structure of truth. Schindler claims that, like Maritain, Balthasar sees knowledge as "a *vital* exchange" in which both the subject and the object come to be what they are through the act of knowledge.[39]

Maritain sought to explain the nature of knowledge: scientific and philosophical, but also religious faith and mysticism in *The Degrees of Knowledge*.[40] Here, Maritain speaks of different "degrees" of knowledge hierarchically ordered according to the nature of the object to be known and the "degree of abstraction" involved. According to him, those objects which are highest in intelligibility, immateriality, and potential to be known, are the objects of the highest degree of knowledge. Like Maritain, Balthasar distinguishes "natural knowledge" from "mystical knowledge,"[41] without considering them to be different "knowledges." In addition, along with Maritain, Balthasar emphasizes faith, rather than reason, as the medium for real wisdom. Balthasar can argue that faith is the means of access to real wisdom because, according to him, "[t]he whole order of reason is theologically embedded in the order of faith, just as the order of creation lies embedded in the order of grace."[42] This means that, in Balthasar, reason is itself entrenched in faith, just as faith is embedded in reason. The description of the dynamic that takes place within the individual mystic, which Balthasar provides in *Theo-Logic* is evidence of this. "If at the moment when [the mystic] is speaking with God, he brings his entire self with him, planting these things in his rational 'I' without thereby intending to diminish the Spirit, his mind acquires a share in the Spirit." On the contrary, if the mystic

37. Henrici, "The Philosophy of Hans Urs von Balthasar," 164.

38. Hunsinger, "Postliberal Theology," 51.

39. Schindler, *Hans Urs Von Balthasar and the Dramatic Structure of Truth*, 213.

40. Maritain, *The Degrees of Knowledge*.

41. Balthasar, *Seeing the Form (TA1)*, 262.

42. Balthasar, *The Theology of Karl Barth*, 325.

fails to plant these things in his rational "I," he or she "will not be able to give an adequate account of the insights and tasks he received in the Spirit."[43]

It is to be expected that anyone using the saints as dependable sources of knowledge and who finds them so persuasive, as Balthasar does, would perceive a link between the saints' expertise in the eyes of others and their own spiritual life, between their adeptness and their own understanding of the Word, between their evident competence and their mystical knowledge. The descriptive nature of the phenomenological method enables Balthasar to state this, precisely because one can see evidence of it, even if it may be difficult to explain how the saints know so much, and express it so well. In Balthasar's theology, the "saints" display exceptional understanding, remarkable knowledge, and an extraordinary ease of access to the truth. Bernard, Francis, Ignatius and Thérèse are compared to "volcanoes pouring forth molten fire from the inmost depths of revelation."[44] In his book on *Prayer*, Balthasar reverses this ascending image with a descending one that is just as powerful: the saints, he writes, have been "overwhelmed by the torrent which pours over and into them," thanks to their proximity to the "total fullness" of Christ.[45] So, we know that saints are epistemic authorities.

The question now arises as to whether the knowledge of the saints differs from that of the members of the Magisterium and, if so, how. Here we have to depend on our own interpretation of Balthasar's theology of the saints. Balthasar would probably say that the knowledge that the saints acquire differs from other knowledge only in that, firstly, it always leads to a transformation of their lives. Secondly, it is based on faith rather than on rational argument, and in that it is attained through the contemplation of the Word of God, rather than through natural philosophy. Moreover, Balthasar would probably say that the knowledge of the saints has an uplifting and revitalizing effect on others. And, finally, it is ubiquitously influential.

In this regard, perhaps it would be helpful to examine the distinction which Balthasar makes between the "two realities" which theology could transport itself to. There is "the realm of pure logical exactness" and there is "experience which leads to contemplation and can become truly mystical."[46] It would seem that the realm towards which the theology of the Magisterium generally transports itself is that of "pure logical exactness," whereas the theology produced by the saints is more contemplative, and perhaps even mystical. As someone who has no enthusiasm for the rational-propositional

---

43. Balthasar, *The Spirit of Truth (TL3)*, 376.

44. Balthasar, *A Theology of History*, 110.

45. Balthasar, *Prayer*, 213.

46. Balthasar, *Seeing the Form (TA1)*, 601.

approach to doctrine, as represented by scholasticism, Balthasar would certainly prefer the latter. I ought to insist that Balthasar never separates and juxtaposes the saints against the Magisterium. However, he does distinguish quite clearly between the theology produced by the saints and that of others, and he does express his preference for the former.

Ratzinger has claimed that, in Balthasar's work, "there is a straight path. . .from the theology of the word to the theology of silence," but not in the sense of abandoning all words in the negation of the worldly and earthly.[47] Balthasar resorts to the *theologia negativa*, without his theology ever detaching itself from its basis in a *theologia positiva*.[48] The apophatic is anchored in the cataphatic.[49] With Balthasar, it is not that theology cannot say anything about God.[50] It is that whatever it says about God will be inadequate.[51] The negative theology which Balthasar is proposing is therefore not a philosophical "negative theology," but "a 'negative theology' within the theology of revelation." Likewise, his saints will not be associated with a "negative theology" in the philosophical sense, but with a negative theology in a theological sense. In a theological sense, "God's incomprehensibility is . . . no longer a mere deficiency in knowledge, but the positive manner in which God determines the knowledge of faith."[52] Balthasar presents two examples of theologians who "relied most consistently on the apophatic method," and yet "never divorced it from the cataphatic approach." These are the Areopagite and John of the Cross, who, according to Balthasar, are the two "most decidedly aesthetic theologians of Christian history."[53]

THE AUTHORITY OF THE INTERNAL MAGISTERIUM

We cannot realistically discuss the authority of the saints unless we situate it within the context of the Augustinian doctrine of the *Magister interior* and the division which emerged after Kant between "immanent experience" and "external revelation." After Kant, the important question became "how to

---

47. Ratzinger, "Christian Universalism," 133–34.

48. Balthasar, *Seeing the Form (TA1)*, 124.

49. Ibid., 448. See O'Donaghue, "A Theology of Beauty," 3. See also Dickens, *Hans Urs von Balthasar's Theological Aesthetics*, 67.

50. *Truth of God (TL2)* could be said to be a defense of positive language about God against neoplatonic apophatic theology and eastern mysticism.

51. Balthasar, *The Spirit of Truth (TL3)*, 358.

52. Balthasar, *Seeing the Form (TA1)*, 461.

53. Ibid., 124–25.

deal with the modern, Kantian interest in the subjective, experiential element of faith without losing the objective character of divine revelation."[54]

Both the phenomenology of the supernatural and the phenomenology
of the subject begin with how an idea is generated within us. Blondel had
studied the mechanism by which our idea of revelation is generated within
us in accordance with the hypothesis that this revelation is supernatural in
its source. Then he had analyzed the way man has to give his assent to this
revelation. And finally, he had shown how faith in this revelation inevitably
expresses itself in an exterior practice, still in accordance with the rational
exigencies of the hypothesis that this way of life is strictly supernatural.[55]
With Tyrrell, revelation received the characteristic of immanence, consisting of internal promptings and guidings of the finite by the infinite will,
so that revelation becomes an anthropological and subjective matter. In
Balthasar, "there is no discrepancy between the one known without and the
one who lets himself be known within: he is one and the same."[56] In the *Aesthetics*, Balthasar tries to reverse the trend of Neo-Thomism[57] by approxi-
mating the external teacher to the *Magister interior*. He presents the latter
as "the theological *a priori* serving as foundation for all other instruction
from outside, whether from the sphere of the Church or of history." Thus,
Balthasar fosters a concept of the *Magister interior* as part of the revelation
process. It is "the *sensorium*, conferred in revelation itself, which perceives
what revelation means . . . in the unique sense of God becoming manifest."[58]
With Balthasar, however, revelation remains a divine initiative and a divine
encounter. In *Theo-Logic*, Balthasar underscores yet again that the Spirit's
testimony is itself both an "inward and outward testimony."[59] Here Balthasar
follows both the Pauline position which emphasized the Paraclete-Spirit's
role within the teaching authority of the church; and the Johannine position which attributes to the Paraclete-Spirit the role of a teacher dwelling
in each Christian.[60] According to Balthasar, a properly exercised external

54. Boersma, *Nouvelle Théologie*, 37.

55. Blondel, *Action* (1893).

56. Balthasar, "Does Jesus Shine Through?," 17. This could be compared to Calvin's
position concerning "the strict correlation between word (Scripture) and the inner testimony of the Spirit." Balthasar, *The Spirit of Truth (TL3)*, 146–47.

57. Neo-Thomism emphasized that the supernatural is extrinsic. Nature is thus
juxtaposed against the supernatural. See Boersma, "Sacramental Ontology," 246; and
Boersma, *Nouvelle Théologie*, 4.

58. Balthasar, *Seeing the Form (TA1)*, 162–63.

59. Balthasar, *The Spirit of Truth (TL3)*, 223.

60. For a discussion of these two positions, see Brown, *The Churches the Apostles
Left behind*, 149.

church authority "recall[s] the individual to that which he from the very depths of his heart has always 'known.'"[61] This is reminiscent of Pascal who had predicted that, once the content of revelation is formulated, it strikes the heart immediately as truth.[62] This focus on the heart also takes us back to what Cardinal Newman once said, namely, that "[t]ruth has the gift of overcoming the human heart, whether by persuasion or compulsion; and, if what we preach be truth, it must be natural, it must be popular, it will make itself popular."[63] The implication, inspired by his image of the aesthetic work, is that truth is its own authority, and has its own supremacy, so that it demands the compliance of the heart without violence.

The discussion continues in *The Christian State of Life*. Here, what Balthasar says about internal and external revelation, and, in particular, about the call, can act as an analogy for understanding the relationship between the internal and the external Magisterium. Balthasar reminds us that "the Church has recognized the finger of God" in various calls, including "the founding of all great religious orders." The church "has also, after appropriate testing . . . recognized the existence and right of a subjective vocation that stems, not from the Church, but from God."[64] Thus, according to Balthasar, God's call comes from within, but it does not "come to an individual *only* from within." It also comes from without so that it cannot "be carried out apart from or even against the Church."[65] If God "calls both exteriorly and interiorly," as Aquinas says, then it is his will that these two aspects work together to establish unity between vocation and mission.[66] Balthasar agrees with Aquinas that God himself cannot permit an ineradicable contradiction between the church and one's personal mission, for we "must be convinced that in Christ our Lord. . .only one Spirit holds sway."[67] Still, Balthasar does grant the possibility

> that a personal call may not be immediately recognized as such by the Church and that one called will, in consequence, be obliged to carry out his mission against strong opposition even though he seeks to the best of his ability to do so in accordance

61. Balthasar, "Authority," 139.

62. Nichols, *The Word Has Been abroad*, 111.

63. Card.Newman, "Preface to the Third Edition," xxiv:15

64. Balthasar, *The Christian State of Life*, 448.

65. Ibid., 439.

66. Ibid., 442. In Balthasar, the two authorities: the external "proclamation and the internal spirit," "must ring out together, must complement one another, must point to each other." See also "Our Shared Responsibility," 143.

67. Balthasar, *The Christian State of Life*, 448.

with the mind of the Church. Despite the Church's resistance, such a mission will be as truly an ecclesiastical one as were the missions of those called to initiate great reforms within the Church, for they, too, had to overcome harsh opposition with the help of God's grace before at last—whether during their lifetime or after it—receiving ecclesiastical recognition.[68]

In the *Theo-Logic*, Balthasar emphasizes the public nature of any personal inspiration. He asserts that, although "[t]he individual believer could receive direct illumination from the Spirit concerning a piece of Scripture or of tradition without the intervention of the external 'teaching office,'"[69] this "direct illumination" never takes place "in a purely 'private' capacity, but with a view to that individual's Christian vocation, which is always related to the Church."[70] Such an emphasis on the social nature of Christian experience is emblematic in Balthasar. Everything must be evaluated within its social context: whether it is vocation or mission, or even obedience and disputation. According to Balthasar, the right to "contest" issues within the church grows, "the more [the individual] allows the Spirit of holiness to hold sway within him."[71] Elsewhere, Balthasar modifies the *right* to contest into an *obligation* "to admonish and advise," claiming that both priest and laity may be called to this.[72]

Needless to say, an over-emphasis on the internal Magisterium has its problems where authority is concerned. For one thing, to write of an internal authority of the Spirit would require that one explain how the diversity or even incompatibility of beliefs within the church is to be resolved.[73] Balthasar would have been aware of this predicament. What he does to overcome this objection is: he maintains, for the saints, the position of the Fathers that the *magisterium internum*—i.e., the teaching which takes place inside the individual—is not bound by the official *magisterium externum*. In agreement with Möhler and with Newman, Balthasar claims that the individual believer may "receive direct illumination from the Spirit concerning a piece of Scripture or of tradition without the intervention of the external

---

68. Ibid., 439. See also 441.

69. Balthasar, *The Spirit of Truth (TL3)*, 328.

70. Ibid.

71. Balthasar, *The Office of Peter*, 343.

72. Balthasar, *The Christian State of Life*, 340. Balthasar proposes practical means–such as dialogue and obedience–that could draw the two sides together. See Balthasar, "Our Shared Responsibility," 146 and "Obedience in the Light of the Gospel," 243–44.

73. Brown, *The Churches the Apostles Left behind*, 121–22.

'teaching office' [of the church]."[74] The Spirit may also "guide the individual in his right action without any truth being proclaimed officially."[75] Concerning the value of "private revelations," Balthasar quotes Adrienne von Speyr. "It may be," he quotes, "that God is speaking to the Church, through someone's prayer, in a *language* that is not understood by the Church at that time; perhaps the Church does not want to and cannot accept it."[76] It is insuch a situation that the roles of the Magisterium and theology are especially important. Balthasar grants that, historically, such private revelations sometimes "had to be first purified and completed by theologians or the magisterium itself."[77] He also emphasizes the responsibility of the visionary him or herself, arguing that, whenever these private revelations "either did not 'succeed' or gained acceptance in a not entirely credible way," this was because of the self-centredness of "the transmitting medium."[78]

While it is clear that the *magisterium internum* is not to be isolated from the *magisterium externum*, it is not as clear whether the *Magister Interior* is the theological *a priori*, serving as foundation for all other instruction from outside, or whether, even when a saint is involved, the *Magister Exterior* is the theological *a priori* serving as foundation for all other instruction from inside. Balthasar does not fail to emphasize that the saints are notorious for their acquiescence to the jurisdiction of the external magisterium. For example, writing about Thérèse, Balthasar commends her for not being "touched by the temptation to substitute an interior certainty for the Church's external authority."[79]

In the *Aesthetics*, the question of certitude is best answered using Aquinas. Balthasar refers to Aquinas's observation concerning the prophet, namely that he "has supreme certainty concerning those things which the prophetic Spirit expressly infuses into him, and also concerning the fact that these things are revealed to him by God."[80] In *Theo-Logic*, Balthasar comes back to the issue: is man able to know whether he is "moved by his natural

---

74. Balthasar, *The Spirit of Truth (TL3)*, 328. See Jean Mouroux, *The Christian Experience.*

75. Balthasar, "Our Shared Responsibility," 143. Balthasar acknowledges God's "right of personal access to souls." According to Balthasar, "all calls to the personal following of the Lord and, indeed, all great and unique missions within the Church come . . . purely from God and, psychologically speaking, are made known directly to the one called." Balthasar, *The Christian State of Life*, 441.

76. Balthasar, *The Spirit of Truth (TL3)*, 376.

77. Balthasar, *First Glance*, 88–89.

78. Ibid.

79. Balthasar, *Two Sisters*, 57.

80. Balthasar, *Seeing the Form (TA1)*, 308.

inclination or by a supernatural impulsion?"[81] Can there ever be certainty that someone is truly a servant of righteousness? Balthasar argues that Montanism and Messalianism "forced the Fathers to confront the issue and adopt positions that, while cautious, are not simply a rejection." He notes that the Reformers and the Council of Trent were at loggerheads on the issue.[82] Balthasar alludes to the reservations which Aquinas held, namely that, while it is quite possible for there to be *certitudo* regarding a *fides informis*, this does not yield any certainty about *fides formata caritate*.[83] Balthasar claims that this uncertainty arises "because of the similarity between natural love and that which is given by grace."[84] Balthasar also refers to Cardinal Cajetan (1469–1534) and to the Spanish theologian and philosopher, Francisco Suárez (1548–1617) on this issue.[85]

The kind of certainty which Balthasar accentuates is the certainty ensuing from "a lived life of faith."[86] Understood in the Pauline and the Thomistic sense, rather than that of the Reformers, the *Magister interior* that is not embodied in a life is no longer an infallible criterion. This means that Balthasar would apply Artistotle, rather than Kant, to argue that—particularly in the saints—knowledge and virtuous activity are inseparable.[87] Balthasar also rests on the Pauline and the Johannine sense, namely that evidence that we are in Christ, "arises solely from the whole thrust of our believing and surrendered existence."[88] In the Johannine sense, the "knowledge" given to us by the Spirit "is always linked to very concrete conditions of Christian living."[89] Balthasar uses Mouroux to argue about the concept of Christian experience of the Spirit. He claims that Mouroux's contribution

81. This was an important question for the early Fathers as well as in the Middle Ages.

82. Balthasar, *The Spirit of Truth (TL3)*, 379–80.

83. Ibid., 380. *Fides informis* would here have to be understood as a faith that is moved by a natural inclination. On the other hand, *fides formata caritate* would refer to the faith that is supernatural, that is permeated by divine love; one that arises from a "supernatural impulsion."

84. Aquinas, *De Veritate*, quoted in Balthasar, *The Spirit of Truth (TL3)*, 381.

85. Whereas Cajetan admits "a *certitudo* regarding the *donum infusum fidei*, but with the restrictions formulated by the Council of Trent," Suárez opposes the assertion of a *certitudo moralis*. He maintains that "there is no sure sign that would permit an "acquired natural faith" to be distinguished from a supernatural infused faith." Ibid., 383.

86. Ibid.

87. For Aristotle, stupidity of a certain kind precludes goodness, whereas for Kant one can be both good and stupid. See MacIntyre, *After Virtue*, 155.

88. Balthasar, *The Spirit of Truth (TL3)*, 381.

89. Ibid., 382.

lies in the fact that he "points us toward the total achievement, the total stance of a life."[90]

THE AUTHORITY THAT COMES FROM LOVE

In the *Apokalypse*, Nietzsche and Kierkegaard (1813–1855) are made to confront each other on the issue of love. Nietzsche's is the "*power* love," while Kierkegaard's is the love that sacrifices itself.[91] With Balthasar, love "plays an indispensable role in thought."[92] In his *Aesthetics*, Balthasar claims that "[a]ll theoretical and practical difficulties of faith as an intellectual act are solved once the deeper level of love is reached."[93] It would seem as if Balthasar is opposed to Aquinas, and in accordance with Augustine. Whereas Aquinas would say that "knowledge comes before love" (giving ultimacy to the intellect), in Balthasar love is "the foundation of knowledge" (giving ultimacy to love).[94] Despite this seeming opposition, David C. Schindler has convincingly argued that Balthasar is not opposed to Aquinas. He is opposed only to a simplistic reading of Aquinas.[95] Schindler claims that, in Balthasar, there is an affirmation of the supremacy of love that nevertheless includes an abiding priority of the intellect over the will.[96]

There is enough evidence in Balthasar to show that love is not unknowing, and blind. Quite the reverse, it is the source of all knowledge. In Balthasar, love precedes knowledge, substitutes knowledge, mediates knowledge, and is the foundation of knowledge. To quote Henrici, "it is the only thing that is truly intelligible, in fact the only thing that is truly 'rational,' 'id quo maius cogitari nequit.'"[97] Balthasar maintains that, in knowledge and in love, "man is open to the Thou, to things and to God."[98] Balthasar uses the saints (for example, Augustine[99] and Bernard[100]) to ratify love as

90. Ibid., 385.

91. Henrici, "The Philosophy of Hans Urs von Balthasar," 160.

92. Nichols, "Theo-Logic," 164.

93. Balthasar, *Seeing the Form (TA1)*, 193.

94. Ibid., 130.

95. Schindler, "Towards a non-Possessive concept of knowledge," 586.

96. Ibid., 580.

97. Henrici, "The Philosophy of Hans Urs von Balthasar," 167.

98. Balthasar, *Seeing the Form (TA1)*, 243.

99. Balthasar, *Man in History*, x.

100. Balthasar, *The Spirit of Truth (TL3)*, 366. O'Donaghue has said that "Balthasar is not concerned primarily with the light in the mind . . . but with the fire in the heart." O'Donaghue, "A Theology of Beauty," 9. This is one of the reasons why Balthasar often singles out Pascal. Pascal is the theologian of the supernaturally enlightened heart.

that which leads to knowledge. He uses Paul's letters to the Corinthians and to the Ephesians to emphasize that love alone mediates the authentic Christian *gnosis* (1 Cor 8:1ff) and that whatever is worth knowing, can only be known by love. With the spiritual theology of the Middle Ages, and on the foundations laid by Gregory the Great, Balthasar claims that "[i]t is through love that we attain knowledge." Indeed, "love itself is knowledge."[101]

I would agree with David C. Schindler that "Balthasar's insistence on the absolute priority of love . . . is not a concession to voluntarism [a perspective in the mind that prioritizes the will over emotion or reason] and the irrationality it entails, but is ultimately due to a significantly different notion of reason than is commonly assumed."[102] The knowledge that this love has is, according to Balthasar, not the "knowledge of itself or of its own work, but of the fullness of Christ."[103] The authority of love is confirmed in his *Christlicher Stand* where Balthasar writes that

> There is no authority higher than love. On the contrary, it is itself the highest authority, holding all else under its sway. Because it is compelled by no necessity, *necessity* and freedom are conjoined in it. When in all freedom it makes its decision to love, it fulfils all that is required.[104]

Brian Daley has said that, in Balthasar's terminology, "*Gnosis* generally means the quest for a cognitive union of the creature with God achieved by asceticism and renunciation," rather than by "a union of love consummated in the midst of the finite world."[105] I agree with Daley's interpretation of *gnosis* in Balthasar, although I am not sure I totally agree with his interpretation of how it is achieved. I do not believe that, in Balthasar, gnosis is achieved by asceticism, mortification, and austerity. In Balthasar, renunciation is not an alternative to the union of love but an essential element of it, as is clear in his hymn to love, found in his first volume of the *Aesthetics*. "Love—indeed, love that partakes in God's love—is the warrant of objective knowledge in the realm of Trinitarian revelation."[106] It is for this reason that Balthasar can argue that authentic love "bears within itself in sensory fashion the quintessence of dogmatics."[107] Likewise, according to Balthasar, "[d]ogmas

---

101. O'Donaghue adds that "the fire in the heart becomes the light of the mind." Ibid., 10.

102. Schindler, "Towards a non-Possessive concept of knowledge," 579.

103. Balthasar, *Seeing the Form (TA1)*, 230.

104. Balthasar, *The Christian State of Life*, 30.

105. See "Balthasar's Reading of the Church Fathers," 192.

106. Balthasar, *Seeing the Form (TA1)*, 618.

107. Ibid., 424.

must be nothing other than aspects of the love which manifests itself and yet remains mystery within revelation."[108]

In one of his essays, Balthasar objects to everything that could lead to *gnosis* rather than to love, and applies Nietzsche's saying God is "dead" to a dogmatics that prefers *gnosis* and reason over and above love and God himself.[109] From what I can observe, this is where the authority of the knowledge of the saints is grounded in Balthasar's case: in its radical difference from simple *gnosis*.

Besides asserting that God can only be known through love,[110] Balthasar also insists that the truth can only be expressed by love. Balthasar builds on John. Here, "love that is practised contains the ability to demonstrate itself as the truth."[111] Balthasar claims that "the task of the members of the Church is precisely to give living and existential [Christian] expression to the truth in the exercise of love."[112] From an epistemological perspective, "whereas the one who does not love is in ignorance,"[113] genuine love enables the Christian saint to interpret, embody, as well as communicate the Christological form which love takes.[114]

Let me recapitulate. In this Chapter, we have so far determined that, in Balthasar, the saints' authority comes from their faith, their knowledge, their love, which gives the saints what I would like to call an *epistemological advantage*. Simply speaking, I have interpreted Balthasar as saying that, in the epistemological dimension, the saints function as an authority within theology, the church and even humanity, because of the quality of their faith, knowledge, and love which enables them to know more, do more and be more. But where does such faith, knowledge and love, derive from, according to Balthasar? What is it that produces such an advantageous epistemological position? In spite of the problems associated with the concept, Balthasar, provides "experience" as the answer.[115] The concept of experience enables Balthasar to provide a good grounding for a theology of the authority of the saints, particularly when he concentrates on the experience of contemplation, on archetypal experience, and on mystical experience, without falling into the Modernist traps of either belittling the intellectual or of over-subjectivizing the subject's experience.

108. Balthasar, *Convergences*, 13.
109. Balthasar, "The Absences of Jesus," 57–58.
110. Balthasar, *The Spirit of Truth (TL3)*, 382, 448.
111. Balthasar, *Seeing the Form (TA1)*, 424.
112. Balthasar, "Our Shared Responsibility," 141–42.
113. Balthasar, *Prayer*, 215.
114. Balthasar, *Seeing the Form (TA1)*, 424.
115. See Maggiolini, "Magisterial Teaching on Experience in the twentieth Century."

THE AUTHORITY THAT COMES FROM EXPERIENCE

Along with other *nouveaux théologiens*, in particular, Johann Adam Möhler (1796–1838), Marie-Dominique Chenu (1895–1990), and Louis Dupré (1926–), Balthasar takes the historical and experiential conditions of human existence seriously,[116] without, however, making them absolute, as Western rationalism and empiricism did. For Balthasar, the theological concept of experience is only "intelligible when shaped by the perception of the basic form of revelation."[117] It is possible to experience Christ's existence, and to participate in Christ's experience. This is much more than an imitation of Christ, or even a conformity with Christ.[118] It is a *being "drawn* by grace into the original work at the place that is reserved" for you.[119] This concept is the Pauline "en Christō,"[120] which, according to Balthasar, could sometimes even take physical form, although it does not necessarily have to do so.[121]

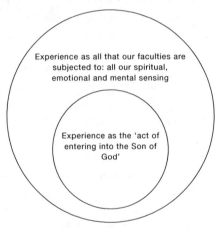

Diagram 02. Experience

Balthasar uses various saints, to describe the authentic "living Christian experience of faith": Ignatius of Loyola, Bernard, Aquinas, and others.[122] Generally speaking, for Balthasar, experience encompasses all that our fac-

116. Boersma, *Nouvelle Théologie*, 22, 36, and 45.

117. Schindler, writing about Peter Casarella's contribution on "Experience as a Theological Category," 109.

118. Balthasar, *Seeing the Form (TA1)*, 330.

119. Balthasar, "The Gospel as Norm," 290; Balthasar, *Engagement with God*, 40. See McIntosh, *Christology from within*, 54 for a discussion of imitation.

120. Balthasar, *First Glance*, 245.

121. Balthasar, *Seeing the Form (TA1)*, 330.

122. Ibid., 412.

ulties are subjected to, all our spiritual, emotional, and mental sensing, so to speak. But, more specifically, experience is narrowed down to refer to the participation in Christ. In Balthasar, the authority of the saints would be grounded in the latter kind of experience, that is, in the surrender to Christ and to his "journey,"[123] and in one's participation in Christ's mission.[124] Pierre de Bérulle (1575–1629) had said that the "Christian experience of existence is the interpretation in faith of all that happens as a modality in the sphere of Christ's life."[125] In Balthasar, it is more a question of actual participation, rather than of an interpretation. In this context, Balthasar utilizes the concept of theological states, and he often alludes to the "christological states of being into which God draws the believer at various moments of life."[126] The authority of the saints would then be grounded in their share in the Christological states, which are dynamic, not static. As an "attitude," faith is interpreted as the surrender of one's own experience to the experience of Christ.[127] Balthasar's best attempt to explain what goes on in Christian experience is probably that found in the *Theo-Aesthetics*. We are told that

> What is here involved is not only an objectless and intentionless disposition (*Stimmung*), but rather a deliberate attunement of self (*sich-Einstimmen*) to the accord (*Stimmen*) existing between Christ and his mandate from the Father, in the context of salvation-history's assent (*Zu-stimmung*) . . . We speak, therefore, primarily of an empathy (*Mitfühlen*) with the Son . . . we speak of a sense for the path taken by Christ which leads him to the Cross; we speak of a *sensorium* for Christ's instinct of obedience.[128]

It is on these grounds that Balthasar can say that, "[t]he Christological experience of God . . . presents two aspects: the *experientia Dei incarnati* as a subjective genitive and therefore, posteriorly, as an objective genitive."[129] The two aspects are: the experience of *God incarnate*, where God incarnate is the subject of the experience, and the *experience* of God incarnate, where God incarnate is the object (the content) of the experience. The experience of the saint is not a replica of the subjective experience of Christ (as a subjective genitive), but a participation in it, an experience of it. In Balthasar's theology, this participation in the experience of Christ is both ontological and

123. Ibid., 228.

124. Ibid., 477.

125. Balthasar, *The Realm of Metaphysics in the Modern Age (TA5)*, 123.

126. McIntosh, *Christology from Within*, 55.

127. Balthasar, *Seeing the Form (TA1)*, 412.

128. Ibid., 253.

129. Ibid., 324–25.

epistemological. And it takes place "by virtue of the inversion." Balthasar describes it as an "intersecting double movement," namely the "descent" of God into the "flesh," and the "ascent" of the flesh into the spirit.[130] Without a doubt, it is, at the same time, an epistemological inversion: where God learns what is human and man learns what is divine.[131]

On his part, Balthasar plays on the two German words "*Einfahren*" and "*Erfahrung*," in order to emphasize that what has the potential of becoming an experience is not inward looking, but rather the "act of entering into the Son of God." These two terms are used to argue that the act of entering into Christ becomes the experience that alone can claim for itself man's undivided obedience. His emphasis is that "*Erfahrung*" (experience) is not "*Einfahren*" (man's entry into himself, into his best and highest possibilities].[132] Balthasar responds to various philosophers and theologians, maintaining that that towards which existence is "travelling" and has always "travelled" (or been made to travel!) is the objective, Trinitarian reality of God,[133] and not his own realization and accomplishment.

Significantly, Balthasar writes of the danger for "the believer . . . to make his own experience . . . almost as if it too were a *credendum*."[134] On the contrary, in Balthasar's theology, the authority of the experience of the saints paradoxically ensues from the saint's detachment from it. Writing about experience, Balthasar insists on "the *renunciation* (of immediate experience)." This, he says, "constitutes the condition for every truly Christian experience of faith."[135] Balthasar insists that regardless of how personal the individual has felt his experience to be, he must nevertheless deprive himself of it for the sake of the church; he must pass it on. As Balthasar puts it, the experience of the individual "was as of one expropriated" and "he must administer it as one expropriated."[136] This is what gives certainty to that experience: the active "self-abandonment."[137] Balthasar justifies this claim by using the

130. Ibid., 473.

131. Ibid., 264. See also Balthasar, *The Spirit of Truth (TL3)*, 204–5.

132. Balthasar, *Seeing the Form (TA1)*, 222.

133. Ibid., 229.

134. Balthasar, *Prayer*, 256–57.

135. Balthasar, "Experience God?," 43–44. Balthasar suggests that Blondel may have been the one who best "understood and described' this point. See Kerlin, "Maurice Blondel: Philosophy, Prayer And The Mystical." See also Balthasar, *Seeing the Form (TA1)*, 257–58.

136. Balthasar, *Seeing the Form (TA1)*, 414.

137. Ibid., 228. D. C. Schindler has argued that, in Balthasar, knowledge is essentially "non-possessive," where "the very act of appropriation is an act of expropriation." See Schindler, "Towards a non-Possessive concept of knowledge," 596.

theological concept of the dark night of the mystics, but with a twist. He again contrasts *"Erfahrung"* with *"Einfahren,"* this time using a totally different rationale. He claims that every *"Erfahrung"* (deeper experience of God) will be a deeper entering into *"Einfahren"* (the "non-experience" of faith, the loving renunciation of experience, the depths of the "Dark Nights"),[138] but in Balthasar, the dark night is the eternal abandonment of Christ *to* God (rather than the abandonment of Christ *by* God). It is an abandonment of the Christian *to* God, rather than his or her abandonment *by* God. The saints participate in Christ's own abandonment *to* God, and this "is greater than all knowledge."[139] Thus, Balthasar does two things: he establishes the authority of the one who reveals,[140] and he establishes obedience as integral to reason. Contrary to the pagans—who "refuse the act of obedience" and "do not place their natural faculties in the service of a believing submission to God,"[141] in Balthasar, obedience is an essential aspect of reason, leading to knowledge.

According to Balthasar "there is no Christian experience of God that is not the fruit of the conquest of self-will, or at least of the decision to conquer it." This is the only thing for which the believer is responsible: the decision to subjugate one's own will. Otherwise, Balthasar condemns the "autocratic attempt of man to evoke religious experiences on his own initiative and by means of his own methods and techniques," claiming, in Ignatian terms, that this is an example of "a *disordinate* self-will" (my emphasis).[142] In Balthasar, "personal religious and charismatic powers" should be relinquished.[143] This is reminiscent of Robert Meagher's reading of Augustine. Meagher claims that, in Augustine, "the search for wisdom somehow involves the renunciation of power, the renunciation of possession, while the search for power somehow involves the renunciation of wisdom, since it presupposes the appropriateness of what it is striving to attain."[144]

---

138. Balthasar, *Seeing the Form (TA1)*, 412–13. These "nights" are an "experience of non-experience," a participation in the total archetypal experience of the Old and New Testaments.

139. Ratzinger, "Christian Universalism," 136.

140. Riches, "Balthasar and the Analysis of Faith," 54.

141. Balthasar, *The Theology of Karl Barth*, 315.

142. Balthasar, "Experience God?," 26.

143. Balthasar, *The Christian State of Life*, 370. Balthasar's words reflect Karl Barth's apprehension concerning humanity's capacity not only for atheism but also for idolatry. Understood in this way, such surrender is laudable. Understood from the viewpoint of political theology, this is very dangerous. Howsare, *Balthasar: A Guide for the Perplexed*, 31.

144. Robert Meagher quoted in Meilaender, *The Theory and Practice of Virtue*, 139

In the *Theo-Logic*, Philip, Magdalen, and John are presented as examples of individuals who had to transcend tangible experience.[145] In Balthasar, the authority of the saints is not necessarily grounded in that which is "consciously perceived," simply because not all experiences which the believer has are necessarily "consciously perceived by him in a subjective and psychological sense." There are experiences—which Balthasar calls "objective"—which are not experienced in such a "subjective and psychological sense," but which are still efficacious.[146]

But our question remains: how does a saint's experience become authoritative? Why has the experience of so many saints been considered so exceptionally authoritative? One attempt at answering this question from an epistemological standpoint is to be found in the *Aesthetics*. Here, Balthasar points to Aquinas's affirmation vis-à-vis the prophet's "supreme certainty concerning those things which the prophetic Spirit expressly infuses into him, and also concerning the fact that these things are revealed to him by God." In writing about the Prophets, Balthasar argues that the divine experiences "had to be considered as universally binding as soon as their authenticity was proven."[147] There are affirmations about two important stages here. The first stage, chronologically, would be the establishment of the authenticity of the experience. This authenticity does not necessarily denote that the legitimacy of the experiences was never contested during the actual lifetime. The people may have initially refused to believe the testimony, or it may even have been aggressively contested, but there was a point when the "authenticity was proven," and when the testimony acquired credibility.[148] There is then the second stage: when this witness becomes universally binding, when the experience of the individual acquires an archetypal (protological) "normalcy," to use Balthasar's term.[149] The best examples for this two stage authentication would be: contemplation, archetypal experience and mystical experience. Let me start with the former.

---

145. Balthasar, *The Spirit of Truth (TL3)*, 384.

146. Balthasar, *Seeing the Form (TA1)*, 258. To speak of "objective experience" sounds contradictory. It is most probable that Balthasar simply means to refer to those experiences of which the individual remains unaware at the conscious level.

147. Ibid., 308.

148. Ibid., 335.

149. Ibid., 412.

The Experience of Contemplation

First of all, it should be said that, with Balthasar, reason and contemplation are not contrary to each other. In Balthasar's case, prayer and worship are actually indispensable to the inner act of reason.[150] So, Balthasar integrates reason and contemplation, which is quite unusual among theologians. Secondly—and we have already alluded to this unusual practice—Balthasar attributes to God several behaviors that other theologians would associate with the finite creature: tasks such as faith and prayer. For Balthasar, prayer is "a participation in the inner-trinitarian prayer of God."[151] Thirdly, Balthasar is very clear as to which contemplation he does *not* support, and is very candid with his criticism. He criticizes the "predominantly individualistic conception of contemplation" which would have been influenced by the "contemplative ideals" of Plato, Aristotle, Stoicism, and Neoplatonism, and he criticizes the contemplation of the medieval mystics which remains centered on the condition of the contemplative himself or herself.[152] He also warns against using contemplation to seek self-knowledge, claiming that many

> engaged in contemplation in order to attain loftier states and illuminations, more subtle theological insights; perhaps, also, simply to get to know the internal laws of contemplation so that they could describe them, on the basis of experience, for the benefit of their fellow believers. They prayed and worshipped *in recto* while at the same time observing themselves *in oblique*, as it were photographing their own transcendence.[153]

In Balthasar, there is only one purpose for the "light and spiritual understanding" given in contemplation, and that is "to enhance and deepen" the contemplative's "sensitivity to the divine will."[154] Balthasar's book on prayer stipulates the characteristics of genuine contemplation, by providing a list of, what I would call, non-doables. First of all, "[c]ontemplation must not get stuck in the intellect . . . for '*gnosis* puffs up, but love builds up.'"[155]

---

150. Balthasar, *Prayer*, 63. Balthasar agrees with Heidegger that "wonder is the element in which thought is always moving." See Kerr, "Balthasar and Metaphysics," 235.

151. Scola, *Test Everything*, 89.

152. Balthasar, *Two Sisters*, 195.

153. Balthasar, *Prayer*, 116–17.

154. Balthasar is careful not to be interpreted as putting forward a "voluntarist" theology of contemplation. "The concept 'will,' here is not used in the sense of a limited faculty of the soul as opposed to the 'reason.'" Ibid., 103–4.

155. Ibid., 135.

Secondly, contemplation must not become a self-contemplation. Authentic contemplation must be a devotional attention to what is essentially the non-I, namely, God's word.[156] Thirdly, in its longing for the "*speculatio majestatis*," Christian contemplation should "not try to bypass Christ."[157] Finally, neither should contemplation "strain away from the earth." Balthasar insists that "the apostles and saints are not daydreamers in flight from the world, living in a fairyland divorced from reality."[158] He maintains that prayer "is not 'ecstasy' in the sense of inspired inebriation or of divesting oneself of created reality, in order to live henceforth in God, beyond one's own self." Inebriation and detachment could be part of the experience of contemplation, but they are not its core. We could say that Balthasar wants to restore to contemplation its original function, namely, worship. This is "a worship which also contains the handmaid's discreet Yes, the consent to be possessed, to be at God's disposal." Therefore, in Balthasar, the "ecstasy" is one of "service," rather than one of forgetfulness.[159] In saying this, Balthasar passes judgment on certain mystics, on particular stages in Christian history, and even on specific faiths which promote such a disposition.

In the epistemological dimension, the authority of the saints is grounded in their contemplation.[160] The saints are credible because their combination of *contemplatio* and *ratio* enables them to provide interpretations which, subsequently, others consider genuine. Balthasar states his position quite clearly: when the Christian emerges from prayer "he appears as someone sent, who has received in contemplation (without being aware of it) all the equipment he needs for his Christian mission: the authority, the abilities and the taste for it."[161] Consequently, the faith, knowledge, and love, the determination that ensues from the contemplative experience of the saints, from their prayer, will become visible to others in one way or another, it will appear credible. The authority of their mission will appear credible. This will subsequently leave an impression on their witnesses, which could range from admiration to a sense of awe and veneration.

---

156. Ibid., 115.

157. Ibid., 272.

158. Ibid., 290.

159. Ibid., 79. Adrienne is of the same disposition. She claims that one should focus on "a person's interaction with God in prayer" and not on visions and prophecies. *Book of All Saints*, 414.

160. The holistic encounter which takes place in "constant contemplation" both transcends, and grounds, every individual act of self-giving. Balthasar, *Seeing the Form (TA1)*, 242.

161. Balthasar, *Prayer*, 122.

Balthasar uses saints such as Thérèse and Elizabeth to both resuscitate the link between action and contemplation—"which the desert monks and Dionysius the Pseudo-Areopagite already knew,"[162]—and to stipulate the kind of contemplation which Balthasar associates with authenticity. According to Balthasar, Thérèse is the first to see quite clearly that "contemplation in itself is a dynamic force and is indeed the source of all fruitfulness, the first impulse in all change."[163] But then how is the difference between saintly contemplation and ordinary contemplation to be understood? In Balthasar, what makes the contemplation of the saint powerful and even efficacious are the "attunement" to, or "consonance" with God,[164] as well as the solidarity with creation, and with Christ's involvement with creation. He writes,

> If the Spirit is to render our prayer effective with God, we need to declare our solidarity with the suffering of creation and with Christ's suffering for creation. In our search for salvation, all that is purely private has been rendered obsolete by the Spirit.[165]

Archetypal Experience

Writing about the "christological constellation," Steffen Lösel claims that Balthasar uses the typological interpretation of the New Testament in order to claim "the authority of divine revelation for the present structural configuration of the Church."[166] This is not exactly how I interpret Balthasar. Balthasar does claim that the church derives from "the dignity and authority" of the biblical archetypes of Old and New Testaments, and that it is "canonized" by these biblical archetypes.[167] But, to my mind, he is using the saints as a criterion for judging the *integrity* of ecclesial structures, not for emphasizing the *legitimacy* of these structures. He is not using the saints to *reinforce* the present structures, to *defend* them and their authority "as divinely instituted."[168] His role is pastoral not statutory. He is using them

---

162. Balthasar, *Two Sisters*, 430. See also *Engagement with God*, 47–48.

163. Balthasar, *Two Sisters*, 195. See also 194, 200. Balthasar prefers the notion of fruitfulness to that of effectiveness.

164. Balthasar, *Seeing the Form (TA1)*, 242.

165. Balthasar, *The Spirit of Truth (TL3)*, 385.

166. Lösel, "Conciliar, Not Conciliatory," 26.

167. Balthasar, *Seeing the Form (TA1)*, 351. In the emphasis he puts on Old Testament types as sacraments that point beyond themselves toward Christ, Balthasar follows de Lubac and Daniélou. Boersma, *Nouvelle Théologie*, 33.

168. Lösel, "Conciliar, Not Conciliatory," 28.

to kindle life back into the church structures. It is a process of reformation based on *ressourcement*.

Moreover, to my mind, in order to understand what Balthasar was trying to do with the concept of "archetype," it is not enough to examine his ecclesiology. One also has to examine his Christology, his exegetical work, and his mystical writings. In Balthasar, that "experience which leads to contemplation and can become truly mystical" always "radiates from the archetype."[169] Although there are other archetypal experiences, Christ is the principal archetype. He is the Übermensch: "the super-form."[170]

Balthasar discusses these "experiences" in the first volume of the *Aesthetics* but he comes back to the same subject in the last volume of his trilogy.[171] The fact that he treats the subject in the beginning and at the end of his great work cannot be without its significance. In Balthasar's theology, the Old Testament Prophets and the Apostles of Christ represent "archetypal Biblical authority through experience," along with Christ.[172] They are "the foundation upon which all Christian faith is built," not just because these experiences are *eye-witness* experiences, nor because they are *mystical* experiences, but because they are "witnesses of Christian *faith*" (my emphasis),[173] when faith entails "the participation in the archetypal faith of the Apostles and in the total structure of experience within the sphere of Sacred Scripture."[174] Balthasar claims that there are other figures who "acquire a kind of secondary archetypicity." These figures, and Balthasar asserts that there are "many" of them, "yield on earth a very clear symbolic image, especially those figures who are manifestly intended to point the way for entire sections of the Church, entire epochs or regions or communities."[175] Therefore, in Balthasar, there is the authority of the archetypal figures (including the patriarchs, whom the Fathers understood as types of Christ),[176] and then there are the post-biblical saints who participate in this original archetypal

---

169. Balthasar, *Seeing the Form (TA1)*, 601.

170. Ibid., 602.

171. See *The Spirit of Truth (TL3)*, 384.

172. Balthasar, *Seeing the Form (TA1)*, 387. The reference to Tyrrell's theology of revelation is clear.

173. Ibid., 301.

174. Ibid., 306, 592.

175. Ibid., 565.

176. We have to "see and abide by this fourfold tradition of archetypal experience in the Church." Balthasar, *Seeing the Form (TA1)*, 351. See Gardner, "Balthasar and the figure of Mary," 68.

experience.[177] They do so through "private revelation and its confirmation by personal sanctity."[178] He writes,

> [s]omething similar is true of the great, fundamental charisms of Church history, above all of the founders of great religious families, from which spiritualities with a clearly defined profile go forth and continue to operate; but it is also true of Doctors of the Church and other personalities who set their mark on the Church . . . who share in giving Christianity its form far beyond the period in which they themselves live.[179]

In the epistemological domain, Balthasar grounds the authority of the biblical figures in their archetypicity, which enables Balthasar to attribute to these figures a diachronic effect that is extensive, stretching back into the past, and carried into the future. On the other hand, Balthasar grounds the authority of the post-biblical figures in their participation in this archetypicity, which takes two forms, namely, personal holiness and private mystical experience, both of which have the diachronic faculty of extending over time.

In "The Gospel as Norm," Balthasar writes about the disciples who act as mediating figures, and of how the form of Christ is impressed on the church through them. According to Balthasar, Peter and John, Paul and James, Martha and Mary of Bethany, Mary Magdalen, the evangelists, and the other less prominent apostles "are the starting point of forms of Christian existence that *continue to operate*."[180] Lösel has said that, in Balthasar, the actions of the archetypes can "amount to a soteriologically relevant action within the theo-drama between God and humanity."[181] On my part, I prefer to see their contribution in terms of uniqueness, depth, symbolism, and efficacy, rather than in terms of soteriological relevance.[182] Balthasar follows Markus Barth (1915–1994) in claiming that what makes the experience of the early constellation "archetypal" is the fact that their "eye-witness" was, by its nature, "exceptional."[183] In Balthasar's theology, in the epistemological

177. Balthasar, *Seeing the Form (TA1)*, 351. Elsewhere, Balthasar states that "every Christian experience is open to the eschatological future." Balthasar, *The Spirit of Truth (TL3)*, 385.

178. Balthasar, *Seeing the Form (TA1)*, 348.

179. Balthasar, "The Gospel as Norm," 296–97.

180. Ibid.

181. Lösel, "Conciliar, Not Conciliatory," 30.

182. One may identify soteriological patterns, but not soteriological efficacy as such.

183. Balthasar, *Seeing the Form (TA1)*, 387. Interestingly, the title of one of Markus Barth's books is *Augenzeuge*.

domain, the authority of the New Testament archetypal saints is grounded in the fact that this "intimate group of chosen persons . . . have been made worthy" of "visibleness," that is, worthy to *see* Christ.[184] There is obviously some danger, as Steffen Lösel has said, in "superimposing a theological typology on one's reading of scripture,"[185] but there is also a lot to be said in its favour, and Balthasar's typological method is not to be ignored.

There is a lot of what Balthasar says about the archetypes that echoes Heidegger, and the way in which past, present and future were disclosed as intertwined in Heidegger's analysis of temporality. There is, in the concept of the diachronic validity of the archetypes, at least a hint of Heidegger's concept of *Wiederholung* (translated as *repetition* or as *retrieving*), whereby it becomes possible for one to appropriate past actions, own them, make them one's own, as a set of general models or heroic templates onto which one may creatively project oneself.[186] Still, Balthasar has developed the concept theologically, and therefore differently. Two points need to be made. First of all, Balthasar claims that the God-experience of Christ's witnesses is only comprehensible if interpreted "as the foundation on whose functional experience the existence in faith of the coming Church can be built up."[187] In some sense, therefore, the experience of the archetypes only makes sense because it builds the church. In the process of acting as the foundation of the church, it gets its meaning from it. Interpreted from the sociological point of view, this universalization, this idea that personal experience no longer has merely private value, has a somewhat utilitarian flavor, and sounds as if it may condone self-sacrifice for the institution, but, from the point of view of faith, it is a poignant notion. Secondly, according to Balthasar, to participate in the archetypal experience is to participate in the archetypal unity between faith and vision that is found in the "eye-witnesses."[188] It is possible that Balthasar is indebted to Möhler in this respect. According to Möhler, the Spirit first communicated the *Lebensprinzip* to the apostles. Consequently, "the new divine life is to flow from those already made alive. Such begetting is to bring about further begetting."[189]

Mary is a special case. Hers is the "more mysterious continuity," namely between her "spiritual experiences in the body and the Church's maternal

---

184. Balthasar, *Seeing the Form (TA1)*, 318.

185. Lösel, "Conciliar, Not Conciliatory," 41.

186. Wheeler, "Martin Heidegger."

187. Balthasar, *Seeing the Form (TA1)*, 306.

188. Ibid., 305.

189. Ibid., 142, 304, and 350. See Möhler, *Unity in the Church*, 77. Quoted in Boersma, *Nouvelle Théologie*, 44.

experience."[190] Mary is "the *Realsymbol* of the (pure) Church."[191] As Lucy Gardner has said,

> Mary is model, type and archetype, symbol and example; there is a Marian principle or profile to the Christian Church and in Christian life; there is a Marian aspect or dimension to all Christian theology, indeed to all creaturely existence.[192]

Like Irenaeus, what Balthasar sees most in Mary is the spiritual power of her obedient consent, which has "archetypal efficacy for salvation."[193] Through her consent, Mary becomes not just an exterior model, but the *prägende Form* for the church, a formative form, a prototype. She is an individual person who is "liquefied" by the power of the Spirit and "universalized" to become the principle of all that belongs to the church.[194] Balthasar describes how Mary "is universalized to a real symbol of the *Ecclesia*, the mediatrix of all grace and the flawless bride."[195] The metaphor of liquification helps to underline how Mary's theological personality extends backwards and forwards in time and incorporates within it the whole of the *communio Sanctorum*.

Bultmann had already assumed that the interpreter in the present has access to the same reality with which those in the past wrestled. He had argued that when we identify ourselves with the human questions within a text, the past becomes intelligible to the present, a position that was also shared by Karl Barth.[196] However, Balthasar intends more than just an existentialist life relation with the subject matter, in the sense of a common human experience.[197] What really counts in Balthasar is that the world in which the Christian stands is governed and inaugurated by the appearance of God and is oriented to that appearance of God.[198] In fact, Balthasar claims that "it is almost a matter of indifference whether [the Christian] possesses

190. Balthasar, *Seeing the Form (TA1)*, 348. See also 341, 539. According to Balthasar, the relationship between Mary and Jesus was intended "to lead into the universal and social relationships between Christ and the Church."

191. Balthasar, *The Office of Peter*, 210–11. See also *Seeing the Form (TA1)*, 669. A symbol, understood in the full sense is "a sacramental reality which corporeally contains the spiritual truth in the sensible image and likeness."

192. Gardner, "Balthasar and the figure of Mary," 66.

193. Balthasar, *The Office of Peter*, 213.

194. Balthasar, "The Gospel as Norm," 295.

195. Balthasar, *Two Sisters*, 461.

196. See Heffernan, *Sacred Biography*, 53.

197. Balthasar, *Seeing the Form (TA1)*, 387.

198. Ibid., 420.

the sensory contemporaneity of the eyewitness." Ultimately, what counts is that we share the same world that has been transformed by Christ.

In his *Aesthetics*, Balthasar claims that the main question is: "In what manner is the archetypal Christian experience incorporated into the Church so that the members who are not graced with it can nevertheless participate in it?"[199] In elucidating the issue, Balthasar uses the concept of re-enactment. He claims that the church "re-enacts on a higher and universal level the part played in God's personal representatives among the people of Israel, that is, that of being the representative of God to the people and of the people to God."[200] In faith, and through the church, Christians of later generations are drawn "into the archetypal experience of the eye-witnesses," on the same footing with these eye-witnesses.[201] Balthasar interprets this not just as a "contemporaneity with the Gospel," but, more importantly, as the "participation of the believer in the eternal aspect of the definitive historical saving events."[202] Balthasar describes the participation of the Christian in the archetypal experiences as both the work of the creative Spirit (who works with "the material" of these "exemplary experiences," and who creates "new and unheard of marvels for each individual believer")[203] and that of Christ (who determines the "sensory environment," so that the Christian "stands in the same space and in the shared time of creation as the Prophets and the Apostles").[204] In spite of everything, the archetypes remain provisional.[205] The witness both of the Apostles and of their successors "possesses only an ostensive, transitory character," and, according to Balthasar, it is "solely as a transitory witness that it can be incorporated in the content of what must be believed."[206]

---

199. Balthasar, *Seeing the Form (TA1)*, 351.

200. The "people" of which Balthasar speaks here is the whole of humanity. See Balthasar, *Engagement with God*, 32.

201. Balthasar, "Experience God?," 42–43. Both the apostolic and the ecclesial kerygma can boast of the presence of eye-witnesses. Balthasar, *Seeing the Form (TA1)*, 305.

202. McIntosh, *Christology from Within*, 17.

203. Balthasar, *Seeing the Form (TA1)*, 418–19.

204. Ibid., 420.

205. Ibid., 364.

206. Ibid., 211.

Mystical Experience

Besides acknowledging the experience of contemplation and of archetypal experience, Balthasar would also claim that the saints become authoritative, and are attributed authority because of their authentic mystical experience. We have already seen that, in Balthasar, archetypal experience in the church and mystical experience within the church are different in their "dignity and authority," but that the mystical experience within the church "participates in the Biblical archetypes." According to Balthasar, mystical experience derives from the former, and "must be canonized" by the former.[207]

The view of mysticism which Balthasar provides is mostly Ignatian. It is a historical, concrete and Christological mysticism. This is in direct contrast with most other approaches, which focus on the sphere of religious needs, on personal mystical experience and on neo-platonic contact with a formless God. It is a mysticism that emphasizes form, a feature which will place Balthasar in conflict even with some of the Fathers and other saints. According to Balthasar, the theory of extreme Origenism that "every form which arises in contemplation" should logically be considered "as a deceptive tactic on the part of the demons,"[208] is incorrect. Evagrius Ponticus, he writes, presses "on towards the borderlands of Buddhism where finitude and form threaten to become merely negative concepts to be abolished."[209] Balthasar is sympathetic with pre- and extra-Christian mysticism, but he emphasizes that authentic Christian contemplation is very different.[210] Diadochus also argues that "it is better to reject these forms even if perchance they should occasionally come from God." Balthasar detects the same "rule" in Aquinas, Eckhart, and John of the Cross.[211] He regrets that "the tradition of Augustine and [of] John of the Cross plays into the hands of all those who would like to do away with all mystical elements in the Church as being an irrelevant private concern."[212] Balthasar, you could say, begins with the claim that mysticism was "misunderstood," "scorned," "exiled and silenced by official theology and proclamation." He asserts that he wants to restore and return mysticism to the center of salvation history. He believes that Adrienne has already done that,[213] and he wants to promote what she has

207. Ibid., 351.

208. Ibid., 315.

209. Ibid., 551.

210. Ratzinger, "Christian Universalism," 136.

211. Balthasar, *Seeing the Form (TA1)*, 315.

212. Ibid., 411.

213. Balthasar, *First Glance*, 89. Balthasar links anti-mysticism to Augustine's "Platonising mystical psychology." Balthasar, *Seeing the Form (TA1)*, 415.

done. Therefore, however indirectly, Balthasar is claiming that, in this regard, Adrienne has corrected the Fathers and other saints. In a sense, Adrienne has also corrected the Magisterium.[214]

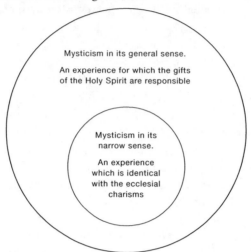

Mysticism in its general sense.

An experience for which the gifts of the Holy Spirit are responsible

Mysticism in its narrow sense.

An experience which is identical with the ecclesial charisms

Diagram 03. Mysticism

In his *Aesthetics*, Balthasar identifies two levels of mysticism. The first of these is that deep "awareness and experience both of the presence within [the Christian] of God's being and of the depth of the divine truth, goodness, and beauty in the mystery of God." This is Christian "mysticism" in its general sense, an experience for which the gifts of the Holy Spirit are responsible. There is then the mysticism which is "identical with the ecclesial charisms (particular vocations and gifts)," which normally presupposes the development of the first level of mysticism.[215] On his part, Balthasar detects "the great mystical theologies" in those theologies where the aesthetic and the mystical converge. Among these "great mystical theologies" he mentions Gregory of Nyssa, Denys the Areopagite, Bernard of Clairvaux, William of St.Thierry, Mechtild of Magdeburg, John of the Cross, Teresa of Avila. These mystical theologians are among his most-favoured authorities.

I would say that Balthasar attributes four characteristics to authentic Christian mysticism, each of which was meant to respond and correct what he considered to be misconceptions concerning mysticism. First of all, authentic mystical experience has its origin within the church,[216] ought to have

214. On the tensions between mysticism and the Magisterium in the history of the church, see McGinn, "Evil-Sounding, Rash, and Suspect of Heresy."

215. Balthasar, *Seeing the Form (TA1)*, 166.

216. Ibid., 414. See also Balthasar, *First Glance*, 101.

an ecclesial "function,"[217] "builds the Church,"[218] and is to be judged within the church. De Lubac had said that "there is no authentic spiritual life which does not depend on the historic fact of Christ and the Church's collective life."[219] Balthasar follows suit.[220] Here, Balthasar's mysticism is diametrically opposed to the existentialism of Sören Kierkegaard, where mysticism is fideistic and individualistic.[221] In Balthasar, even the experience of the dark night "is always an ecclesial event."[222] Balthasar grants that the authentic mystic may need to justify him or herself before the church on the grounds of compatibility with Revelation. He or she may have to demonstrate that they are "vitally integrated into the communion of love of all the members, this communion constituting the total ecclesial archetype."[223] Balthasar himself did all he could to integrate Adrienne and get the church's approval for her mystical writings. This means that although Adrienne was already authoritative for him—with or without official approval—he believed that her mystic experiences were meant for the church, and he would have liked to see the rest of the church appreciate their value.

Secondly, in Balthasar, authentic Christian mysticism is an experience within faith, and complements the theology of mission. He identifies what he calls a "radical homogeneity" between mystical experience and faith. For him, "faith in Christ is *already* a genuine and objective encounter of the whole man with the incarnate God" [my emphasis], which means that it is already mystical, and that extraordinary mystical experience is not necessary.[224] Wherever such mystical experience does occur, faith is always the basis of it, faith is its object, and faith is "renewed" and "enriched" by it.[225] Christian mysticism also happens when, "instead of a self-designed plan of life, [the individual] accepts a commission from God, a divine piloting in commandments and counsels, and carries out these directives through every temptation from without and within."[226] Both faith and the ecclesial concept of mission are integral to Balthasar's theology of mysticism. They

217. Balthasar, *Seeing the Form (TA1)*, 411.

218. Balthasar, *The Office of Peter*, 326.

219. De Lubac, *Catholicism*, 101.

220. See Balthasar, "Tradition," 127; *Seeing the Form (TA1)*, 300–31; and *The Christian State of Life*, 380.

221. Balthasar, *First Glance*, 86.

222. Balthasar, *Prayer*, 272.

223. Balthasar, *Seeing the Form (TA1)*, 409–10.

224. Ibid., 300–301, 309, and 412.

225. Balthasar, *First Glance*, 86.

226. Balthasar, "Experience God?," 26.

would also be integral to a theology concerning the authority of the saints. This is yet another reason why Balthasar's theology could aptly be used to navigate through a theology concerning the authority of the saints.

There is a third characteristic. According to Balthasar, authentic mysticism, is accompanied by "bitterness and the humiliations of the Cross."[227] In Balthasar's theology, the intimacy of one's share in the Cross is always the yardstick for the intimacy of one's share in Jesus' destiny and mission.[228] This is one reason why Balthasar could have been so attracted to Adrienne. In Adrienne, the theological content of the work is made tangible. It is often accompanied by psychological distress or even physical pain.[229] When Adrienne writes her *Treatise on Purgatory,* "one could almost say she suffered it."[230] In her case, what is involved is not the *spiritual understanding* of the truths of Christian revelation, or the *living* of the truths of Christian revelation "in a spiritual-mystical way." but the actual sensing of Christian revelation in one's own existence, "even bodily."[231] For Balthasar the authority of Adrienne's experience becomes indubitable. He even claims that Adrienne "filled in" gaps in revelation where Christ's suffering was concerned.[232]

The fourth and final characteristic is selflessness. Balthasar maintains that "neither the Church nor the Christian should ever aspire to mystical graces" since the form of revelation is already sufficient.[233] Through Christ, "we are made free of the imposed, heteronomous law that had continually led us to attempt to capture God and his free light in the nets of our wisdom and praxis."[234] On the contrary, it is only possible for us to receive the "totality of being, the divine mystery" if and "when we renounce every partial experience and every subjective guarantee of possessing what is experienced."[235] The saints of the baroque period, most particularly, Francis de Sales, Pierre de Bérulle, and François Fénelon (1651–1715)[236] are criticized openly. The implication is that theirs is not authentic mysticism. The

227. Ibid., 44–45.

228. Balthasar, "The Absences of Jesus," 56.

229. Kilby has expressed a few remarks concerning Balthasar's fascination with suffering. *Balthasar,* 115.

230. Balthasar, *First Glance,* 56. One could mention other examples. For instance Adrienne's "nocturnal introductions" to John's Gospel, which were begun in 1943. Ibid., 36.

231. Ibid., 94.

232. Balthasar, *First Glance,* 35.

233. Balthasar, *Seeing the Form (TA1),* 416–17.

234. Balthasar, *The Office of Peter,* 7.

235. Balthasar, "Experience God?," 44.

236. Balthasar, *Convergences,* 34–35.

exceptions, according to Balthasar, are Blaise Pascal (1623–1662), Marie de l'Incarnation (1599–1672) and Ignatius of Loyola (1491–1556), being saints who went "beyond the preoccupation with the pious self toward an apprehension of the gospel as a whole."[237] According to Balthasar, the weakness of the baroque period "lies in the fact that it is no longer a central meditation on the biblical revelation." It ignores the eschatological, the openness to the world, and the soteriological, and is characterized by introversion and anthropocentricity.[238] On the contrary, on the epistemological level, the self is called to depersonalize itself and to ecclesialize itself.[239]

It should be remembered that, in Balthasar, the terms "mystic" and "saint" are not univocal,[240] and yet "[t]hose who above all have undergone and enjoyed such [mystical] experience have in every age been the saints."[241] Where authority is concerned, one may need to distinguish between the concept of authority attributed to the mystical experiences in themselves, and the concept of authority being attributed to the saints who happen to have had authentic, mystical experiences. G.M.Jantzen is of the opinion that—along with Bernard of Clairvaux, Eckhart, Ruysbroeck, and the author of *The Cloud of Unknowing*—Balthasar does not seek the basis of mystical or spiritual authority in visionary experience.[242] However, although Balthasar would rather speak about "vision" than about "visions," at least in the context of faith, Balthasar does attribute some authority to visionary experience because of his emphasis on form. Adrienne's "visions" certainly played a role in convincing Balthasar of the authenticity of her theology. Balthasar makes extensive use of Adrienne's mystical knowledge as a resource in his theology, thus legitimating the use of mystical theology in constructive theology, but also legitimating Adrienne's authority through her visions. Her knowledge was mystical both because it was acquired mystically, and because its content was mystical. According to Balthasar, it is the biblical nature of Adrienne's visions that legitimizes them. It is for this reason that he attributes authority to her visions as well as to her. The question of the legitimacy of such visions remains, as Karen Kilby and Kevin Mongrain have maintained. Is it ever valid for a Christian intellectual to be fundamentally

237. Ibid., 35–36.

238. Ibid., 34–35.

239. Balthasar, *Seeing the Form (TA1)*, 355. See also 556. Writing about theology, Balthasar claims that it "must be as open as possible . . . towards the full sweep of the church's thinking, even if such depersonalization imposes on the individual scholar an ascetical renunciation of his own opinions and fancies."

240. Balthasar, *First Glance*, 88–89.

241. Balthasar, "Tradition," 125.

242. Jantzen, *Power, Gender and Christian Mysticism*, 191.

guided in his or her own writings about God by the charismatic mystical teachings of a living contemporary, and hence to write in the voice of one who is called by God to a special teaching vocation? Where Balthasar is concerned, the answer to this question would clearly be "Yes."

THE AUTHORITY OF THE SCRIPTURES AND ITS INTERPRETERS

There is then the issue of scriptural interpretation. We know that authority is needed to attest to the authority of the Scriptures, to transmit the knowledge of the truth that is contained in the Scriptures, to teach us the skills we need to read Scripture correctly, as well as to authorize the individual believer who reads the Scriptures.[243] With Balthasar the authority attributed to the Scriptures and the authority attributed to the Magisterium are distinguishable, but not incongruent.[244] Balthasar would approve the one source theory advanced by the Vatican document *Dei Verbum*, where God is the one source of revelation, where both the authority of the Scriptures and ecclesial tradition are totally dependent on the facts of revelation, and where the Magisterium is there to serve the Scriptures.[245] Moreover, "the canonical validity of Scripture does not exclude, but rather includes an ecclesial teaching authority."[246] Whereas Modernism had questioned the historical reliability of Scripture and the church's authority to interpret it,[247] in Balthasar's theology, Scripture is reliable, and the authority of the Magisterium is not questioned. However, in Balthasar—and this is crucial—the ecclesial teaching authority does not consist solely of the official teachings of the Magisterium and of the representatives of the hierarchy alone. The Magisterium also includes the saints and their teachings. In the *Two Sisters*, Balthasar states that although it may be

> true that the tradition is animated by the Holy Spirit, which in every age prompts those in apostolic office or in the hierarchy to interpret the scriptural revelation of Christ, but we should not

243. Austin, *Up with Authority*, 108, 116.

244. Augustine's own practice was to speak of post-scriptural and ecclesiastical authority separately from the authority of the Scriptures. Congar claims that it was the "desacralizing of the medieval imagination," which made it possible to play off the "juridicized authority of the Church" against the authority of the Scriptures. Quoted in Boersma, *Nouvelle Théologie*, 16.

245. Vatican Council II, *Dei Verbum*, 1.

246. Balthasar, *Seeing the Form (TA1)*, 552.

247. Pope Pius X, *Pascendi Dominici Gregis*, 1907.

forget that this prompting is equally urgent in the saints, who are the "living gospel."[248]

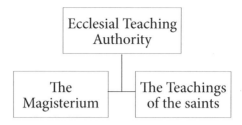

Diagram 04. The Teaching Authority of the Church

We have to remember that, with Balthasar, the starting point for the *fides quaerens intellectum* is not the "*desiderium naturale visionis Dei*, as the creatures' core *existentiale*," but the Scriptures.[249] In addition, Balthasar's view is that faith seeks understanding and that we need an authority that can help us understand. The saints in Balthasar's theology are absorbed by the Word of God.[250] Being absorbed by the Word is one of the more important signs of their credibility.[251] The saints are not just fascinated by, and immersed in, but also capable of interpreting the Word of God. In fact, they are the ones most proficient in transmitting the real content of the Scriptures, the ones who have attested to the Scriptures sometimes with their blood, the ones whom we should trust to teach us the skills we need to interpret the Scriptures. The saints interpret the Scriptures, and demonstrate skills for reading the Scriptures. It is therefore understandable that, in Balthasar's theology, the saints function as a means for resolving issues related to exegesis. Balthasar's is an intra-textual interpretation. But he is not just saying that the Bible should be read within the *communio*. He is also saying that the saints can interpret the Bible *for* the *communio*. In this regard, Balthasar is not averse to criticising the saints either. For instance, as has already been said, he criticizes quite harshly "the so-called affective theology of the baroque," represented by de Sales, de Bérulle, and Fénelon. His justification is that its mystical, introverted and anthropocentric manner is non-biblical.[252]

248. Balthasar, *Two Sisters,* 26.

249. Balthasar, *The Spirit of Truth (TL3)*, 365. See also "The Gospel as Norm,"285.

250. Balthasar, "Obedience in the Light of the Gospel," 241.

251. To take one example, Balthasar tests John of the Cross by checking whether he reserves the religious value of all the figures of revelation, namely, the Incarnation, the Church and the Scriptures.

252. Balthasar, *Convergences,* 35.

Secondly, Balthasar emphasizes "the *pneuma* within the letter," that is, the "spiritual sense which is embedded in philology."[253] He wants to emphasize the literal and to show that the interest in the literal is not just modern, but that, both in ancient and in medieval times, priority is given to the literal sense.[254] This is reinforced in the *Theo-Logic*, where Balthasar maintains that the Spirit, who is infinite, "is in the word itself." But then he also insists that it is in the very presence and action of the Spirit, who leads us into this depth dimension of the Scriptures, that the "word is truth".[255] Thus, the depths of the word are to be found in the Spirit who is in the word.[256] As Ratzinger has said, though "unafraid" of philology, Balthasar refuses to be "swamped" by philology.[257] In Balthasar, the Scripture which is the body of the Logos becomes "spirit," just as the incarnate Logos "wholly becomes *Pneuma*."[258] The implication in this context is that not everyone can read and interpret the Logos which has become "spirit," and that it is the saints who come closest to the genuine interpretation of the Scriptures. In Balthasar, the Spirit is the primary author, the "*auctor primarius* behind the word, ready to lead to deeper levels of divine truth those who seek to understand his word."[259]

Clearly, in Balthasar's work, the saints are no naïve realists where the interpretation of Scriptures is concerned, precisely because they interpret the Spirit within the Word, rather than provide a historico-critical analysis of the Word.[260] Neither is theological truth "abstracted" from Scripture in a kind of theological sensualism. It is only under the influence of the Spirit that "Scripture must be interpreted and grasped."[261] The interpretation of the Scriptures is interpreted as "the Holy Spirit's delivery of testimony."[262] It is not like the interpretation of other literature.[263] For this reason, according to Balthasar, "[t]he purpose of the word is of course, not attained by

253. Balthasar, *Seeing the Form (TA1)*, 544.

254. Dickens, *Hans Urs von Balthasar's Theological Aesthetics*, 37, 47.

255. Balthasar, *The Spirit of Truth (TL3)*, 195.

256. Ibid.

257. Ratzinger, "Christian Universalism," 143.

258. Balthasar, *Seeing the Form (TA1)*, 549. See Potworowski, "An Exploration," 83.

259. This is Balthasar's definition of inspiration. See Block Jr., *Glory, Grace, and Culture*, 13.

260. It should be said that De Lubac and Daniélou had already recovered spiritual interpretation. As Boersma puts it, "[T]heir *ressourcement* of pre-modern methods of exegesis relied on a sacramental understanding of Scripture." *Nouvelle Théologie*, 33.

261. Balthasar, *The Spirit of Truth (TL3)*, 325. Balthasar claims that the "standpoint of faith" is "the only one which does justice to the phenomenon of the Bible." *Convergences*, 80.

262. Balthasar, *The Spirit of Truth (TL3)*, 74.

263. Dickens, *Hans Urs von Balthasar's Theological Aesthetics*, 69.

those who read the Bible out of curiosity or study it scientifically."[264] He also maintains that if exegesis "wishes to be scientific, [it] is faced with the fundamental decision of belief or unbelief."[265] With Balthasar, the implication is that the authenticity of the interpretation relies on the genuineness of the faith, and that what is correct—dogmatically and spiritually—is nothing but the fruit of a deepened understanding of the Bible.[266]

Furthermore, because, for Balthasar, a proper interpretation of Scripture requires a dynamic theological and spiritual life,[267] he expresses great appreciation for the life of the saints which is, in itself, even more credible than any exegesis, or rather, which is an embodied form of exegesis. According to Balthasar, it is the saints who "are the great history of the interpretation of the gospel, more genuine and with more power of conviction than all exegesis."[268] In Balthasar, "the saint is aptly recognized as a theological wellspring that reflects scripture and tradition."[269]

Also significant is Balthasar's emphasis that the Spirit's testimony in the Scriptures is realized incessantly, not only by increasing the comprehension of the Scriptures, but by transforming those who contemplate it. Scripture is the vehicle used by the Spirit in order to constantly actualize, "with grace and as grace, this total historical form of the revelation of salvation."[270] The *abstractio* is carried out by the Spirit "in a continual '*conversio ad phantasma*,'" which Balthasar understands as "a continual re-conversion to the sensible reality of the Gospel."[271] In Balthasar, this *conversio* takes the form of a reciprocal movement from the *logos-sarx* into *logos rēma* and from the *logos rēma* back into the *logos-sarx*. The saints reverberate this when their whole being becomes the word of God.[272] There is then, in Balthasar, a dynamic reciprocation between the *analogia entis* and the *analogia linguae*.[273]

Therefore, in Balthasar's theology, the theology of the church is, and ought to be, a continuation of the inner-biblical theology. It is very probable that Balthasar wants to criticize Ritschl and Harnack, who drew a sharp line

264. Balthasar, *Prayer*, 94.

265. Balthasar, *Convergences*, 79.

266. Balthasar, *Cosmic Liturgy*, 54.

267. McIntosh, *Hans Urs von Balthasar's Theological Aesthetics*, 30.

268. Balthasar, "Tradition," 125.

269. Nussberger, "Saint as Theological Wellspring," Abstract.

270. Balthasar, *Seeing the Form (TA1)*, 548.

271. Balthasar, *A Theology of History*, 93.

272. Ibid.

273. Balthasar, *Truth of God (TL2)*, 81. See also "God Speaks as Man," 84–85.

between the Bible and the theology of the early church.[274] There is a lot that Balthasar wishes to do. He clearly presents the saints as the best interpreters of the Scriptures, and as a means for resolving issues related to exegesis. In the process, Balthasar also offers an alternative to the historico-critical method which claimed to be the supreme explorer of biblical truth.[275] Evidently, Balthasar also wants to put faith back into the theological process. He wants to establish the genuineness of the faith as the foundation for the authenticity of interpretation, the saints being the ones who can understand the *Pneuma* who is in the Word. Proper interpretation of Scripture requires a dynamic theological and spiritual life, which only the saints can provide. This also means that Balthasar wants to emphasize the self-involving nature of biblical interpretation, as well as the necessity of holiness for understanding and for authentic explanation.

The issue that arises now is: what is it that takes place in the act of interpretation of Scripture according to Balthasar? Balthasar wants to avoid both the extrinsicist model and the immanentist model of biblical interpretation. In the immanentist model, represented by Bultmannian Protestantism, the risk is that of having the object vanish within the subject.[276] Bultmann had claimed that the only way in which we can understand texts is insofar as they confront us with an existential decision.[277] Balthasar claims that Bultmann's theology is not faithful to the biblical core, because, in his work, objective theology loses its importance for the believer whereas the existential and subjective aspect gains significance.[278] On his part, Balthasar maintains that the interpretation of Scripture involves bringing "to light 'treasures' that are 'hidden' in the enfleshed figure of the Word."[279] He claims that, what really requires interpretation is not the written text *per se*, but the Son, that is, the "enfleshed figure of the Word," which is "permeated by the Spirit."[280] This would mean that Balthasar emphasizes revelation as that which "must set the criteria and norms for its own interpretation."[281] It is

---

274. Riches, "Von Balthasar as Biblical Theologian and Exegete," 38.

275. Oakes, "Balthasar's Critique of the Historical-Critical Method," 163. See Balthasar, *The Dramatis Personae: Man in God (TD2)*, 106–30.

276. Dickens, *Hans Urs von Balthasar's Theological Aesthetics*, 35.

277. Quash, "Hans Urs von Balthasar," 118.

278. Balthasar, *Convergences*, 38–39. According to Balthasar, in the Scriptures, the issue is the community and the church, rather than the self.

279. Balthasar, *The Spirit of Truth (TL3)*, 239.

280. Ibid. As Ratzinger describes it, in the Bible, one stumbles on the humanity of God, on man, "on the *analogia entis* in the *analogia fidei*." Ratzinger, "Christian Universalism," 134.

281. Dickens, *Hans Urs von Balthasar's Theological Aesthetics*, 46.

for this reason that, in Balthasar, only the saints, or those "who themselves live in the world of the saints,"[282] are able to understand and authentically interpret the Scriptures. Only they have this authority, only they can be credible, only their interpretation is reliable, because they draw the criteria for their interpretation from revelation itself. In his *Aesthetics*, Balthasar explains this in phenomenological terms, "[t]he purity and clarity with which the Word of God presents itself in the world is in direct proportion to the transparency and purity of the medium of faith that receives it and from which it creates its own form."[283] This daring statement reflects Balthasar's recurrent attempts to link the objective with the subjective elements within the exegetical exercise.

The fact that the saints whom Balthasar chooses to use are the ones whose exegesis he believes is the most reliable goes to show that, for him, the authority of the saints is grounded in their capacity for interpreting the Scriptures. Adrienne is certainly included among the saints in this regard. Balthasar describes the difference between the way a professional exegete listens to the biblical text and the way in which Adrienne listened to it. In Balthasar's view, Adrienne had a gift for interpreting the Scriptures.[284] Adrienne's listening to the word of God was more radical, and her living of it more exclusive than in anyone else.[285] Blankenhorn has acknowledged that "Balthasar consistently gives Speyr's mystical understanding of the New Testament a great deal of authority."[286] Riches even points out that Balthasar allows Adrienne's reading of the *triduum mortis* to assume "pride of place over the canon."[287] Whether Balthasar can be justified in attributing such authority to her will remain a matter of controversy. Was Adrienne the typical exegete in the historico-critical method? Certainly not, but the mystical exegesis which she provides is certainly an exegesis Balthasar approves.

What I have said so far does not mean that, according to Balthasar, the saints would always agree on the interpretation or on the exegetical method. This is the advantage of spiritual and mystical exegesis. It lends itself to more creativity, and a more polyphonic reading, than the historico-critical method. As Jeffrey A. Vogel has said

282. Balthasar, *Two Sisters*, 26.

283. Balthasar, *Seeing the Form (TA1)*, 539.

284. Chantraine, "Exegesis and Contemplation," 137.

285. Balthasar, *First Glance*, 247. Concerning her contemplative hearing of the word of God, see also 101.

286. Blankenhorn, "Balthasar's Method of Divine Naming," 260.

287. Riches, "Balthasar and the Analysis of Faith," 41.

there are always new directions in which [the Spirit] is able to go. At one and the same time, his interpretation is pure repetition and continually surprising, bound to the revelation in Christ and as free as the love Christ reveals. Though the Spirit imparts no new truths, his interpretation never approaches closure, because the object he interprets—the divine life—is itself always new, essentially creative, always more than can be grasped.[288]

Balthasar acknowledges the differences in exegetical styles among the saints. Gregory of Nyssa's "exegetical method corresponds exactly to the antiplatonist theory of real becoming." Origen's method preferred the separation of the literal and material meaning from the spiritual meaning.[289] For Maximus, the theological act of meditating on Scripture was "one with the act of spiritual or mystical contemplation."[290] But what is specific about the way in which the saints read and interpret the scriptures? Balthasar claims that to accept that a passage of Scripture is the word of God is to accept that one cannot fully understand it.[291] And this is what seems to be generic among the saints: the fact that they approach the Word of God with humility, reverence, and a sense of awe.[292] In his *Two Sisters*, Balthasar claims that contemplation and adoration of the Word are essential.[293] Balthasar thus seems to want to put the record straight by implying that the verbose method of the modernist theologians may be less helpful than they may think. In his book on prayer, he claims that the pursuit of theology and exegesis should be accompanied with "a disposition to worship," a "habitual adoration" and, "a liturgical attitude" of the mind. St Anselm is used as a good example of this reverent exegesis.[294] So is Mary. "Mary . . . . does not speculate: she worships and obeys, opens her womb to the Spirit."[295]

Balthasar claims that one of theology's main responsibilities is that of interpreting the Bible as authoritative for Christian life and thought. He has the theologian saints in mind: "Who can withdraw his attention from those interpreters whom the Holy Spirit itself sets before the Church as

---

288. Vogel, "The Unselfing Activity of the Holy Spirit," 20.

289. Balthasar, *Presence and Thought*, 57–58.

290. Balthasar, *Cosmic Liturgy*, 54.

291. Balthasar, "The Word, Scripture, and Tradition," 21.

292. For Balthasar, dogmatics itself is "a theory of rapture" (*Entruckung*). Balthasar, *Seeing the Form (TA1)*, 126.

293. Balthasar, *Two Sisters*, 217.

294. Balthasar, *Prayer*, 94.

295. Ibid., 195.

authentically representing the meaning of Scripture?"[296] In his *Two Sisters*, Balthasar claims that the motive for the church's interest in Thérèse should be the new vistas onto the Gospels that are opened up through her,[297] although she "never acquired a genuine contemplation of the Scriptures."[298] Elizabeth of the Trinity, on the other hand, "seems to take each of the 'teachings' of Thérèse and reset them into their framework in revelation."[299] She is "a faithful expositor of the finest and most profound passages of [Paul's] letters."[300] Balthasar has high regard for Elizabeth's "scriptural thought." He says that

> She does not perceive herself to be a theologian. In no sense is it her task to speculate or construct theories out of revealed concepts. Her power lies in reflecting (*speculari*), in gazing (*theōrein*), in glimpsing the depths of the simple word. These glimpses fully satisfy her, for she could never fully chart the depths of the word by taking soundings. She permits the word to stand, and, as she adores, its unforeseen dimensions reveal themselves . . . She desires not theology, but adoration; yet adoration of the word in its revealed character. This requires contemplation of the word, contemplation born of "the mind of God" as it is implanted in the believer.[301]

One could interpret Balthasar's emphasis on the authority of the saints in the exegetical domain as contrary to the established belief that the revelation of Christ was concluded with the death of the last apostle (the last historical witness). Balthasar would use his pneumatology to clarify his position. He would maintain that the Spirit's revelation is never concluded.[302] This would be simply a repetition of Catholic belief, except that Balthasar interprets his theology of revelation in terms of mission. According to him, "the Scriptures contain special sayings appropriate to each mission" and it is the mission that will interpret it.[303] Balthasar acknowledges that this does not make it a straightforward process. He claims that

296. Balthasar, *Two Sisters*, 26.

297. Ibid., 30. See also 217.

298. Ibid., 92.

299. Ibid., 413–14.

300. Ibid., 487.

301. Ibid., 376. See also 488.

302. Balthasar, *The Spirit of Truth (TL3)*, 199.

303. Balthasar, *Two Sisters*, 84.

All these concrete norms in which the Holy Spirit expounds the Word of God to the Church are subject to many kinds of perils and contingencies: resistances in those who are thus chosen; resistances in their environment which hinder their work; resistances, finally, in the Church, who may not listen to their message, or only listen sceptically.[304]

What is Balthasar trying to do here? Steffen Lösel has accused Balthasar of placing the Magisterium above Scripture and tradition.[305] On my part, I believe Balthasar is trying to avoid an impression that the critical exegete is autonomous.[306] Balthasar follows Ignatius, and insists that "[t]he relative independence of the exegete does not. . .exempt him from the 'ecclesiastical sense' (*sentire cum ecclesia*)."[307] Thus thinking *with* the Holy Spirit (my italics) (*sentire cum Spirito Sancto*), is closely linked to *sentire cum ecclesia* (thinking with the church).[308] The model for this "ecclesially appropriate hermeneutics" is to be found in other saints besides Ignatius: in Irenaeus, Origen, Augustine, Anselm, and Bonaventure.[309] In Balthasar's theology, there is a profound relationship between the church's official dogmatic and doctrinal exegesis and the saint's own exegesis. Both of them are at the service of the Scriptures. The former bases its authority on the latter, the latter are measured by their faithfulness to the former, the Spirit is the same.

it is never possible to apply the "pneumatic" norms independently of the more "formal" norms of Scripture, tradition, and the teaching and pastoral office. The saints themselves have to allow themselves to be measured by these norms, and if the Spirit of God is in them, they will not try to avoid such judgment; for he is the Spirit of the Church. But it is nonetheless true

304. Balthasar, *A Theology of History*, 110–11.

305. Lösel, "Conciliar, Not Conciliatory," 26, 39.

306. The issue of autonomy for the critical exegete was one debated by Alfred Loisy (1857–1940) and Adolf von Harnack (1851–1930). See Boersma, *Nouvelle Théologie*, 19.

307. Balthasar, *Convergences*, 70.

308. Balthasar, *A Theology of History*, 104.

309. De Lubac had used Hilary of Poitier to argue that the spiritual meaning of the Scriptures is essentially an "ecclesiastical" meaning: "[T]he meaning of the *praefigurationis significantia* is equivalent to the *spiritualis praeformatio*, and the *spiritualis praeformatio* alternates the *Ecclesiae praeformatio*." De Lubac, *Catholicism*, 93–94. Balthasar "regard[s] Holy Scripture as an inspired whole—one that is, moreover, interpreted in the essential tradition and history of the Church." Balthasar, *The Christian State of Life*, 16.

that in the final analysis, these formal norms exist for the sake of the living norm of holiness.[310]

Dickens is right to say that, in his emphasis on the importance of interpreting the Bible within an ecclesial setting, Balthasar is in agreement with the pre-moderns.[311] A few questions arise, however, as to what Balthasar is actually claiming, whether he is claiming that the authority of the saints arises from the fact that they feel with the church (this would be an ecclesiological question), whether he is trying to establish that saints who are considered authoritative, always feel with the church (this would be an apologetic question), or even whether he is claiming that the saints require the help of theologians to establish them within the church (this would be a methodological question). The apologetic question is especially evident in his attempts to integrate Adrienne's work. He wants to prove that Adrienne is not "withdrawn . . . from the authority, guidance, and watchfulness of the sacred Teaching Authority." She is totally an *anima ecclesiastica*.[312]

But to get back to our main argument: I have so far argued that the authority of the saints comes from their Scriptural interpretation, and that the saints function as authorities within the context of biblical interpretation, both because of the quality of the interpretation which they provide and because of the trust which their holiness elicits from others. Naturally, we cannot ignore the fact that, in Balthasar, a proper understanding of the Bible is self-involving and dramatic. Biblical interpretation requires a living faith which involves a radical Yes to the offer of grace made through the Bible. Thus, ultimately, the theologian-saint acquires his authority from the fact that he or she responds to God's Word (and often interprets it for others) and accomplishes in his or her life that which has been heard and understood in contemplation of God's Word.

CONCLUSION

The question throughout this Chapter has been: in the epistemological dimension, where is the authority of the saints grounded? In this Chapter, I argued that, in the epistemological dimension, the authority of the saints is grounded in the faith, the knowledge and the love of the saints. I deduced that, in Balthasar, the faith, knowledge and love of the saints is quantitatively or qualitatively different from that of others, thus enabling the saints to have

---

310. Balthasar, *A Theology of History*, 111.

311. Dickens, *Hans Urs von Balthasar's Theological Aesthetics*, 71.

312. See Roten, "The Two Halves of the Moon," 72.

better access to the truth and to understand more. In Balthasar, it is experience that grounds the epistemological advantage enjoyed by the saints, since the quality of one's contemplation, the saints' participation in archetypal experience and the sharing of the saints in the mystical experience of the church, enables the saints to grow in knowledge, and to impart it, in acting as a testimonial to others. I also maintained that, in Balthasar, the authority of the saints is also grounded in the saints' very lack of attachment to the mystical understanding and grasp of the truth, which humanity has such a thirst for.

My argument has been that, from Balthasar's theology, it is possible to infer that the saints are epistemologically proficient, that it is holiness which furnishes the saints with epistemological authority (both for theology and for the church), and that the saints are assigned authority on epistemological issues precisely because they are saints. Furthermore, in the epistemological dimension, the saints function as an authority whom one invokes when there has been a failure to know and to whom one submits in the process of learning.[313] This makes the authority of the saint analogous to that of the Magisterium.

So far I have looked at two of the dimensions which act as a grounding for the authority of the saints, namely the existential and the epistemological. These two dimensions are essential, but not sufficient on their own. My next Chapter will discuss the ecclesiological dimension.

---

313. Austin, *Up with Authority*, 46.

CHAPTER 5

The Ecclesiological Dimension

INTRODUCTION

IT IS BEST TO establish our presuppositions for this Chapter. First of all, in Balthasar, God's power is communicated by Christ to the church, and above all to Peter, to the Twelve, and to their successors.[1] Secondly, in attributing authority to the saints, Balthasar does not intend to assume an anthropocentric approach to authority, at the expense of the divine. Balthasar is willing to accept a *propter auctoritatem ecclesiae* because, according to him, ecclesial authority and proclamation pronounces and exacts *the auctoritatem Dei*.[2] Thirdly, in Balthasar, ecclesial authority is not reserved to the hierarchy, although it is associated with office understood in a wide sense. In Balthasar, besides ordination, there are other offices and other missions which are authoritative in the church. Fourthly, authority in Balthasar may take the form of the *sensus fidelium*, but more often than not, it derives from the wider concept of the *communio sanctorum*, rather than from the narrower concept of a theological consensus, or *consensus fidelium*. Finally, it is also important to draw attention to the two elements which Balthasar favors for describing the church: namely the Marian and the Petrine components. Balthasar claims that Mary is the first member of the church in whom the

---

1. Balthasar, "Authority," 130–33. See also *The Office of Peter*, 197; and Balthasar, *Seeing the Form (TA1)*, 140.

2. Balthasar, *Seeing the Form (TA1)*, 140–41.

subjective and the objective elements in the church become fully unified.[3] Finally, Balthasar also claims that others within the church can share in this all-rounded holiness of hers.

Balthasar identifies two sources for the assistance of the Christian community (the *communio sanctorum*), namely the "holy Church" or the "Church of the saints" and the apostolic succession of the pastoral and magisterial office.[4] Here, it is important to clarify that, besides the trend whereby the Marian principle is expansive enough to include everyone, including the official side, there is evidence in Balthasar, of a second trend, that of positioning Mary alongside Peter.[5] Both of these descriptive models feature in my own discussion, but I hope that clarity will not be sacrificed.

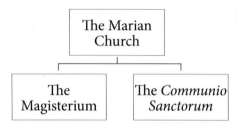

Diagram 05. The Marian Church

THE AUTHORITY THAT COMES FROM ECCLESIAL HOLINESS

Before the issue of authority can be treated, it is best to put Balthasar within the context of the conversation concerning individual holiness and the ecclesial context. Pieter De Witte has argued that, in their attempts to respond to criticism and accusations of hypocrisy, Catholic leaders have failed to convey a credible understanding of the church's holiness. De Witte draws upon the Joint Lutheran-Roman Catholic Declaration on the Doctrine of Justification by Faith, to point to the need for renewed reflection on the church as *simul justus et peccator*, maintaining that this would help resolve

---

3. Some would disagree that Mary is prior to the church chronologically. Zizoulas is one example. In Zizoulas, Christ is corporate from the beginning. McPartlan, "Who is the Church?," 282.

4. Balthasar, *The Office of Peter*, 228.

5. Ibid., 221. Because of Balthasar's double-stance, this chapter will at times deal with the Marian office as distinct from, and possibly in contrast with, the Petrine, and at times with the Marian office as encompassing the Petrine office.

the troubling pattern of the systematic abuse of pastoral authority.[6] As Dominic Robinson has pointed out, in this regard, Balthasar learns from Barth and Luther. For Barth, Luther's *simul justus et peccator,* the doctrine that we are, after the Fall, at one and the same time sinners yet justified, propels us not to look at ourselves as sinners, nor to look at some future hope. Rather, Barth focuses on Christ in the midst of human lives in the present. Balthasar's own preoccupation with the challenge of correlating individual failure with ecclesial holiness is relentless. What he does, on his part, is he provides a more explicit understanding of how the human person is "involved in this relationship with Christ in ontological terms."[7] However, this must be seen in the light of his main contention that the property of holiness is primarily a mark of the whole community before it is the attribute of an individual.[8] It is the "collective consecration" which leads to the members of the New Testament church being called "saints."[9] This is not the same as attributing holiness to "the central administration of the Church."[10] In his view, the church will never succeed in making her structures "transparent to Christian love" because of "the sinfulness of man."[11] The risks of such ecclesial structures being misused is too great.[12]

Balthasar identifies a series of what he calls ecclesial "objectivizations" which are intended "to guide the subjective spirit of believers through the process of self-surrender,"[13] namely, the Scriptures, Tradition, the episcopate, the sacraments and canon law.[14] Such "objectivizations" are always

6. De Witte, "The Church as *simul justus et peccator?,*" 96.

7. Robinson, *Understanding the "Imago Dei,"* 102–3.

8. Balthasar, *Two Sisters,* 39.

9. Balthasar, *The Office of Peter,* 205.

10. Ibid., 67

11. What Balthasar grants is that the structures of the church "are more easily permeated" by the sacred than the structures of the world. Balthasar, *Engagement with God,* 89.

12. Balthasar, *Engagement with God,* 89. See also Balthasar, *Seeing the Form (TA1),* 603.

13. Balthasar, *The Spirit of Truth (TL3),* 153–54. Balthasar describes "subjective spirit" as "the individual consciousness, which . . . gradually . . . by means of the renunciation of self-surrender . . . discovers the true dimension of spirit and, hence, the authentic freedom proper to it."

14. Ibid., 311–12. In Balthasar, the various aspects of objective holiness can be given the title "holy," although this must not be interpreted as referring to them subjectively. For instance, we may speak of "Holy" Scripture, of the "holy" sacraments, of the "Holy" synods and councils. The expression "Holy Father," however, does not refer to the person who bears it. It refers to the office he holds. See also Balthasar, *The Christian State of Life,* 141.

prior to the individual, and they are "superior to all personal holiness."[15] Balthasar's approach of prioritizing the objective over the subjective, collective holiness over individual holiness, and holiness over sinfulness is certainly a matter of theological controversy. Concerning the second of these pairs, Elizabeth Johnson has said that the symbol of the communion of saints "does not in the first instance refer to paradigmatic figures, those outstanding individuals traditionally called 'saints,' but rather names the whole community of people graced by the Spirit of God."[16] The third of these pairs: the prioritizing of holiness over sinfulness would be especially risky if it involved the concealment of sinfulness. As John McDade has noted, if you omit the sinners from within a communion called to holiness, "you create the Church of the righteous elect," whereas even "the presence of Judas requires constant acknowledgment."[17] The consequences of hiding the sinfulness within the church can have grave consequences, as the pedophilia scandal has made evident. Writing about the church in the New Testament, Raymond E.Brown has said that "an emphasis on the holiness of the Church can be a weakness if it begins to mask faults that exist" and that "oppression, veniality, and dishonesty . . . may need to be exposed and spoken against," because of the harm they do to the church.[18]

Davies has accused Balthasar of hiding the sinfulness. Davies claims that the "critique of the particular narrative tradition from within" is "substantially lacking in von Balthasar's work."[19] This is not entirely correct. I tend to support Nicholas M.Healy's position. Having analyzed Balthasar's theodramatic form of ecclesiology, Nicholas M. Healy points out that Balthasar often assesses the tradition and expresses disapproval wherever necessary. Healy claims that Balthasar's assessment embodies the belief that all people and all institutions, including the church are sinful.[20] He maintains that the struggle for and against God does not just take place between the world and the church. It also takes place within the church.[21] Thus Balthasar acknowledges the paradox of individual sinfulness and the

15. Balthasar, *The Spirit of Truth* (TL3), 337. This means that, in Balthasar, the underlying concept could ultimately be described as a postliberal one, that is, as one that emphasizes the individual as a product of a religion understood in a cultural-linguistic manner.

16. Johnson, *Friends of God and Prophets*, 1. I have tried to clarify this by distinguishing between the *communio sanctorum* and the *Communio Sanctorum*.

17. McDade, "Von Balthasar and the Office of Peter in the Church," 102.

18. Brown, *The Churches the Apostles Left behind*, 56.

19. Davies, "Von Balthasar and the Problem of Being," 15.

20. Healy, *Church, World and the Christian Life*, 151.

21. Ibid., 65.

problematics of structure, while still appreciating and maintaining the holiness of the church.[22]

Thus, Balthasar takes the Augustinian view and emphasizes that the church is one body, but that it is a *corpus permixtum*.[23] It is a thoroughly mixed body (not a divided one).[24] Balthasar goes one step further, he *accepts* a church where "the saints . . . retain their weaknesses, perhaps even their sins,"[25] where saints "are to be taken seriously when they insist on their inadequacy,"[26] where the saint must "love" his or her "imperfection and not long to escape from it,"[27] where the liability often rests with the greatness.[28] So there are no clear boundaries between saints and sinners. Balthasar actually presents a church where not only is the church a *corpus permixtum*, but each individual is also composite. We have here two different interpretations of the *simul justus et peccator*. One is of us being entirely saints (in Christ) and entirely sinners (on ourselves), and the other of being partly saints, and partly sinners. At the same time, one is envisioning one of two things. First is the possibility of some kind of grading among the saints. D.M.Matzko has said that "[a] devotion to saints requires inequalities among persons in a hierarchy of goodness."[29] The inequalities would have to be part and parcel of the theology concerning the authority of the saints. For, how is it possible to maintain the authority of the saints, without drawing attention to the distinctions among human beings? Secondly, one is also envisioning the possibility of having saints being authoritative at times and not at others.

There is also the issue as to whether Balthasar is trying to defend the prestige of the institution at the expense of that of the individual? The answer to this is "no." In Balthasar, each individual must consciously work towards the holiness of the church first, and let individual holiness follow, if it will. Balthasar's intention is to embolden individuals to sacrifice their own ideals—even that of sanctity—for the sake of the community.[30] Just as

22. Ibid., 107–8.

23. Augustine, *City of God*, 1:35.

24. Healy, *Church, World and the Christian Life*, 55

25. Balthasar, *Two Sisters*, 38.

26. Ibid., 27.

27. Ibid., 281. Within the genre of hagiography, "a saint who vaunted holiness was not only an imposter but a contradiction in terms." Weinstein and Bell, *Saints and Society*, 154.

28. Howsare, *Balthasar: A Guide for the Perplexed*, 166.

29. Matzko, "Postmodernism, Saints and Scoundrels," 19.

30. Balthasar gives the example of the Curate of Ars, "who lived wholly by the spirit of the religious life without ever entering a religious order, although the thought was

with Paul, "[t]he rule that governs what we do and what we do not do" will be "only what is most beneficial for the community" and what will not "give scandal to its weaker members," and not "what is permitted the individual as a private person, what he can allow himself to do on the basis of his own conscience."[31] In Balthasar, subjective holiness "is only holy if it serves as the path and goal of this objective holiness."[32]

In his essay on "Foundations of Christian Ethics," Marc Ouellet highlights that which distinguishes the theology of the *communio sanctorum* in Balthasar: it is "at once divine and human," and it "resembles the Trinitarian communion" in that, what becomes common property—their very personhood—is more than just what belongs to each one.[33] Ouellet argues that "by recovering the essential implication of community in the occurrence of grace," Balthasar "advances beyond the Protestant individualism of justification by faith and the Catholic individualism of merit."[34] According to Ratzinger, the model of church as *Communio* enables Balthasar not only to take the church's call to holiness seriously, but also to recognize "the consolation of this holiness," since it takes the form of solace to the weak, of guidance and of nurture.[35]

There are four advantages to using the *communio sanctorum* as a model for the church. The first of these is that it makes it possible to contemplate the whole while deliberating on the individual, and vice-versa, which is otherwise a real *coincidentia oppositorum*.[36] The second advantage is that the concept of the *communio sanctorum* enables Balthasar to transcend the limitations of church and the limitations of time. As he says in the *Theo-Logic*, through the supratemporal understanding of the *communio sanctorum*, "the elements of tradition—the saints, the Fathers, Doctors of the church, and so on—maintain a kind of presence and currency that abolishes much of the historical distance between us and them."[37] The third advantage is that the concept of the *communio sanctorum* makes it possible for Balthasar to develop a proper economic pneumatology and a Mariology which pres-

always present to him as a temptation to lighten his superhuman ministry." Balthasar, *The Christian State of Life*, 377–78.

31. Balthasar, *The Christian State of Life*, 339.

32. Balthasar, *The Spirit of Truth (TL3)*, 311.

33. Ouellet, "Foundations of Christian Ethics," 238 and 241.

34. Ibid., 241.

35. Ratzinger, "Christian Universalism," 141.

36. See "Who Is the Church," 191. The neoplatonic Latin term, attributed to Nicholas of Cusa, is used to describe a revelation of the oneness of things previously believed to be different. See his essay *De Docta Ignorantia*.

37. Balthasar, *The Spirit of Truth (TL3)*, 327.

ents Mary as an exemplar, but not necessarily as a personification of the church.[38] And finally, it enables Balthasar to allocate an authoritative place to each and every saint, and to each and every mission, since the mission is evaluated within a communal context, rather than individually.

Balthasar does not give a full account of the historical development of the doctrinal symbol of the *communio sanctorum*. Nor does he give a full account of the devotional practice accompanying this doctrine. It would have been good had he written more extensively about it, but we do know that the concept is very important for Balthasar. And we can safely say that we have enough to be able to understand what he means by it.[39] Balthasar simply refuses to describe the communion of saints as "a *closed* circle of those who exchange their merits and rewards among themselves," as it is generally understood. On the contrary, he maintains that it is "an *open* circle of those who 'give without counting the cost.'" (my emphasis).[40] It is not the "collective understanding, collective will and collective feeling of the community," to which the individual intellect must submit, as it is with Tyrell.[41] It is rather that "the self is opened toward the Church and toward the most intimate fellowship of the saints."[42] In terms of its identity, the *communio sanctorum* incorporates all those who are seeking to praise God's glory.[43] In terms of its effectiveness, it extends to "unbelievers" as well.[44] Balthasar writes of a "mystical communism" where "individuals receive things which are kept from the rest." For Balthasar, the *communio sanctorum* is built up and fostered, "not through the levelling-down of privileges (as Protestantism practiced on Mary) . . . but rather by the distinguishing of different vocations, which only in their interconnectedness yield a qualitatively integrated unity."[45] Balthasar agrees with Aquinas that "this spirit which circulates through the organism causes the members not only to care 'horizontally' for one another but also . . . to love the whole more than themselves, the parts."[46] Balthasar also adds that it is this life-giving spirit that "gives every

38. McPartlan, "Who Is the Church?," 285.

39. See Balthasar, "Catholicism and the Communion of Saints"; and Balthasar, "The Communion of Saints."

40. Balthasar, "The Communion of Saints," 96.

41. Balthasar, *The Office of Peter*, 112.

42. Balthasar, *Two Sisters*, 461–62.

43. Sicari, "Hans Urs von Balthasar," 127.

44. Balthasar, *Two Sisters*, 40. This is a concept Balthasar owes to De Lubac. See De Lubac, *Catholicism*, 118; Balthasar, *The Theology of Henri de Lubac*, 39; and Balthasar, "The Communion of Saints," 96, 99.

45. Balthasar, *Seeing the Form (TA1)*, 342.

46. Balthasar, "The Communion of Saints," 98.

member its form and function and consequently at the same time relates it internally to the whole."[47] The significance of all this is that, for Balthasar, the authority of the saints would arise from the very fact that they are the best "protectors and inspirers" of this *communio*.[48]

THE AUTHORITY THAT COMES FROM OFFICE

What about the issue of office? It is difficult to prove the correlation between the authority of office and that of holiness. This is probably the most problematic concept with which I have had to deal. Office is a position of authority or service, typically of a public nature, whereas holiness is generally understood as the sanctification of the individual who has encountered God. Moreover, it can be difficult to relate Balthasar's view of the penitential character of office—where office is understood as one of the consequences of sin, and as a cross for the community to carry[49]—with his theology of office as a charism. Before I can delve deeper into these issues, it is necessary to elicit, in very concise form, the main tenets of Balthasar's theology of office. First of all, unless otherwise stated, when Balthasar refers to "office," it is generally the priestly or the Petrine office that he intends. Secondly, in Balthasar, as in the official Catholic point of view, office is an aspect within the organism which takes its mission from Christ (*jure divino*).[50] It "does not emanate *from* the community but is instituted in the Church from above."[51] Thirdly, office is associated with the authority "to teach, to consecrate and to shepherd,"[52] "to make present sacramentally, to govern legitimately."[53] Fourthly, office is not merely reserved for those in the priesthood, and the Petrine office is not the only office within the church.

---

47. Ibid.

48. Balthasar, *Two Sisters*, 40.

49. Balthasar, *The Office of Peter*, 388. See also Balthasar, *The Christian State of Life*, 368.

50. Balthasar, "Catholicism and the Communion of Saints," 167.

51. Balthasar, "Obedience in the Light of the Gospel," 244–45. See also Balthasar, *Seeing the Form (TA1)*, 226–67.

52. Balthasar, "The Church as the Presence of Christ," 90.

53. Balthasar, "Obedience in the Light of the Gospel," 242. One could perhaps explain this emphasis on office as one instance of Irigaray's "phallocentric model," where "only a male body can represent God, in a way which comes close to an idolatry of the masculine." Beattie, "Sex, Death and Melodrama, 164. However, I believe that the issue ought to be read from within sacramental theology, rather than from the point of view of sexual ethics, if it is to be understood at all.

Now that that has been said, I have to identify the other offices which Balthasar proposes. Besides Peter—who represents the official ministry, the secular priest,[54]—there is John, who represents evangelical life, love, the religious priest, the saints;[55] Paul, who represents the apostolic office;[56] and Mary whose "perfect subjective holiness" is itself an office.[57] Office is fourfold. Moreover, these offices are all authoritative. McDade analyzes "the Apostolic Foursome," which includes James.[58] Peter exercises pastoral care.[59] John exercises the office of love, an office exercised by the saints of the church. James represents the dimension of Tradition and law. Paul represents the dimension of universalism and inculturation. McDade describes how, through these figures, Balthasar develops the foundations for different offices, different ecclesiologies, and different models of authority.[60] I understand Balthasar as implying that, just as each sacrament has its own grace, so each office has its own special kind of authority. As McDade has also pointed out, Balthasar identifies different ways in which each principle—the Johannine, Jamesian and Pauline no less than the Petrine—could go wrong,

> each principle in the fourfold office can become distorted. Johannine love can weaken into a mere "universal humanitarian benevolence"; Pauline flexibility can become a fashionable assimilation to cultural mores; the tradition of James can give rise to an "anxiously integralist, reactionary clinging to obsolete forms."[61]

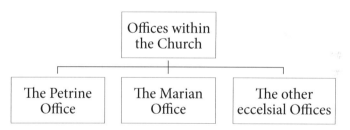

Diagram 06. Offices within the Church

54. Balthasar, *The Christian State of Life*, 287.

55. Ibid., 282, 287, 289. Balthasar, *The Office of Peter*, 242.

56. Balthasar considered Paul's apostolic authority in the Christian communities to be "overwhelming." Scola, *Test Everything*, 55.

57. Balthasar, *The Spirit of Truth (TL3)*, 314,

58. McDade, "Von Balthasar and the Office of Peter in the Church," 104–5.

59. Balthasar, *The Office of Peter*, 62.

60. Balthasar uses the various principles not just to answer the question "Who is the Church?" but also to provide a more ideal model of the church.

61. McDade, "Von Balthasar and the Office of Peter in the Church," 105.

The office of John is particularly significant to us, because, in Balthasar, the saints are the continuation of the Johannine church. "It is the Johannine principle, the ideal of holiness and unitive love for Christ, towards which the interaction of the other three principles must be directed . . . The goal of the fourfold office is the holiness of the Church."[62] This Johannine church "is not a 'third,' spiritual Church, supplanting the Petrine and the Pauline, but the one that stands under the Cross in place of Peter and on his behalf receives the Marian Church."[63] In Balthasar's theology, the saints are those who fill in for Peter, and who receive "the Marian Church." They "have, as it were, an unofficial ecclesial mission," which is also authentic. Thus, according to Balthasar, the saints support both the Marian and the Petrine in the church.[64] The "Johannine principle" also synthesizes the Petrine (representing the hierarchical and institutional form of the church), and the Pauline elements (representing the charismatic-missionary dimension) and combines them. For Balthasar, as for the Fathers of the church, John is the theologian, not in the sense of being a "bold explorer" or "fearless critic" but in the sense of being a man of the church.[65]

In his exploration of church history, Edward Schillebeeckx has referred to the "gradual sacerdotalisation of the vocabulary of the church's office."[66] Schillebeeckx understands church office as pastoral leadership of an ecclesial community. According to him,

> the tension between an ontological sacerdotalist view of the ministry on the one hand and a purely functionalist view on the other must therefore be resolved by a theological view of the Church's ministry as a charismatic office, the service of leading the community, and therefore as an ecclesial function within the community and accepted by the community. Precisely in this way, it is a gift of God.[67]

He has also referred to "the contemporary and alternative forms of office which are arising everywhere today and which deviate frequently from the valid order in the church and discover the possible theological value of these ways of exercising office."[68] He proposed "a non-sacral, but

---

62. Ibid., 109.

63. Balthasar, *The Office of Peter*, 242.

64. Ibid., 170.

65. Saward, "Mary and Peter in the Christological Constellation," 131.

66. Schillebeeckx, "The Christian Community and its Office-Bearers," 105 and 113.

67. Shillebeeckx, *Ministry*, 70.

68. Schillebeeckx, "The Christian Community and its Office-Bearers," 97.

nonetheless sacramental meaning of office."[69] Schillebeeckx even anticipated that practice with regards to office will be "ultimately sanctioned canonically."[70] Balthasar does not go this far, but he does, so to speak, *desacerdotalize* office. And he associates this broadening of the term with the saints. Balthasar reminds his readers that Thérèse does not hesitate to compare the contemplative vocation to that of the priesthood. She believes that her office is "no less dignified than that of the priest."[71] According to Balthasar, Thérèse shares just as much as—if not more than—men, do in the existential priesthood of Christ. Likewise, Balthasar maintains that God calls every woman, just as he calls every man, to imitate Christ in a thoroughly unique way.[72] Elizabeth of the Trinity, also emphasizes the place of office within the monastic framework. Those in monasteries "fill an ecclesial office."[73] Balthasar is amazed by the way in which Elizabeth places her office as a Carmelite nun side by side with that of the priest and permits her office and that of the priest to interpenetrate and complement each other.[74]

In Mary's regard, Balthasar also writes of holiness as an office.[75] He claims that, "[a]s a fruitful charism of the whole body of Christ, [holiness] has, in the economy of that body, a function that is just as much an official ministry as is the official ministry of the priest."[76] Where the ministerial priesthood is concerned, authority is given for ministry, as stated in *Lumen Gentium*. "For those ministers, who are endowed with sacred power, serve their brethren."[77] On the other hand, there is an authority, and there is a ministry, that follows from holiness. Balthasar maintains that the 'perfect subjective holiness' that is found in Mary "is of a qualitatively different kind' from ministerial office, and 'does not in any way tend toward ministerial office."[78] In not so many words, Balthasar establishes a theology of holiness that incorporates office, but is not necessarily of the "ministerial office" type. The issue is not without its problems. It is difficult to envisage a theology of

69. Ibid., 117.

70. Ibid., 98.

71. Balthasar, *Two Sisters*, 196.

72. Balthasar, *The Christian State of Life*, 374.

73. Balthasar, *Two Sisters*, 485.

74. Balthasar claims that the evangelical state "must borrow from the priesthood the concept of ecclesial office, extending it to include also the office of abbot, provincial or other major superior." *The Christian State of Life*, 371.

75. Balthasar, *The Spirit of Truth (TL3)*, 314.

76. Balthasar, *The Christian State of Life*, 380.

77. *Lumen Gentium*, 18.

78. Balthasar, *The Spirit of Truth (TL3)*, 314.

holiness which is understood as both the underlying reality (or the ultimate end) for all offices, and, at the same time, as an alternative form of ministry.

Where authority is concerned, various questions remain unanswered. First of all, does Balthasar intend the authority which we associate with the office of subjective holiness to act as an authority in the same way as the authority of someone in ecclesial office? Does the fact that authority is bestowed (from above) with every office make every authority bestowed (including that of office) equally authoritative? And what happens if an ecclesial office is bestowed on someone who already has the office of holiness? Is it the case that the saints who are given authoritative roles—whether it is the priesthood, or something else—receive a different authority in addition to the authority that comes from their holiness? Is their original authority increased? Does a holy person who is ordained become more holy; whereas a priest who becomes holy becomes more of a priest? And what about the saints who do not have such recognized authoritative roles? Does their office of holiness have to compete with other authoritative roles? There seems to be no evidence that Balthasar made any attempt to analyze these issues.

Ultimately, there is a lack of clarity on Balthasar's part concerning at least three fundamental matters: Firstly, concerning how we are to understand holiness as an office. Secondly, concerning whether a charism in the form of an office adds anything to the authority that comes from holiness, and, thirdly, whether the saints who are *in* authoritative roles—whether it is the priesthood, or something else—have more authority than the saints who do not have such authoritative roles. Though not formulated by Balthasar, these are questions which logically arise out of any attempt to formulate a theology of the authority of the saints, using Balthasar's theology. To my mind, the best way to explore these issues is to take one example. This will be our next step.

The Authority of the Priestly Office

In the *Theo-Logic*, Balthasar refers to various saints and theologians who instructed on the subject of ordination: John Chrysostom (c.347–407), the French Catholic priest and the founder of the Sulpicians, Jean-Jacques Olier (1608–1657), the theologian and mystic Matthias Joseph Scheeben (1835–1888), as well as Möhler, Newman, and others. He emphasizes that the priesthood "is much more than a moral duty toward God and men,"[79] but that it "confers authority in matters of Church leadership,"[80] it "implies

79. Ibid., 349.
80. Ibid., 347.

an absolute and definitive appointment and authorization for service," it entails "an automatic and analytic requirement" that this appointment and authorization for service be carried out,[81] and it "demands a life *in accordance with*" this service (my italics) and not just a life of service.[82]

Balthasar is not alone to think that there is an authority that is grounded in the (objective) priestly office. Most Catholic theologians would agree that the priestly office is "the preeminent *situs* of the presence of Christ in the Church."[83] However, Schillebeeckx has pointed out that office—as originally envisioned—did not depend "on a private and ontological qualification of the individual person bearing office and is also in no way separate from an ecclesial context."[84] Schillebeeckx claims that the priesthood has been "personalised and privatised," and we have, as a consequence, "the *plenitudo potestatis*," that is, "authority as a value in itself, isolated from the community."[85] Raymond E. Brown offers an evaluation of the priesthood through a discussion of its evolution.

> Precisely because much of Protestantism ceased to designate Christian ministry as priesthood (on the grounds of biblical silence), Roman Catholic theology buttressed the ordained priesthood. It was emphasized that the one ordained to the priesthood was metaphysically changed and indelibly marked by the sacrament; even Vatican II insisted that the difference of the ordained from the non-ordained was one of kind and not simply of degree.[86]

Balthasar does not acknowledge any oversight in tradition which has led to an inaccurate interpretation of the authority of the priest. What he does is he chooses to emphasize two things. First of all, he emphasizes the distinction between the "ineradicable character" that is given in priestly ordination and the personal holiness of the ordained person.[87] He maintains that one does not necessarily entail the other. Here, Balthasar is in agreement with Walter Kasper's principle that there "remains a permanent distinction between the objective mission of the priestly office and its subjective

81. Ibid., 348.

82. Ibid., 310.

83. Balthasar, *The Christian State of Life*, 369.

84. Schillebeeckx, "The Christian Community and its Office-Bearers," 102.

85. Ibid., 113–14.

86. Brown, *The Churches the Apostles Left Behind*, 80. Brown is writing about 1 Peter.

87. Balthasar, *The Spirit of Truth (TL3)*, 347.

realization."[88] Secondly, Balthasar attributes authority to the priesthood *per se*, not to its subjective realization. Where the priesthood is concerned, it is not that authority ensues from a *pointing to* Christ, but rather that the priest is meant to use his authority to point to Christ. Whereas in the first of these, the authority follows from the pointing to Christ, in the latter, the authority comes first, and the pointing to Christ is what should follow. This is an authority *in order to*, not an authority *because of*. If we apply the argument to authority, we could say that Balthasar is distinguishing between an authority that follows from authenticity (that is, from the subjective realization of the objective mission), and the authority that is not authenticated, but is an authority just the same (an objective mission that is not yet subjectively realized, or never will be). In the logical order, there is, therefore, the possibility of an authority which comes from "priestly ordination," irrespective of the subjective realization. In the order of the real, this distinction is more difficult to prove. It is difficult to have someone claiming authority as a consequence of the priesthood without in actual fact realizing that authority in terms of holiness. In the real order, the ecclesial office must also be able "to actualize, re-present, what it points to."[89] When the bearer of office in the church goes "about his business in a 'purely official' way, his actions will practically have no claim on the authority imparted by such office."[90] Thus Balthasar would agree that there is an authority that is grounded in the sacrament of ordination itself, that this authority is not the same as the authority that comes from holiness, and that each one can exist without the other. Perfection is not required before ordination and the priestly order is not itself a state of perfection.[91] Ordination is still valid, even without holiness, and holiness does not depend on ordination. However, this does not mean that, with or without holiness, the degree, or the extent, of the authority of the priesthood will remain the same. Whereas it is possible, logically speaking to separate objective and subjective holiness, separating them in the real world "would lead to a purely functional or administrative priestly ministry."[92]

88. Ibid., 347–48.

89. Balthasar, "Obedience in the Light of the Gospel," 241–42. See also "Authority," 130.

90. Balthasar, *The Spirit of Truth (TL3)*, 322.

91. According to Balthasar, whereas perfection, is "the internal disposition of an individual before God," the state of perfection is "an external social state established by canon law." *The Christian State of Life*, 301. Like Aquinas, Balthasar did not believe the priestly order to be a state of perfection. See Aquinas, *Summa Theologiae*, "The State of Perfection in General," Q. 184.

92. Balthasar, *The Spirit of Truth (TL3)*, 348.

In *The Office of Peter*, Balthasar uses Augustine to argue that the sacrament of ordination is located "in the innermost domain of ecclesial holiness, so that even in failure (in a bad priest) the fundamental effectiveness of the office was not allowed to be lost."[93] Balthasar also emphasizes that any authority that the ordained person exercises is, strictly speaking, a "communication" of the divine, paternal *potestas* of God, and not of his or her own.[94] In the *Theo-Logic*, however, Balthasar does add that "the merely objectivist, merely anti-Donatist priest of the *opus operatum*, the priest who fails to fill this *opus* inwardly with the whole strength of his person, is not the priest he should be."[95]

An important question would be whether authority is a quality that arises automatically out of holiness (as if simultaneously), or whether it is a quality that is attributed by others to those who are holy (as if subsequently). It would seem to me that, whereas with the office of the priesthood, the authority is attributed from outside, in arguing for the authority of the saints, we would have to claim that authority arises out of the internal holiness, and that every saint—whether canonized or not—emits, radiates and displays authority, concurrently with his or her growth in holiness.

The Authority of the Episcopate

Similar arguments to those above can be made concerning the episcopate. Here, the first question is: does someone who receives the ordination to the episcopate receive the office of holiness along with it? This would be very difficult to maintain. A second question is: if holiness is itself an office, does a charism in the form of the episcopate add anything to the authority that comes from holiness? Thirdly, does a saint who is a bishop have more authority than a saint who does not have such an authoritative role? And finally, when someone who is a bishop subsequently receives the office of holiness, does this add anything to his episcopate?

I should say that although the first question (does someone who receives the ordination to the episcopate receive the office of holiness along with it?), sounds rather simplistic, it is an issue that was hotly debated over the centuries. Balthasar himself refers to the Areopagite and to Aquinas, who had held that the bishop "is in the 'state of perfection' because his office expropriates [him] totally for the service of love to his flock." Balthasar concurs, but adds that once "the objective expropriation . . . has taken place,"

93. Balthasar, *The Office of Peter*, 188.

94. Ibid., 197.

95. Balthasar, *The Spirit of Truth (TL3)*, 305.

the one in office then "has a duty to realize subjectively [this] objective appropriation."[96] In the *Summa*, Aquinas tackles the issue as to whether all ecclesiastical Prelates are in a state of perfection. According to Aquinas, we should say that parish priests and archdeacons "have an office pertaining to perfection, rather than that they attain the state of perfection."[97] In Balthasar, office already tends towards subjective holiness, and requires it.[98] Balthasar does not hold that "election to the episcopal state" enables "the candidate to achieve, simultaneously and *ex opere operato*, the personal perfection necessary for fulfilling his office in a manner befitting that state."[99] According to him, neither Aquinas, nor the Fathers of the church ever maintained this. Balthasar prefers Cajetan's interpretation, and distinguishes between the state of perfection of the religious, and that of the bishop. According to him, the former is "the state of perfection for oneself [*status perfectionis propriae*], whereas the latter is the state of perfection for others [*status perfectionis alienae*]."[100]

With regards to our second question above, it could be said that Balthasar distinguishes between the two authorities—that of office and that of holiness—when he states that the hierarchy is "the successor to the Apostles with respect to the authority of their office but not with respect to their archetypal role as eyewitnesses."[101] An office in the form of the episcopate does add something to the individual in the form of authority, but it does not add the authority that comes from holiness (which can only be increased the deeper the holiness of the individual becomes).

Concerning the third question, we should repeat that the authority of office is to be distinguished from the authority of personal holiness, even the personal holiness "which is appropriate to such an office."[102] The saint who becomes a bishop now has an additional authority that is different from the authority that comes from holiness itself. As Francis A. Sullivan has said, bishops are authoritative teachers (*doctores authentici*). They teach authoritatively (*authentice*).[103] In this sense, one could say that the saint who is a bishop has more authority than someone who is not in such an authoritative role.

96. Ibid., 348. See also "Obedience in the Light of the Gospel," 245.

97. See Aquinas, *Summa Theologiae*, "The State of Perfection in General," Q. 184.

98. Balthasar, *The Spirit of Truth (TL3)*, 314.

99. Balthasar, *The Christian State of Life*, 305.

100. Ibid., 308.

101. Balthasar, *Seeing the Form (TA1)*, 337.

102. Balthasar, *The Christian State of Life*, 305.

103. Sullivan, *Magisterium*, 27.

And finally, were someone who is a bishop to receive the office of holiness, would this add anything to his episcopate? Balthasar would probably say that it would. Holiness bestows on the individual the authority that comes from holiness. Moreover, both logically, and realistically, it can be assumed that with the office of holiness, and particularly, the personal holiness that is appropriate to the episcopate, the authority of the episcopal office will also be increased. On the other hand, according to Augustine, it is possible to have a bad bishop in the real world. Logically speaking, his title would be "empty." Such a person [whether a priest or a bishop] may retain the *jus dandi*, and his official acts may be valid, but he is a "sham" (*fictus*).[104] He would be a *contradictio in terminis*.

The Authority of the Petrine Office

The modernist approaches focus away from the papacy and from any authority whatsoever. Balthasar will not follow in their wake. On the contrary, as John McDade has pointed out, in *The Office of Peter*, Balthasar presses the church to examine authority within the church, and the papacy in particular, and "to examine the bias in its nature against its central focus of authority."[105] Balthasar rules out Protestantism and Papolatry "because they dissolve the differentiated character of the Church."[106] His stance is that "the life of the Church is constituted by different elements or principles involved in a dynamic interchange and tension between the figures who are archetypal dimensions in its 'individuation."[107] Consequently, Balthasar insists on two things: first that the office of Peter cannot "be treated in isolation," since "in the *mysterium* of the Church . . . no element makes sense if it is isolated from the whole."[108] And secondly, that the role of the Petrine office is unity. In the ecclesiological dimension, Peter alone has "the right to demand unity,"[109] and he alone has the authority that facilitates unity. Balthasar writes,

> As shepherd who has to pasture the whole flock, [the Pope] has a right to claim authority (in doctrine and leadership) and to demand unity. This prerogative is his alone. But it does not isolate

104. Balthasar, *The Office of Peter*, 190.

105. McDade, "Von Balthasar and the Office of Peter in the Church," 97.

106. Ibid., 98.

107. Ibid., 99–100.

108. Balthasar, *The Office of Peter*, 138.

109. Ibid., 167–68.

him from the others who have founding missions and who, in their own way, have no less a continuing life and representation in the Church.[110]

John McDade has justifiably argued that Balthasar's aim is "to restore an ecclesiological balance which an over-juridical, ultramontane approach to papal authority has disturbed." The ultramontane approach had put a strong emphasis on Papal authority and on centralization of the church. Balthasar restores that balance by displacing the Petrine office from the "center" or "top" of the church, and placing it within the "larger unity" of the church, "relativizing" it without marginalizing it.[111]

There is a lot which Balthasar says that relates specifically to the Petrine office, particularly in *The Office of Peter*. One of the more radical things which he claims, and which is especially significant in our case, is that "many representatives of the papal ministry have failed terribly to unite their office and their own lives of discipleship," whereas "[t]o be a successor of the Good Shepherd in the Spirit of Christ demands harmony between the office and one's personal way of life."[112] Balthasar is saying that, although ideally the office of holiness and the office of Peter should go together, and although both logically and theologically one cannot be without the other, in reality, authority has often been unsupported by holiness. I have already established that, in Balthasar, the authority of Peter is distinct from the Marian-Johannine kind, which is that of the authority that comes from subjective holiness, and from the Pauline kind, which is that of the authority that comes from "deep or specialized theology."[113] Whether the Pope is personally exemplary and holy, or whether he is theologically outstanding is a distinct charism from the actual Petrine charism to which he is called. The authority that arises out of holiness is distinct from the authority that arises out of the office of the Papal episcopacy, although not separate. In fact, with Balthasar, there is a holiness that is specific to the office of Peter. As with Christ's ministerial authority (the "high priesthood"), the Petrine ministry consists of the "privilege and ability to give [one's] life for his sheep."[114] This is a far cry from the understanding of the Petrine ministry as a triumphalist papalism.[115] Balthasar suggests that the best way to understand the office of Peter is to understand it sacramentally and analogically. "[L]ike the saints,

110. Ibid., 158.

111. McDade, "Von Balthasar and the Office of Peter in the Church," 104.

112. Balthasar, *The Office of Peter*, xx.

113. Ibid., 260–61.

114. Ibid., xv.

115. Ibid., 134.

his whole existence is to be a sign, but," he adds, "the charism and prerogative of the saints (or of some of them) was not put into his cradle at birth!"[116]
As desirable as it would be that the holder of Petrine authority be a spirit-
filled saint, the office of holiness does not always complement the office of
Peter. Balthasar claims that it should be obvious that the Pope

> will err again and again at this intersection of time and eternity.
> Either he will betray the eternal for the sake of the temporal by
> trying to imprison it (putting eternal statements in "infallible
> statements") or he will betray the temporal by clinging to illu-
> sory formulas that seem to be eternal, thus missing the ongoing
> reality of his own time.[117]

Still, in Balthasar, it is Peter alone who has "the prerogative" to *claim*
authority in doctrine and leadership,[118] irrespective of other charisms he
may have received, or not received, even irrespective of his personal holiness. Balthasar does not diminish the authority of Peter due to lack of personal holiness.[119] Neither does he claim that the office of holiness has any
entitlement to authority.

Nouvelle théologie had reacted against neo-Thomist theology because
of its "authoritarian ecclesiology."[120] Balthasar also attributes to the Pope a
great deal of authority. He denounces all kinds of heresies: Gallicanism,[121]
Jansenism,[122] and integralism,[123] and emphasizes the ministerial authority
of Peter (rather than the administrative and the judicial), just as he had
emphasized the pastoral office (rather than the teaching office) of the episcopate.[124] Petrine authority is a ministerial authority, like Christ's, whose
ministerial authority (the "high priesthood") consisted of his "privilege and

116. Ibid., 39.

117. Ibid., 385–86.

118. Balthasar, *The Office of Peter*, 167–8.

119. The risks of having a Petrine office that is supreme (that is, where everything
is ultimately subject to it: the Marian and the Johannine principles, even Scripture and
its interpretation), has been articulated by Lösel. See "Conciliar, Not Conciliatory," 40.

120. Boersma, *Nouvelle Théologie*, 20.

121. Balthasar, *The Office of Peter*, 69. Gallicanism attempts "to qualify every papal
decision, be it by an appeal to a council or by a stipulation that the directives must be
accepted by the whole Church (bishops and flock) to be valid."

122. Ibid., 69. Jansenism supports papal authority only as long as it does not clash
with a higher form, e.g., the authority of St Augustine.

123. Ibid. Balthasar condemns integralism, claiming that "when a community
within the Catholic Church refers to a dictate of its collective conscience against a final
papal decision, it has already lost the sense of the Church communion."

124. Balthasar, *The Spirit of Truth (TL3)*, 326. See also 314.

ability to give his life for his sheep."[125] At the same time, Balthasar restricts Petrine authority by denoting that it is occasional, and that its application is sporadic. He states that "the Petrine function asserts itself [or should assert itself] only . . . when the 'unity in love' is imperiled or when people turn for advice or arbitration to [Rome as] the acknowledged center of unity."[126] Moreover, in Balthasar, the authority of the Petrine office does not lie in the capricious giving of orders, judgments, verdicts, dogmas, and *imprimaturs*. The Petrine office "is an indispensable, visible service, mediating unity."[127] Balthasar insists that

> as representative of the norm, [Peter] more than all the others
> has the duty to make his life coincide as closely as possible with
> his official mission. He has to represent not only formal author-
> ity but also a humanly credible authority, not by identifying
> himself with Christ or with the gospel—the pope is not the suc-
> cessor or representative of Christ, but of Peter—but by pointing
> to Christ in an existentially convincing manner.[128]

Balthasar insists that, inherent in the nature of discipleship, but particularly in that of the individual exercising the Petrine office, are two elements: the actual following, but also the consequences of that following.
In Balthasar, suffering is an integral part of the function of office, and the
Cross is the paradigm for the explanation of authority. Not only is office
made possible only and entirely by the Cross,[129] it is also "modeled" on the
Cross.[130] Authority in itself is a reconfiguration of the individual into the
cross. Death on the Cross is therefore an essential part of the exercise of
this authority. It is not optional, or superfluous to the function, and it is not
private, but "essential," part of the very nature and function of the office.[131]
With Paul, Balthasar claims that the "state of being crucified" is required of
someone who holds ecclesiastical office. With Peter, he claims that the "sin-
gular participation in Jesus' authority and responsibility obliges him also to
participate specially in Jesus' spirit of service and his readiness to suffer."[132]
On the part of the holder of the Petrine office, there is "a distinctively Petrine

---

125. Balthasar, *The Office of Peter*, xv.

126. Ibid., 263.

127. Balthasar, *The Office of Peter*, 245. See also 230, 311.

128. Balthasar, "Obedience in the Light of the Gospel," 242.

129. Balthasar, *The Office of Peter*, 191.

130. Ibid., 386.

131. Ibid., 382, 386.

132. Ibid., xv, 150.

effacement of personality."[133] This is in agreement with what Balthasar says in the *Aesthetics*. Concurrently with the elevation to office, "humiliation strikes." The Petrine form is established upon this "simultaneity" of elevation and humiliation.[134] Balthasar is convinced that "the ever-renewed humiliation of the office also contributes to its purification and clarification." He repeats that "it is God who puts the officeholders in the 'last' place; it is not they themselves who voluntarily take it, nor does the community have any mandate to put them there."[135]

These thoughts are repeated in Balthasar's essay on obedience. Balthasar states that Peter is given two things "at his installation in office: the command 'follow me' (containing the grace needed for following) and the rich promise of 'the kind of death by which he would glorify God.'" Balthasar thus emphasizes that it is "crucifixion" that draws "the ecclesial office into the Lord's most primordial authority."[136] How is one to explain this? Is Balthasar saying that one's authority originates in one's suffering? Is he claiming that only that authority which has the *forma Christi* (including the Cross) is authentic authority? Is he saying that authority should be attributed to those who suffer? Or even that the more a Pope suffers, the more authoritative he becomes? So what does Balthasar really mean when he associates authority with suffering? As I understand it, what Balthasar means to say is that once an office is bestowed upon someone, a process begins (led by the Spirit), whereby that individual is transformed into an authentic form of that office. Since office is modelled on Christ and has his form, suffering is part and parcel of this process. There is also a sense in which the higher the office, the more Christ-like it is, so that one is obliged to do three things: to prepare oneself for the objective sanctity to which he has been called, conform oneself to this objective sanctity,[137] and also accept the depths of suffering that are related to that objective sanctity, just as one assumes the authority that is implied in it. Unfortunately, this has begun to sound very much like the scholastic nit-picking that Balthasar himself loathed. Still the alternative would be to accept Balthasar's statements at face value, and to ignore what sometimes seem like marked contradictions. It is now time to direct our attention to the more important aspect of ecclesial authority for my study, namely, the authority of the individual Christian.

133. Ibid., 316.
134. Balthasar, *Seeing the Form (TA1)*, 566.
135. Balthasar, *The Office of Peter*, 388.
136. Balthasar, "Obedience in the Light of the Gospel," 246.
137. Balthasar, *Two Sisters*, 19.

THE AUTHORITY THAT COMES FROM SUBJECTIVE HOLINESS

Despite the "absolute demand for subjective holiness,"[138] at no point does Balthasar claim that the authoritative role that ecclesial office has can be attributed "to the superiority of [one's] own personal qualifications or 'perfection' over those of others."[139] Neither does Balthasar claim that one commanding ought to "measure the authenticity of his claim to authority" by his own personal holiness. According to Balthasar, one can never institutionalize "[t]he synthesis of authority and witness." Likewise, "ecclesial obedience cannot depend on the degree of this synthesis."[140] What is Balthasar trying to do? Balthasar is certainly not saying that the authenticity of one's claim is independent of one's holiness. What he is saying is that the link between one's holiness and one's authority cannot be institutionalized, that the authenticity of one's claim to authority cannot be *measured* by one's holiness, and that obedience cannot be contingent on the combination between authority and holiness. Balthasar should be interpreted as saying that the authority that comes from holiness is a different authority to that which comes with ecclesial office, and not to be confused with it. Secondly, he is emphasizing the "important absoluteness of the subjective commitment [*das Sollen*]," alongside the absoluteness of objective ministry [*das Sein*].[141] Thirdly, he is thereby fostering his theology of nature and grace. Already, in *Two Sisters*, Balthasar had made the distinction between what one *should* do and what one *can* do (with the aid of grace). Balthasar recognized the danger of thinking that the two were the same.[142]

In fact, you could say that Balthasar uses three doctrines—the doctrine of grace, the doctrine of surrender and the theological metaphor of fruitfulness—to deliberate on the kind of authority that personal discipleship has,[143] on the authority which ecclesial office has, and on the kind of authority that subjective holiness adds to the individual who holds ecclesial office. (Please note: adds to the individual, not to the ecclesial office itself).[144] In *The Christian State of Life*, Balthasar grants that

138. Balthasar, *The Spirit of Truth (TL3)*, 348.

139. Balthasar, *The Christian State of Life*, 365.

140. Balthasar, "Obedience in the Light of the Gospel," 246–47.

141. Balthasar, *The Christian State of Life*, 371–72. See also 277.

142. Balthasar, *Two Sisters*, 382.

143. Personal discipleship is described as "a real participation in the official redemptive act of Christ." Balthasar, *The Christian State of Life*, 371–72. See also 277.

144. Balthasar does not consider the other issue, namely, the kind of authority that ecclesial office adds to the individual who has the office of holiness.

a good priest transmits more grace than a bad one, not only because a bad priest causes scandal and turns the faithful away from the path of salvation, but also because, in the very nature of things, a priest in the state of grace receives more grace than one who is not.[145]

In the *Theo-Logic*, Balthasar claims that the distinction between the *opus operatum* and the *opus operantis*, is only "necessary as a result of sin." He claims that "from the perspective of God's redemptive plan" (and here he is possibly playing God!) such a distinction ought not to be made, in the real world. "It *does* exist, in an anti-Donatist sense, for the benefit of those who receive grace through it; but it remains fruitless for the unprepared sinner who distributes or receives it."[146] According to Balthasar, in a sinful world, to equate the authority that comes from office with the authority that comes from subjective holiness would be a mistake, because, at least with the priest, "the contrast between office and person is dominant to the end—a static dualism that no existential effort can overcome or weaken." Thérèse's "period as novice mistress teaches her what every priest learns in the exercise of his office," namely, "the complete discrepancy between his office and his achievement."[147]

For Balthasar, the authority "to teach, to consecrate and to shepherd"— "is independent of the worthiness or unworthiness of the one who exercises it."[148] But this is only because we live in a sinful world. Against Tertullian, the Donatists, "spirituals" like Jean-Jacques Olier (1608–1657) and others, and along with Cyprian and Augustine, Balthasar maintains that the basis of office is not "personal holiness" as the Donatists would have said. Balthasar maintains that the basis of office is "primordial love."[149]

> If—as the Montanists, the Messalians, the Donatists, the Spiritualists, and many contemporary Pentecostals hold—only a man who has the Holy Spirit were able to bestow it, and then only in the measure that he himself has the Spirit, Jesus' presence would be dependent on the person's degree of holiness, and we would

---

145. Balthasar, *The Christian State of Life*, 277.

146. Balthasar, *The Spirit of Truth (TL3)*, 310.

147. Balthasar, *Two Sisters*, 172.

148. Balthasar, "The Church as the Presence of Christ," 90.

149. Balthasar, *The Office of Peter*, 287. Ultimately, what Balthasar is saying is what Healy also says, namely, that it would not be good news if the truth of the gospel "depend[ed] upon our righteousness." Healy, *Church, World and the Christian Life*, 14.

have no certainty at all that this presence was being transmitted to us pure and intact.[150]

OFFICE AND CHARISM

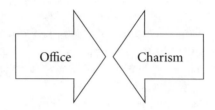

Diagram 07. Office and Charism

In Balthasar, the relationship between "objective ministry" and "subjective commitment" is closely related to that between office and charism. David J.Stagaman makes a distinction between "charismatic, or *an* authority" and "official or *in* authority."[151] He has pointed out that the conflict "office-versus-charism" is not peculiar to religion. It pervades other institutions besides the churches.[152] Stagaman also writes of a "paradigm shift" which has occurred in the Catholic Church since the Second World War, from "an almost total preoccupation with official authority," or "status" to "a recognition of the necessary role charismatic authorities play in the Church."[153] He claims that the two authorities "justify their actions and themselves according to quite different and sometimes conflicting logics," but that both are needed if the church is to function healthily.[154]

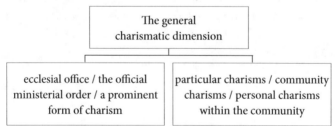

Diagram 08. The Charismatic Dimension

150. Balthasar, "The Church as the Presence of Christ," 90. See also Balthasar, *The Spirit of Truth (TL3)*, 313, 348.

151. Stagaman, *Authority within the Church*, xv.

152. Ibid., 5.

153. Ibid., xv, 3.

154. Ibid., xv.

The doctrine of office and the doctrine of the charisms were unmistakably a concern for Balthasar. Already in the 1950s, in his writings on Thérèse and on Elizabeth, office and *charisma* are intimately linked, and not only in the Pauline sense of "apostles and prophets" both being necessary for the church, but also on a personal level, with the emphasis that "office should not be without *charisma*" and that the office-bearer is also to seek "charisma" because of his proximity to the church.[155] In Balthasar, "[f]ar from being opposites, office and charism actually coincide."[156] Every office is a charisma and every charisma is an office. In the *Theo-Logic*, he claims that there is a "general charismatic dimension" to Christian existence under which both office and particular charisms are subsumed. The ordinary Christian life is charismatic in itself, even anterior to the distinction between "office" and "charism" in the narrower sense. Office and charism are two effects of the one Spirit.[157]

Balthasar's intention is clearly one of reconciliation and integration of office and charism, but not of confusion between the two.[158] In *The Office of Peter*, he even expresses frustration at the fact that this seems to be an unexplored field. He raises the question as to

> who has taken the trouble to look at great personal sanctity (the charism that is unique and a gift but that has to be genuinely accepted and lived) in its theological tension with the principle of ecclesiastical office? Who has looked at it, not polemically, but constructively, so as to integrate it into the total theology of the Catholic Church?[159]

The question is not just: what would such an analysis contribute to the theology of the authority of the saints? But, more importantly, why does Balthasar himself not pursue the issue further? One could perhaps explain it by saying that he did pursue it, but only in his "radiating manner," which is always difficult to analyze. Certainly, the rendering of holiness as an office is a significant attempt—however imperfect—especially since it puts holiness at least on a par with other offices, enabling the reader to correlate authority with holiness, and to avoid a situation where the ecclesial offices benefit from positive prejudice.

155. See Scola, *Test Everything*, 63–65.

156. Balthasar, *Two Sisters*, 484. They would coincide in an ideal world, but not in a sinful world.

157. Balthasar, *The Spirit of Truth (TL3)*, 315–16

158. Balthasar, *The Office of Peter*, 19, 27.

159. Ibid., 20. This comment alone is enough to justify my own endeavor.

Within Christian groups, the concept of charism has mostly been understood "as a spectacular personal gift or a miraculous phenomenon."[160] Extraordinary charisms could easily portray an individual as authoritative, but authentic authority requires authentic charisms. Furthermore, as Austin says, because charisma is grace, authentic charisma "cannot be separated from morality, obedience, authority."[161] In Max Weber's work, the charismatic ruler is heeded because those who know him believe in him. The ruler may not necessarily have actual power or capabilities, but his or her followers believe that such power exists. This would require the followers to continue to legitimize the authority of the leader if the leader's authority is to be maintained.[162] Certainly, Balthasar does not wish to encourage the notion of the personality cult, nor to depersonalize charism. Balthasar prefers to use the charisms to emphasize the Spirit's work within the church, and the church's Catholicity, that is, its unity in variety, rather than to emphasize the individual personality. In this, Balthasar is not too distant from Schillebeeckx. Although Schillebeeckx discusses charisms within the context of his theology of ministry, there is the same emphasis on "the solidarity of Christians equipped with different charismata of ministry."[163] Neither does Balthasar wish to portray the simplistic interpretation that associates the saints with the charismatic element within the church, while associating the Magisterium with the official element.

Balthasar's theology of the charisms[164] is quite comprehensive, in the sense that he distinguishes multiple combinations. He distinguishes between the ordinary charisms and the "higher" or less ordinary charisms,[165] between the charisms which "point outwards," and those which "point inwards,"[166] and between the strictly charismatic charisms,[167] and the "unmystical" or "natural charisms," which may still have "a role to play within the narrower field of salvation history." Among the natural gifts, Balthasar includes

160. O'Meara, *Theology of Ministry*, 201.

161. Austin, *Up with Authority*, 39. Referring to Rieff, *Charisma*.

162. Weber, "The Nature of Charismatic Authority and Its Routinization." In *Theory of Social and Economic Organization*.

163. Schillebeeckx, *Ministry*, 46.

164. For a definition, see "The Gospel as Norm," 296.

165. Balthasar, "Obedience in the Light of the Gospel," 253.

166. Balthasar claims that those charisms that point inwards will "exert their force, and their effect even without being registered externally," whereas the others will have to "be recognised as such for them to have an effect." See Balthasar, *Seeing the Form (TA1)*, 410.

167. A tautology Balthasar considers it necessary to use.

the leaders' political ability in Joshua, judicial talent in the judges, artistic gifts in those who made the Ark of the Covenant, economic enterprise (such as Pharaoh praised in Joseph), the art of government (thus Saul, moved by the Spirit, joins in the dancing of the prophets).[168]

On the other hand, among the "charismatic charisms," Balthasar mentions "the profound intuitions of great Church Fathers" like Origen, Basil, and Augustine, or the mystical charisms of great "mystics" like Hildegard of Bingen, the two Mechthilds, and Lady Julian of Norwich.[169] The first question that occurs is: are all charisms equally important? The second question is: what is it that establishes the importance of a charism or the lack of importance? In the *Theo-Logic*, Balthasar claims that what makes some charisms "great," is the fact that they provide more clarity with respect to Christ, and have a more lasting influence. Balthasar claims that "[p]eople with great charisms, like Augustine, Francis, and Ignatius, can be granted (by the Spirit) glimpses of the very center of revelation, and these glimpses can enrich the Church in the most unexpected and yet permanent way."[170] The charisms which hold a special place for him are

> the charisms of famous founders (such as the world vision of St Benedict, the all-embracing vision of salvation in St Ignatius of Loyola and the experiences of St John of the Cross and St Teresa) which are commonly called "mystical" but which are just as charismatic, being given "for the common good" . . . of the whole Church and in particular for the benefit of the particular Church family being equipped.[171]

Balthasar distinguishes between the official ministerial order and community charisms (or personal charisms within the community), claiming that the Spirit is "in and above" both of them.[172] The Spirit is "in" the official ministerial order

> insofar as he completes and ratifies the official ministerial orders that Christ began; he is "above" insofar as his divine order (which is beyond our grasp) is continually shattering our purely

168. Balthasar, *The Spirit of Truth (TL3)*, 425.

169. Ibid., 317.

170. Ibid., 21.

171. Ibid., 317.

172. Ibid., 248.

human order that tends to ossify, in order to refashion it after his own free vision.[173]

On the other hand, the Spirit is "in" the community charisms

insofar as he genuinely bestows them upon individuals for their use, giving them the spiritual qualities necessary; he is "above" them insofar as no member of the Body of Christ can stubbornly insist on his own charisma and try to wield it against the comprehensive ecclesial order of the Body.[174]

In the meantime, Balthasar expresses support for the idea that charisms attribute authority to those who manifest them because they "give their recipients a semi-official function in the community."[175] The authority of the saints would thus lie not only in the clarity of the saints' theological charism but also in the appreciation of the worth of their charism by the members of the community. The church has a "high regard for charismatic grace." Balthasar states categorically, however, that whenever the church singles out for public honour an individual member, either during his lifetime or posthumously, the authentic charismatic "will always look at such a show of honour as a misunderstanding." Balthasar's argument is that "grace was not intended at all for this member but for the Church as a whole, through the mediation of his service."[176]

Balthasar concedes that the church may not be quick to approve new charisms. New religious communities often have to suffer "strong opposition from the Church." However, Balthasar maintains that, "[w]hen one of these orders succeeds in opening the closed mind of the mind of the Church—the Church recognizes the finger of God *ex post facto* in this work, lets it prosper and in the end praises and approves it."[177] The alternative, that is, the naïve acceptance of a vision, audition, or stigmatisation, is not at all desirable. Balthasar considers the latter to be an "abuse," and claims that saints such as Augustine and John of the Cross have rightly protested against such a lack of discernment.[178] The abuse is the lack of discernment, not the avid discernment. Balthasar reminds us that Thérèse wanted "her

---

173. Ibid.

174. Ibid.

175. Ibid., 315.

176. Balthasar, *Seeing the Form (TA1)*, 414. The attribution of the term "mediators" is more properly associated with Rahner. See Sullivan, "Saints as the 'Living Gospel.'"

177. Balthasar, *The Christian State of Life*, 379–80.

178. Balthasar, *Seeing the Form (TA1)*, 411–12.

illuminations, presentiments and desires tested by the irrevocable standards of the Church."[179]

Despite his emphasis on the ecclesial aspect of the charisms, however, Balthasar states quite clearly that

> it is quite possible for a charismatic "spirit" to be found to be genuine even when it criticizes situations in the Church or when it is charged with introducing something new into the Church in response to the contemporary situation, that is, something that is not immediately obvious to the Church's office-bearers and is perhaps ahead of its time.[180]

The two examples which Balthasar gives, namely, Mary Ward and Ignatius, reveal a lot of what Balthasar leaves unsaid.

THE AUTHORITY THAT COMES FROM ONE'S MISSION

In Balthasar, authority is closely associated with the mission that one receives. Missions are ultimately "different modes of sharing in [Christ's] temporal sufferings and in Calvary's profound mystery of judgment."[181] They are the means by which the disciples are "drawn by grace into the original work at the place that is reserved for them."[182] In Balthasar, mission is not something reserved for the few. Everybody is called to it. One could almost consider it a transcendental, in the sense that it qualifies all living creatures. In the *Theo-Drama*, it is Jesus Christ who plays the role of yielding "the principle for allotting roles to all the other actors" and so "it is from this center that human conscious subjects are allotted personalizing roles or missions (charisms)."[183] In the *Theo-Logic*, this mission is "equally a result of the imparting of [the] Spirit."[184] In Balthasar, the conferring of mission [*Sendung*], which occurs at a particular historical moment in the life of the one called, is but the starting-point of what will, thereafter, be a constant *being-led by the Holy Spirit*.[185] It is a mission that will only be realized if the

---

179. Balthasar, *Two Sisters*, 55–56.

180. Balthasar, *The Spirit of Truth (TL3)*, 317–18.

181. Balthasar, *Prayer*, 297.

182. Balthasar, "The Gospel as Norm," 290.

183. Balthasar, *The Dramatis Personae: The Person in Christ (TD3)*, 257–58.

184. Balthasar, *The Spirit of Truth (TL3)*, 291.

185. Balthasar, *The Christian State of Life*, 406.

Christian truly becomes this form which has been willed and instituted by Christ.[186]

There is an advantage to developing a theology of mission over a theology of ministry, as Balthasar has done. For Schillebeeckx, ministry is a function for a community, rather than a status. For Balthasar mission is more than just a function. It is also a status. It is not a status in the sense of a position of prestige, but it is a status because mission puts the individual in a position of influence. With a theology of mission, Balthasar is able to set the focus of authority on three levels: God, the individual Christian, and the church. As Potworowski has said, in Balthasar, mission "is received from God as something which corresponds structurally and objectively to my being."[187] Balthasar maintains that

> The mission that each individual receives contains within itself the form of sanctity that has been granted to him and is required of him. In following that mission, he fulfills his appropriate capacity for sanctity. This sanctity is essentially social and outside the arbitrary disposition of any individual. For each Christian, God has an idea that fixes his place within the membership of the Church; this idea is unique and personal, embodying for each his appropriate sanctity.[188]

Once man responds to it, however, it becomes man's responsibility (*Verantwortung*).[189] The authority of the saints, their reliability, trustworthiness and steadfastness would then be grounded in their resolve to serve God's mission to the best of their ability, on the existential and dramatic involvement in this mission, and on the recognition by the church of the divine origin of such a mission.

Something should be said about the double vocation, or the "special union between one to whom [God] reveals his mysteries and one able to interpret them objectively." Balthasar claims that God often "calls two by two those whom he has chosen so that there are no longer two persons with separate vocations, but [a] 'two in one vocation.' Such unions" he adds, "can have the same necessity and urgency as the call itself."[190] Evidently, Balthasar would include his partnership with Adrienne among these double vocations. As we said in our introductory chapter, the relationship between them could easily be compared to other such relationships in ecclesial history.

186. Balthasar, *Seeing the Form (TA1)*, 28.
187. Potworowski, "An Exploration," 83.
188. Balthasar, *Two Sisters*, 20.
189. Babini, Babini, "Jesus Christ: Form and Norm of Man," 222.
190. Balthasar, *The Christian State of Life*, 450.

The example which inspires Balthasar the most is probably that of Francis and Bonaventure.[191] Balthasar reports on the common mission, and on the complementarity of their work in his *Unser Auftrag,* in 1984. One gathers from this that Balthasar is expressing approval towards a relationship that could be compared to a professional collaboration but is also more than that. The saint (particularly the mystic) can thus actualize the potential of the theologian, and the theologian can actualize the potential of the saint. The implication is that, where the theologian is not him or herself a saint, he or she may still produce good theology through a close connection to a saint. Johann Roten has written in depth about the common mission of Balthasar and Adrienne, mentioning thirteen themes that reflect Adrienne's "direct influence on von Balthasar's opus."[192] In claiming that such vocations are from above, it would seem that Balthasar is using the *auctoritas Dei* to justify his relationship with Adrienne. Clearly, Balthasar wants this mission to be judged by the same criteria as those used for other missions, namely on its participation in Christ's own *Sendung* from the Father, on the resolve of the will to expropriate itself and to serve the mission indicated by God, on the existential and dramatic involvement of the individual in the actual mission, and on the subsequent recognition of the mission by the community.

The doctrine of mission as developed by Balthasar has a lot to contribute to a theology about the authority of the saints. For all its attractiveness, however, this doctrine poses some serious challenges. For example, Balthasar would say that everyone is called to a mission. As a consequence of this huge quantity of missions, one would have to claim that the fulfilment of God's will entails the pursuit of an "individual" rather than a "universal law."[193] The ethical consequences of such a statement are not to go unnoticed. With such a view, each mission would require its own distinct ethical criteria. Secondly, there is Balthasar's contention that personhood depends on the accomplishment of one's mission,[194] an issue that has certainly not been properly tested philosophically. Finally, in claiming that all missions are vital, Balthasar is levelling all ecclesial vocations, our established hierarchy of values, our presuppositions concerning spiritual fruitfulness, and other no-

191. In developing his Christology and trinitarian theology, Bonaventure the theologian learns from Francis the saint, and Francis has his spiritual vision elucidated by Bonaventure.

192. Roten, "The Two Halves of the Moon," 76–78. See also Štrukelj, *Teologia e Santita'*, 319–43.

193. Balthasar, *Two Sisters,* 21.

194. In Balthasar's theology, the saints, become fully incarnate, fully persons, to the extent that their spiritual mission becomes transparent in them. Balthasar, *The Spirit of Truth (TL3),* 193.

tions which have traditionally been associated with holiness. Because of all this, one has to concede that Balthasar's theology of mission could not, on its own, be used to resolve the issue of authority as attributed to the saints. Despite its potential, using it as the principal doctrine to explain either the *anthropos* or the *hagios* would be problematic. It will have become clear, therefore, that, in arguing for the theology of the saints, there is no one single doctrine developed by Balthasar that incorporates all the essential aspects. To insist on identifying one central idea is unhelpful.

THE AUTHORITY THAT COMES FROM ONE'S CALL

Dominic Robinson has described "Balthasar's dramatic picture of human identity" as "vocational."[195] There is in Balthasar, as in Enda McDonagh, a "vocation structure" to human existence.[196] Some work has been done on Balthasar's theology of vocation, but to the best of my knowledge, no one has genuinely assessed his work.[197] One thing which Balthasar has emphasized is that the "call" is not reserved to a few.[198] The call is for everybody, just as the mission is. Some may be "*more* called" than others,[199] some may be "called later" rather than now.[200] But everyone is called. Clearly, Balthasar wants to avoid the distinction which one finds in the Syriac *Liber Graduum* between "the righteous" (Christians in the world) and "the perfect"(monks, who have left all things), between the special church and the general church.[201] Balthasar does not wish to create a spiritual hierarchy within the Christian "ecclesial life-form."[202] As part of this same attempt to avoid divisions and hierarchies, Balthasar interprets the evangelical state as normative for all states of life within the church, and at the same time, as a complement to the lay state.[203] Clearly, Balthasar is fascinated by the special vocations on the level of ministry, but he wants to avoid all elitism on the level of

195. Robinson, *Understanding the "Imago Dei,"* 119.

196. McDonagh, "The Theology of Vocation," 292–97.

197. Goulding, "Hans Urs von Balthasar's Theology of Vocation," 115–38. See also Secomb, *Hearing the Word of God*, 44–83.

198. In Balthasar, election and vocation are the first step (the vertical aspect of the call), whereas the call is the horizontal aspect. *The Christian State of Life*, 410, 141.

199. Ibid., 428.

200. Ibid., 411–12.

201. Balthasar, "Obedience in the Light of the Gospel," 248.

202. Among the ecclesial life-forms, Balthasar mentions the sacramental, the hierarchical structure, ecclesiastic discipline, the life of the counsels. Balthasar, *Seeing the Form (TA1)*, 600.

203. Balthasar, *The Christian State of Life*, 19–20. See also 210–11.

mission.[204] He prefers to write about the demands common to both: about the readiness, the renunciation, the sacrifice of one's being, the placing of oneself at the disposal of God's entire will, which is required for the laity as well as for those in religious life.[205]

Where does authority feature where the call is concerned? In Balthasar, the authority of the saints would come from the conviction experienced by the saints that their call has a divine source, that God's dominion is infinite and should be abided by,[206] and that it is totally undeserved. Using several figures as examples—Moses, Jeremiah, Amos, Samuel, Saul, David, Elijah, Balaam, and Job—Balthasar emphasizes that there is a spontaneity in God that is unpredictable. "God chooses whom he will."[207] Balthasar insists that the call of God does not depend on "determinants inherent in the natural order," even if it can make use of them.[208] God's election and vocation is

> completely independent of all that is natural in man—neither the existence nor the nature of the new call can be determined or evaluated on purely natural premises. Far from being a neces- sary precondition for this grace filled call, the creature's whole nature is, in fact, inconsequential to it.[209]

The authority of the saints would also come from the recognition and the confirmation of the community, which could even be represented by the Spiritual Director. According to Balthasar, "the touchstone of a genuine sub- jective call is one's readiness to submit oneself to the objective interpreta- tion and guidance of a director 'called' by the Church." Balthasar recognizes the risks involved when the subjective mission is not integrated into the objective mission. When this happens, the call "will degenerate" into a the- matization and an aggrandizement of oneself and one's mission, a state of affairs which Balthasar describes (in his typical overstated manner) as "the beginning of all heresy."[210] In Balthasar, the "ecclesiastical mediation" both "precedes and follows" the act of choice.[211] Balthasar does grant, however, that there can even be "charismatic" vocations, whose official recognition

204. Lösel, "Conciliar, Not Conciliatory," 43.

205. Balthasar, *The Christian State of Life*, 172.

206. Ibid., 81.

207. Ibid., 398, 414–15.

208. Ibid., 419–20. He mentions forms of poetic inspiration, and of rapture, that resemble "the forms of supernatural inspiration or mystical experience of God within a genuine mission."

209. Ibid., 396.

210. Ibid., 450.

211. Ibid., 492.

and acceptance in the office are, so to say, compelled by divine evidence.[212] Balthasar's vision of the call is therefore ecclesial as well as mystical, where the process of discernment becomes one of aligning oneself to the will of the church. In other words, it remains a matter of attuning one's interior life to the interior life of Jesus, but with the emphasis that sharing in the self-effacement of Christ may require that one accept the church's rejection.

THE AUTHORITY OF THE EXTERNAL MAGISTERIUM

In *The Office of Peter*. Balthasar even discusses the issue of how truth is NOT determined within the church. The church, he says, does not determine truth either by questioning "the *sensus fidelium*, followed by an authoritative decision of the Church leadership." Nor does it determine the truth by taking "a poll to find the truth by majority vote."[213] If this were the case, he says, "the place of the ruling hierarchical authority would be taken by the authority of the expert," and obedience would only be "rendered to a 'superior' . . . insofar as he is able to show his competence." Balthasar expresses disapproval at such an approach, claiming that, if this were to become the norm, then one "particular consequence . . . would be the downgrading of the mystery of faith to the level of rational-theological comprehensibility." Balthasar fears that, if this were to occur, "the differences in theological opinion would be negotiated between the so-called 'ecclesiastical teaching office' and the theological profession," something that Balthasar would reject.[214]

212. Balthasar suggests that the ordination of Origen to the priesthood may have been one of these. Balthasar, *The Office of Peter*, 169.

213. Balthasar, *The Office of Peter*, 31. Along with Cardinal Newman, Balthasar attributes "indefectibility in faith" to the *sensus fidelium*, understanding it as a "consensus," but only in its original meaning, i.e., a "feeling with," a "being of the same-mind." However, Balthasar thinks that the *sensus fidelium* may not always be helpful. This is because "the opinion that one really possesses this *sensus fidelium* can likewise be subject to all sorts of illusions, traditional or progressive." Balthasar, "Obedience in the light of the Gospel," 244.

214. Here, "the extent and degree of this competence [would be] determined by one who is to obey: the pastor's by the parish community, the pope's by the community of the faithful." Balthasar, *The Office of Peter*, 31.

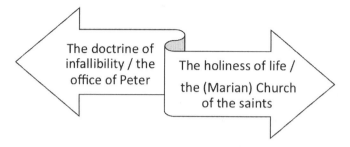

Diagram 09. Petrine Office and Marian Holiness

And yet, it should be clear by now that Balthasar's theology supports the idea that holiness attributes to the individual an authority, and that this authority is different from that which other ecclesial offices bestow, although analogous to it. The question then arises as to what happens when there is a conflict between the saints and the church, or the saints and the Magisterium of the church, or even when the Magisterium of the church is in crisis. Does Balthasar give the saints a *higher* authority? A second issue is, what kind of balance does Balthasar provide with regards to the internal and the external Magisterium?

In the *Aesthetics*, the office of Peter and the holiness of life within the (Marian) church of the saints are "intimately bound up with one another" and "continually oriented toward and pointing to one another," with Balthasar insisting that "neither of them can replace the other and claim solely for itself the re-presentation of the whole Christ."[215] In this sense, the office of Peter and the Magisterium does not, on its own, represent Christ. But neither do the saints on their own. Both require each other. This means that Balthasar hesitates to give either of them the *higher* authority. The whole issue is best viewed within the context of Balthasar's pneumatology, where, as with Yves Congar, the Spirit is working within the whole of the church.[216] It should also be viewed within the context of Balthasar's theology of revelation, where the concept of authority which Balthasar works with has a "penitential" character. Balthasar argues that mankind is "constrained to submit its authentic or alleged interior inspirations to the authority of an external inspiration." He claims that the *locutio interna* was first, but that this *locutio interna* had to become a *locutio externa* "because of man's deafness." It had to become a "word from God which is spoken to man from outside."[217] With Balthasar, the implication is that a return to a God who has exterior-

---

215. Balthasar, *Seeing the Form (TA1)*, 212–13.

216. Groppe, *Yves Congar's Theology of the Holy Spirit*, 85–114

217. Ibid., 452.

ized himself should itself require an external authority. Consequently, with Balthasar, missions and experiences, even the special archetypal ones will submit to Peter who is to judge their authenticity or their lack of it.[218] In this light, the "authentic apostolic authority" does not just have a say on "external things and regulations." Its authority also extends to the consciences of individuals.[219] It can even intervene "in internal operations."[220] Needless to say, one could criticize Balthasar heavily for subordinating so much to the church's teaching office, even the *foro interno*. Balthasar seems to be challenging the supremacy of conscience, which is almost unthinkable nowadays. However, Balthasar does not ignore the primacy of conscience,[221] but rather attributes to conscience a more social nature.

Balthasar insists that the reason why we ought to listen to the Magisterium, is that only the church can give the "sublime buoyant certainty that we are not straying from the right path and are not subject to the risks and dangers that threaten lonely seekers."[222] Balthasar maintains that the Magisterium is not only "rooted in Scripture and tradition, but also in the Church community, which it must consult with regard to its faith."[223] The Magisterium itself feels the need to consult the communal conscience, the *sensus fidelium*, or what the Council of Trent called the *universum Ecclesiae sensum*, and Aquinas called the *congregatio fidelium*. This follows the principle of Vincent of Lerins (*Quod ubique, quod semper, quod ab omnibus creditum est*) and of Cardinal Newman (*securus judicat orbis terrarum*). At times when the Magisterium has forgotten its rootedness in Scripture and Tradition, saints have arisen to revoke the balance of authority. In his essay on "Our Shared Responsibility," Balthasar maintains that God's presence accompanies the church "not only from above . . . but from within,"[224] and he provides examples from the history of the church of extreme situations, when, sometimes the hierarchy and sometimes the laity, were responsible for upholding the faith.[225] The office of Peter is full of examples of saints who

218. Ibid., 355.

219. Balthasar, *Seeing the Form (TA1)*, 590.

220. Ibid., 255–56.

221. Balthasar asserts that, although "the teaching Church can set forth the truth; she cannot force believers to accept it in their hearts . . . the individual is free to obey or not to obey." Ibid., 212–13.

222. Balthasar, *The Office of Peter*, 12.

223. Ibid., 255. Balthasar reminds his readers that Vatican I itself had emphasized this (DS 3069) and that Bishop Gasser had underlined it even more explicitly.

224. Balthasar, "Our Shared Responsibility," 149. See also "Tradition," 116–17.

225. He quotes Newman's Rambler affair as a moment in history when it was the people who upheld the faith, and he mentions Athanasius and Maximus as saints who suffered martyrdom because they were misunderstood by the authorities. Balthasar, "Our Shared Responsibility," 149.

strengthened the Popes:[226] Athanasius, Ambrose or Maximus Confessor.[227] Balthasar mentions Catherine of Siena's protest against Avignon and her appeal to Gregory XI,[228] John of Chrysostom's opposition to the infringements of the "divine Christian Empire," Peter Damian's protestations against the simony and unchastity of the clergy, Ignatius of Loyola's struggle against the excesses of the Inquisition, Bishop Georges Darboy of Paris's admonition of the pope, Francis of Assisi's chastisement of the Pope with his silent example.[229] We also have a reference to the "predictions and threats of St Hildegard and St Brigid against the Roman abuses."[230] One could interpret such balance-of-power-situations in one of two ways. It could be said that the saints have served the Magisterium for the good of the church. It could also be said that the Magisterium has served the saints for the good of the church.

So, does Balthasar then resolve the issue concerning the *higher* authority, whether it is the Magisterium or the saints who act as the higher authority in the case of conflict? Moreover, what kind of balance does Balthasar provide with regards to the internal and the external Magisterium?

In his essay on obedience Balthasar sets down the criteria for disputation. Here, he describes a situation where someone who is meant to obey sees a disparity between a directive given by the authorities and the gospel norm. According to Balthasar, "if the command prescribed something culpably deviating from the gospel norm," then the disagreement is justified. There is no justification for such contesting, however, when it is simply a case of the authority prescribing "something less good than what I conceive on my own."[231] Balthasar grants that the acceptance of the hierarchy's decisions—the "(*réception*)"—is a "delicate problem."[232] As Austin has said, "to exercise authority is to be acknowledged as one who has authority."[233]

---

226. Needless to say, the authority of the saints has mostly been revealed in the absence of effective leadership.

227. Balthasar, *The Office of Peter*, 272.

228. Ibid., 66.

229. Ibid., 343–44.

230. Ibid., 66. Here, Balthasar quotes the German theologian and church historian,Ignaz von Döllinger (1799–1890), who rejected the dogma of papal infallibility.

231. Balthasar, "Obedience in the Light of the Gospel," 243. Balthasar could actually be repeating Rev 2:26 and the maxims of various saints that describe the benefits of obedience. See, for instance, the maxims of St Philip Neri, http://www.liturgialatina. org/oratorian/maxims.htm.

232. Balthasar, "Are There Lay People in the Church?," 182.

233. Austin, *Up with Authority*, 21.

Balthasar grants that the fruitful exercise of authority cannot take place un-less the pope is "recognized and loved in a truly ecclesial way, even in the midst of *paraklesis* or dispute."[234] In this regard, Balthasar can be situated within the shift which Stagaman has identified, namely from imposition on the part of church officials, and obligation to accept on the part of the members, to persuasion on the part of the officials and ratification on the part of the members and humanity generally.[235] Balthasar describes it in pneumatological terms. Whenever the Spirit himself wants the external Magisterium to propagate a truth, there is actually a double operation that is taking place simultaneously: within (through the internal Magisterium), and without (through the external Magisterium). So, Balthasar resolves the issue concerning the internal and the external Magisterium by emphasizing that the two cooperate to propagate the truth.

But what happens with regards to the other issue concerning the *higher* authority, namely, whether it is the Magisterium or the saints who act as the higher authority in the case of conflict? The answer is to be found in his es-say on authority. Here, Balthasar refers to the analogy between the authority of the *laos hagios* and the authority of those in the hierarchy. According to Balthasar, in this analogy, "the presence of the authority of God in Christ is made concrete (incarnate) for the people in their differentiation." Ana-logically, therefore, it is possible to speak of a "double" concrete presence of God's authority: one pertaining to the hierarchy, and one pertaining to the holy people.[236] McDade writes about how the hierarchy and the laity can balance each other through a recognition of "lay holiness."

A sense that the core of the church is lay holiness, which precedes hierarchical structuring, is a corrective to any exaggerated estimate of pa-pal authority, and should condition how the papacy conducts itself in the church. If Petrine authority is to avoid destructive patterns of authoritar-ian isolation, it must acknowledge other, equally valid dimensions of the church, and serve them and listen to them with respect.[237]

Lucien Laberthonnière can help us understand this better. According to Balthasar, it was Laberthonnière who "came up with the most profound and prophetic insights" on the question of authority within the church.[238] Laber-thonniére claims that, "in the Church of God authority can never instruct,

234. Balthasar, *The Office of Peter*, 343.

235. Stagaman, *Authority within the Church*, 3. Stagaman observes that this is a shift that occurred after the Second World War.

236. Balthasar, "Authority," 134. See also 135.

237. McDade, "Von Balthasar and the Office of Peter in the Church," 113.

238. Balthasar, *The Office of Peter*, 282. This is very significant, considering that the works of Lucien Laberthonnière (1860–1932) were prohibited under Pius X.

'from outside,' nor can it impose the truth on anyone; and neither should the Christian submit himself to be led and instructed purely passively."[239] Especially significant is the question which Laberthonnière seems to have asked, namely "How should people like us act, so that, spiritually deepened by the acceptance of authority, we can contribute to the spiritual deepening of authority itself?"[240] This question expresses quite clearly the spiritual dependence of those who command on those who obey, and the other way round. Those who obey are spiritually deepened by the acceptance of authority, and those who are in authority are, in turn, spiritually deepened by those who, having obeyed, are holier than before. Thus, in the same way that "the same obedience in faith to the Divine Word is demanded from both the one who commands and the one who obeys," [241] The same thing applies where ecclesial authority is concerned.[242] John McDade speaks for many when he says that, "[f]or authority to work well, the one *in* authority and the one *under* authority must be in accord; either of them can cause the process to break down" (my emphasis).[243]

THE THEOLOGIAN AND THE AUTHORITY OF ROME

In Balthasar, the Petrine and the Pauline offices are distinct, but they serve each other. The relationship of the theologian with the Magisterium remains a central issue.[244] As Francis Sullivan pointed out, the clear distinction made by Aquinas between the *Magisterium cathedrae pastoralis* of pope and bishops and the *Magisterium cathedrae magistralis* of the doctors (i.e., the university professors of theology) only appeared with the rise of the universities.[245] On his part, Avery Dulles has described the dialectic, even the "mutual assistance" between the institutional authority of the Magisterium and the non-institutional authority of the individual theologian.[246] You could say that Balthasar would agree with most of what Dulles says. Most

239. Laberthonnière, *La notion chrétienne de l'autorité*, 79. Quoted in Balthasar, *The Office of Peter*, 283.

240. Balthasar, *The Office of Peter*, 286.

241. Ibid., 42.

242. Ibid., 61.

243. McDade, "Von Balthasar and the Office of Peter in the Church," 110.

244. Balthasar attributed the title "theologian" to one who was "a doctor of the Church whose office and mission consist in explaining revelation in its fullness and completeness and thus in considering dogmatics as the central point of his activity." Quoted in Sicari, "Hans Urs von Balthasar," 121–22.

245. Sullivan, *Magisterium*, 181. Cf. Aquinas, "Of the Ministers of the Keys."

246. Dulles, "Teaching Authority in the Church," 21.

importantly, according to Balthasar, the theological activity is an ecclesial office and mission, but theology "cannot claim divine authority," or presume infallibility.[247] Balthasar is critical of theologians that claim "infallibility." According to him, such a claim "often seems to be a more stubborn sickness than the defined infallibility of the papacy," which he says "is applied with incomparably greater discretion" than the former.[248] However, a problem arises when the theologians are also saints. Although it may not be the role of the Magisterium to follow the guidance of theologians, but, surely, the same cannot be said of the Magisterium vis-à-vis the theologian saints.

Before any attempt to provide answers, one ought to investigate the significance of Peter (ecclesial office) and Paul (the gifted theological writer). As Raymond E. Brown has put it, Paul's role is not one of doctrinal authority, but that of a "missionary witness."[249] In Balthasar, Peter's attitude to Paul is "not unfriendly," but it is a "reserved official attitude."[250] According to Balthasar, Peter alone has "the prerogative" to claim authority in doctrine and leadership, and the right to demand unity.[251] Balthasar would therefore insist that the Magisterium and the theologians "differ in the quality of the authority with which they carry out their tasks." This means that he does not deny that both have authority. It also means that he would have agreed with the Statement of the International Theological Commission published in 1975, which recognizes that "the authority that belongs to theology in the Church" is "a genuinely ecclesial authority, inserted into the order of authorities that derive from the Word of God and are confirmed by canonical mission."[252]

Balthasar refers to the "long list of unnecessary human tragedies" which reflect "the uneasy and unclarified relationship between theology and the Magisterium," calling it a "sickness [that] had three crises": the first was around the time of the "Syllabus" (1866), the longest and most important was that of Modernism, which outwardly was put down by the encyclical *Pascendi* (1907); and finally, the false alarm concerning the *nouvelle théologie* to which *Humani generis* (1950) intended to put an end.[253] Still,

247. Balthasar, *The Office of Peter*, 115. See also Olsen, "The Theologian and the Magisterium," 310; and Eno, "Authority and Conflict in the Early Church," 49.

248. Balthasar, *The Office of Peter*, 286.

249. Brown, *The Churches the Apostles Left behind*, 61.

250. Balthasar, *The Office of Peter*, 171.

251. Ibid., 167–68.

252. http://www.vatican.va/roman_curia/congregations/cfaith/cti_documents/rc_cti_1975_magistero-teologia_en.html.

253. Balthasar, *The Office of Peter*, 280.

Balthasar is impatient with contemporary theologians who moan about the sufferings undergone by theologians in the past.[254]

Writing about what he terms the "fateful" Modernist period, Balthasar argues that "what stands out most is perhaps the limited nature of the Petrine charism of leadership." He argues that "it could deliver hard blows to those who departed from the center line but was unable to contribute much that was constructive toward solving the problems presented by the times." Having said that, Balthasar goes on to say that "things could be very different now," as well as cites "the great positive impulses that have come from several strong encyclicals of Leo XIII and Paul VI, which were themselves products of collaboration."[255]

Balthasar is adamant in his claim that Rome's pronouncements remain unsurpassed, despite accusations concerning its slow progress. He writes,

> We might be inclined to think that Rome . . . was always behind the times in its interventions, which were all the more embarrassing, the more they were presented with the weight of authority; but the astonishing thing is that these interventions (which were by no means frequent initially) prove the very opposite: Rome's responses, although they refer back to the faith handed down, regularly point beyond the ecclesial horizon of the "committed" and "speculative" theologians.[256]

In fact, Balthasar envisages the theologian-saints supporting the Magisterium, but he also envisages the Magisterium supporting the theologian. He even gives examples of instances when the theologian-saints fed the Magisterium, and where the Magisterium claimed for itself the conclusions of the theologians. One example which he gives is that of Maximus. As he puts it, at Constantinople, in 681, Maximus the Confessor's Chalcedonian Christology was declared to be identical with the faith of the Catholic church.[257] Please note that it is not the other way around.

THE AUTHORITY OF CANONIZATION

The term "canonization" refers to that Papal declaration whereby an individual or individuals are officially registered in the official canon of saints

254. Ibid., 286.

255. Ibid., 281–82.

256. Ibid., 264.

257. *Definition of the Two Wills of Christ, against the Monothelites,* during the Council of Constantinople III. See Denzinger-Schönmetzer, *Enchiridion Symbolorum,* 289–93.

within the church. The canonization process was revised in 1983 by Pope John Paul II's Apostolic Constitution *Divinus Perfectionis Magister*, and now consists of the following stages: the inquiry, the *positio*, the verification of a first miracle, the Beatification, the verification of a second miracle, and finally, the canonization. Most Christians would ground the authority of the saints within their official recognition through canonization. Matzko states that "the practice of naming saints is . . . a process of naming what social (moral and religious) practices are held to be constitutive of common life."[258] Josè Maria Castillo asserts that "[t]he saints whom the Church canonizes or intends to canonize express the type of Church which it wishes to promote and build." Elizabeth Johnson claims that "the right to name the community's exemplars reinforces the authority of the one who canonizes."[259] In Balthasar, there is a pneumatological turn. It is the Spirit who chooses for canonization those who in his judgment express the type of church he wants.[260]

The issue of canonization is often associated with controversy, particularly when the question of infallibility arises. According to the doctrine of infallibility, there are specific circumstances when the Pope is incapable of error in pronouncing dogma. This is evidently relevant to us since, if the authority of the saints is to be understood as the consequence of their canonization, the next important question would be whether the church and the pope can err in proposing a particular person as an object for veneration.[261] The best discussion of the issue of inerrancy and canonization, it seems to me, is that provided by Eric Waldram Kemp in the 1940s. In a chapter entitled "Canonization and Papal Infallibility," Kemp offers a chronological synopsis of the pertinent questions involved, identifies the major figures who contributed to the issue, isolates the most significant documents, as well as provides actual examples. Aquinas had claimed that, hypothetically, both the pope who decides and the human testimony on whom canonization relies, can err in canonizing. However, the Holy Spirit would not allow the Pope to make a wrong judgement, or the church to be deceived. According to Cesare Carbone, the church cannot err in venerating saints who are celebrated in Holy Scripture, and cannot err in the canonization of saints *intercedente espresso vel tacita Pontificis approbatione*.[262] On his part, Suárez

258. Matzko, "Postmodernism, Saints and Scoundrels," 22.

259. Johnson, *Friends of God and Prophets*, 100–101.

260. Castillo, "The History of Canonization in Christianity: Its Real Meaning," 70–77.

261. Kemp, *Canonization and Authority in the Western Church*, 151.

262. Ibid., 158.

argued that the pope cannot err in canonization which is *pars quaedam materiae moralis*, and that the pope orders the veneration of a saint *sub praecisa obligatione*. Consequently, that command ought not to be subject to error. Suárez argues that papal infallibility in canonization is not *de fide*, but it is "sufficiently certain for the contrary view to be impious and temerarious."[263] The issue is considerably complicated. So many questions emerge: whether it is the *papal* approval that makes a canonization infallible, whether the pope is infallible in beatifying as well as in canonizing, whether beatifications which were announced by local bishops, or declarations of sainthood by public acclamation, are valid, whether the popes themselves (as popes, not as theologians) ever put forward any claim to infallibility in canonization, and how one should deal with the saints whose case was examined, but whose canonization was never approved. And what about the canonized saints whose names are themselves unknown?[264] This is not to mention the political and theological reasons that the Magisterium may have for proclaiming particular saints at one stage rather than another.

Balthasar himself seems to have complete trust that the church does not err in this regard. For instance, in *The Office of Peter*, he refers to the several cases of "imposters," including certain stigmatics, who, he says, "were, *of course*, not canonized" [my italics], although they may have been "considered from a distance as being fairly holy."[265] In Balthasar, "it is the prerogative of the Holy Spirit to have his demands and inspirations accepted and followed, [not just by the individual], but by the Church as a whole."[266] It seems to me, however, that, in Balthasar's case infallibility does not just mean: the church cannot be mistaken in presenting this individual as a model for imitation. It also seems to mean that you would be infallible if you walked in this individual's footsteps. In the latter case, infallibility is not an attribute of the church or the Pope who is responsible for approving and canonizing, nor is infallibility an attribute of the saint, but rather an attribute of the individual Christian (the *sensus fidei* as opposed to the *sensus fidelium* of Newman). Perhaps Balthasar is emphasizing all aspects: the demands of the Spirit, the responsibility of the church and the obligation of the individual Christian.

The issue of canonization often brings the argument for the authority of the saints to an impasse. How can one attribute an authority to the saints, when the authority of the saints depends on the Magisterial decision for

263. Ibid., 159. Quoting Polanco, *Tractatus de fide theologica*.
264. The martyrs of Uganda are a case in point.
265. Balthasar, *The Office of Peter*, 343–44.
266. Balthasar, *The Christian State of Life*, 442.

canonization, and therefore on the Magisterium for the official recognition of the authoritativeness of that saint? But this is the wrong question to ask. After all, the authority of the saints does not depend on the Magisterial decision for canonization. In his essay "The Gospel as Norm," Balthasar claims that it is the Spirit who carries out the effective "publicity" for the saints who are canonical in each age (and therefore are to be canonized by the church).[267] This would mean that, in Balthasar, the Spirit will find ways and means of making the saints shine, so that their lives may serve as "the criterion" for others, and so that their lives and teachings may be considered authoritative. The Spirit is able to draw the church's attention to the teaching and the life of the saints and to make universal concepts out of them.[268]

CONCLUSION

Part of Balthasar's contribution lies in the fact that what could be reduced to a struggle for power becomes a collaboration of the holy among each other. For one thing, for Balthasar, it is the saints who make up Tradition. Secondly, for Balthasar, the Magisterium incorporates more than just the uppermost ecclesiastical officials. The Magisterium is the teaching authority of the church, and the teaching authority is not reserved purely to the official Magisterium. In Balthasar, the saints are also directly involved in teaching, and therefore, we can deduce, that the Magisterium also includes the saints, or rather, there is also a Magisterium of the saints. Ultimately, the authority of any noteworthy theologian is not just grounded in his literary gift of writing theology. It is also grounded in his or her involvement with the church, and therefore in ecclesial holiness, as well as in his or her personal holiness.

267. Balthasar, "The Gospel as Norm," 293–94.

268. Ibid., 292–94. Balthasar claims that a mission may develop "only after the death of the one to whom it was entrusted—sometimes even long after, as in the case of Angela Merici and Mary Ward." Balthasar, *The Christian State of Life*, 449.

CHAPTER 6

General Conclusion

IT IS NOW TIME to start the process of closure. My intention is to conclude
with a double critique. The first of these concerns the inconsistencies which
are evident in any attempt to attribute authority to the saints. I want to
demonstrate that the emphasis in Balthasar on unity and on the equality of
the saints within the *communio sanctorum* is often inconsistent with, and
even counter-productive to his emphasis on the exceptional character of
the individual saints who are part of the *Communio Sanctorum*.[1] I want
to demonstrate that, in Balthasar, it is difficult to harmonize the portrayal
of the individual saints as outstanding individuals and his own vision of the
church as a community of equals, just as it is difficult to harmonize his portrayal of the church as a conversing community with his emphasis on the
Magisterium as the teaching and governing body *par excellence*. I will also
provide some reasons why I believe such inconsistencies exist, and why, in
my opinion, Balthasar fails to argue overtly for the authority of the saints. It
will be determined that, despite everything, no doubt can be cast on the fact
that, *de facto*, Balthasar gives to the saints an extraordinary prominence in
his own theology, and that he not only recommends the saints as a resource
for theology and for the church, but attributes to them an authority that
is analogical to that generally attributed to the Magisterium. The second

---

1. Dalzell has argued that Balthasar is more concerned with the individual subject,
than with the social aspect. He comes to this conclusion because of Balthasar's emphasis on the freedom of the individual and on his or her mission. Dalzell, *The Dramatic
Encounter of Divine and Human Freedom*, 285. My argument would be that the emphasis on the *communio sanctorum* serves to balance this prominence on the individual,
but also to justify it.

critique will deal with the authority of the saints in general and the consequences for the church of attributing—or not attributing—such authority
to the saints.

RESUMÉ

Before we can present our critique, it is best to provide a resumé of what
has been argued so far. This book began with an emphasis on Balthasar's
remarkable sensibility to the theology of the saints (that is, the theology for
which they were responsible), both individually and *en masse*. It was stated
that, from what Balthasar has said about the theology for which the saints
were responsible, it is possible to elicit a theology *about* the saints, from
Balthasar's perspective. It was argued that Balthasar considered this theology of the saints (the theology for which they were responsible), authoritative
for him on a personal level and as a theologian, but he also recommended,
sometimes implicitly, that their theology be considered authoritative to
theology in general. He did this by developing a theology *about* the saints,
claiming that this theology was mandatory for theologians and for the
building up of the church, and by continually pointing to the theology *of*
the saints (that is, the theology produced by them). It was determined that
Balthasar does not evoke the memory of the saints by mentioning supernatural evidence, miracles, and visions. On the contrary, he avoids the more
supernatural, and rather vain aspects, and things like "worldly power" and
"miraculous intercession" are absent from Balthasar's list.[2] Balthasar de-
picts the saints as authoritative by incorporating the saints as an integral
part of his theology, and by using them to substantiate his claims, to address
particular theological issues, or for other theological reasons mentioned
earlier. He establishes their authority by making them known, by actively
providing new translations and new anthologies of their works, by dedicat-
ing whole monographs to them. He establishes their authority by bringing
their ideas to life, by continually discoursing with them, by involving them
in his discussions, by amplifying their voice, so to speak.

I also referred to what Balthasar calls, the "various degrees and holders
of authority in the Church,"[3] and to the various forms which ecclesial authority takes in Balthasar: from governing, to commanding, creating laws,

---

2. According to the official procedures for canonization established by Pope Urban
VIII in the early seventeenth century, "all the candidates except martyrs must satisfy
three general requirements: doctrinal purity, heroic virtue, and miraculous intercession
after death." Weinstein and Bell, *Saints and Society*, 141.

3. Balthasar, "Obedience in the Light of the Gospel," 244.

imposing sanctions on those who fail to obey.[4] It was noted that some of these authoritative practices are, generally speaking, only associated with those in office, and are only required from those "saints" who hold authoritative positions, but who may not necessarily be holy in the narrow sense of the word. I then inferred that, in Balthasar, irrespective of their state, role or function within the church, the "true" saints, those who are holy, are authoritative, precisely because of what holiness entails, and how it is perceived by others, and that this authority is analogical to that of the Magisterium, both in its nature and in its consequences, because it makes the saints credible, reliable, worth considering, their memory worth preserving, just as, traditionally, the Magisterium has been perceived. Consequently, the saints trigger esteem, even veneration, in those who encounter them. It was therefore ascertained quite early in our argument that, according to Balthasar, the saints' life and work is not just useful, but authoritative, and that it demands a response. In Chapters 3 to 5, I then focused on three dimensions which helped to elucidate the issue of the grounding of the saints. In these chapters, I dealt with the different settings in which the saints function authoritatively, as well as with the *why* it is that the saints are so authoritative, so useful, credible, persuasive and demanding of a response. I maintained that it is Balthasar himself who generates this focus on the *grounding* of the authority of the saints, choosing to focus—in contrast with the postmoderns—on the more hidden causes of this authority, rather than on the external expressions of it, or on the evident response of others to it. It was determined that the saints have existential, epistemological, and ecclesial authority precisely because they are saints, and that there is something about holiness, or characteristics that accompany holiness, that makes the saints authoritative, influential, in all of these dimensions, so that the saints are deemed (or, perhaps, to be deemed) an authority for theology and for the church.

I also argued that the authority of the saints denotes different things in different dimensions, but that it is always, in some way or other, analogous to that of the Magisterium. Whereas in the existential dimension (Chapter 3), the saint is an authority because he or she exemplifies the essence of existence, and because he or she is someone whom one consults on existential issues, in the epistemological dimension (Chapter 4), the saint is an authority because he or she perceives, comprehends and assimilates more, because others invoke him or her when there has been a failure to know, and because others submit to them in the process of learning. Finally, in the ecclesiological dimension (Chapter 5), the saint is an authority because

4. Balthasar, *Christian State of Life*, 264.

he or she is in-formed by the church and esteemed within the church, and because he or she is someone to whom one appeals, perhaps even to whom one submits in obedience, when there has been a disagreement on issues of theology or discipline. The analogy between the authority that is attributed to the saints, and that which is attributed to the Magisterium is very clear. Clearly, Balthasar wanted to repair the flawed assumption that only the official Magisterium has access to the truth, and that it is sufficient on its own and requires no assistance. On the contrary, Balthasar uses the saints, not only to teach other theologians but also to teach the official Magisterium, and thus handling the saints as if they were themselves a Magisterium.

CRITIQUE 1

At the beginning of this Chapter, I promised to provide two critiques. The first critique was to focus on the inconsistencies which are evident in Balthasar's attribution of authority to the saints.

The first thing I would like to say is that, because of his tremendous preoccupation with the unity of the church, Balthasar downplays the distinctions that one finds within the church—something that is required if one is to argue for the authority of some, not all—and thus fails to argue explicitly for the authority of the *Communio Sanctorum*. My argument is that there is a contradiction in the way in which Balthasar *de facto* uses the saints (the *Communio Sanctorum*) as the experts and the real *connoisseurs*, in the way he recommends them to theologians and to the church as a whole, in the way he attributes an authority to them, but then *de jure*, when it most matters—in his discussions of authority within the church—emphasizes and underscores the authority of the priestly office, and the authority of the official Magisterium, rather than the authoritative contribution of the saints. My critique thus focuses on the fact that Balthasar does not make the next step and argue overtly for the authority of the saints. I attribute this contradiction, not to Balthasar's aversion to having the centrality of Christ being contested (and therefore to his scaling down of the saints)—although it could be argued that this is also a cause—but to Balthasar's preoccupation with ecclesial unity. I believe that Balthasar wanted his theology of the saints to support his emphasis on unity, rather than to work against it, and he is not willing to argue for the authority of the few (the *Communio Sanctorum*) out of fear of dividing the church. Balthasar does not approve any of the dialectical divisions of the church of the past. For example, he radically disapproves of Tyconius.[5] He says that this "creates a kind of structural

5. For Tyconius, the church was simply a bipartite body, consisting of a body of

fracture in the body of the Church," which is painful for the church (*gemitus columbae*) and for Christ.[6]

The second point I would like to make is that Balthasar's maturity of the theology of the saints may have been cut short because of the Second Vatican Council. There is some evidence of development in Balthasar, particularly where office is concerned. Before the Vatican Council, he was more willing to downplay the differences, to widen the significance of office and to argue for the office of holiness. But he was less willing to do that after the Council. In his *The Christian State of Life*, which is Post-Vatican II, Balthasar criticizes all attempts to remove the distinction between laity and clergy by a continual interchange of services, ministries and even "offices" and "functions," claiming that it was "unbiblical" to remove this distinction.[7] And he affirms that "[t]he dogmatic, theoretical form of Christian truth belongs in a special way to the serving offices, that is, the 'apostles,' 'prophets,' 'evangelists,' 'shepherds,' 'teachers.'"[8] Likewise, in the late Balthasar, authority, in terms of leadership, but also of teaching, is generally reserved to the apostolic succession. In the third volume of the *Theo-Logic*, Balthasar insists that the mission to preach and interpret the mystery "cannot be divorced from ecclesial office, which comes explicitly from Christ's command."[9] This means that he contradicts his earlier work, insisting, in his later work, that it is ultimately the Magisterium that carries the responsibility, as well as the institution which claims the right to lead and to teach. This brings with it a real risk, as Raymond E.Brown has said, which is that of having holiness attributed to the ordained.

> In relation to the equality of Christians as disciples, it is especially difficult for the ordained priesthood to be kept in the category of service (to God and to the community), for the ordained will frequently be assumed to be more important and automatically more holy.[10]

In this regard, it would probably have been so much more helpful had Balthasar been more clear about the teaching and leadership roles of the different offices and functions within the church, rather than focusing so

---

saints and a body of sinners. See Mueller, "Christian and Jewish Tradition behind Tyconius's Doctrine of the Church as Corpus Bipertitum," 286–317.

6. Balthasar, *The Office of Peter*, 191.

7. Balthasar, *The Christian State of Life*, 16.

8. See Eph 4:11.

9. Balthasar quotes Clement of Rome, Ignatius, and Irenaeus. Balthasar, *The Spirit of Truth (TL3)*, 326.

10. Brown, *The Churches the Apostles Left behind*, 100.

much on the apostolic roles. Avery Dulles had distinguished three kinds of succession, corresponding to the Pauline functions singled out in the first letter to the Corinthians: namely, the apostles, the prophets, and the teachers (1Cor.12:28).[11] All of these are leadership roles, and therefore authoritative. According to Dulles, those who succeed the apostles enter into the leadership functions of the Twelve. The prophets, on the other hand, are not attached to any office or to particular skills, and they teach "by proclamation and example," rather than by "juridically binding decisions" or by "probative arguments."[12] The teachers are the theologians and the scholars who teach through "reasoned argument."[13]

What relevance does this have for us? For one thing, in spite of everything, authority has still kept its narrow significance of leadership, and is still mainly attributed to the Magisterium. In over-emphasizing the hierarchy, Balthasar could be interpreted as canonizing the members of the hierarchy, rather than setting the 'real' saints as the standard to be followed. In this respect, the authority of the authentic saints has been undermined. In fact, some of Balthasar's statements concerning the authority of the ordained priesthood are especially distasteful to members of the laity.[14]

The third point I would like to make concerns the issue of gender. Needless to say, the issue of gender is highly relevant, both where Balthasar is concerned, and where sainthood is concerned. For instance, more recently, we have had reflection on whether holiness may be embodied and expressed by same-gender relationships, as well as on whether the martyrdom suffered by gays and lesbians deserves recognition.[15] Some work has even been done on "embodied authority" as evident in the spiritual autobiographies of women.[16] There is always some difficulty arising when one attempts to associate women with official authority.

Balthasar's theology obscures the wider reality within the church concerning women, as well as disregards the overall impression which his own theology leaves on feminist readers. Concerning the first of these, evidence

11. Dulles, "*Successio,*" 61–67. It should be noted that the apostolic succession of bishops and their authority as protectors of the faith was rarely debated by the Church Fathers.

12. Ibid., 62.

13. Ibid., 63.

14. See, for example, Balthasar, *Christian State of Life,* 260, 270.

15. During the CTSA's 66th Annual Convention, Cyril Orji, from the University of Dayton, convened a session entitled "The New Forms of Martyrdom and Sainthood in Africa." His Paper examined "the martyrdom of gays and lesbians in many African societies."

16. Cloud, "Embodied Authority."

shows that women in the church have received less recognition than men. Steffen Lösel has said, in Balthasar, it is "the masculine Church" that "is invested with exclusive jurisdictional and teaching authority." On the contrary, women are offered a very "restricted" and "unattainable" ecclesial life script.[17]

The reception of women has often been problematic, even when it involved holy women. From a feminist perspective, there is a lot one could say. For one thing, depictions of holy women are generally male-authored. For this reason, they often "reveal more about men's idealized notions of female sanctity and its embodiment in women's lives than they reveal about the female saints themselves,"[18] and such an interpretation necessarily involves some injustice.[19] Another thing is that many more males than women have historically been pronounced holy, so that sanctity is made to seem more difficult for a female that it is for a male.[20] Thirdly, male saints were often members of the church hierarchy,[21] and were consequently considered more authoritative than women. One can indicate at least one instance where Balthasar may have made an additional effort to make the voice of the women mystics sound more authoritative than that of the more established masculine saints.[22] This was in the book *Dare We Hope 'That All Men be Saved?'*. But except for his references to Adrienne, such instances are not very common. Historically, many female mystics had to depend on male confessors in order to make their work public. Adrienne herself is an example of a woman who required a man (Balthasar himself) to thrust her forward, to transcribe, publish, and publicize her work. Furthermore, various feminist scholars have judged Balthasar's representation of women as insufficient, if not unjust.[23] Therefore, for him to be arguing for the authoritativeness of female saints—or rather, for me to be contending that Balthasar argues for an authority of the female saints—may be considered spurious. Tina Beattie has accused Balthasar of taking "a non-gendered view of humanity." According to her, this shows, either that Balthasar finds reference to gender

17. Lösel, "Conciliar, Not Conciliatory," 41.

18. Mooney, "Voice, Gender and the Portrayal of Sanctity," 3.

19. See, for instance, Dillon, "Holy Women and Ttheir Confessors or Confessors and Their Holy Women? Margery Kempe and Continental Tradition," 115–40.

20. See Weinstein and Bell on "Men and Women," *Saints and Society*, 220–38.

21. See ibid. on "The Occupational category by Gender," *Saints and Society*, 221.

22. Balthasar, *Dare We Hope.*

23. Some examples could be Beattie, "Sex, Death and Melodrama," 160–76; and Nussberger, "Review Symposium, 95. See also Lösel's criticism of Balthasar's interpretation of Mary. Lösel, "Conciliar, Not Conciliatory," 40.

unnecessary, or that for Balthasar, *Mensch* is equivalent to *Mann*.[24] Despite all that has been written by feminist theologians—some of which I would agree with—Balthasar's theology can be used to navigate through a theology of the authority of the saints. With reference to discourse about sanctification, Balthasar finds reference to gender unnecessary. Hopefully, this is not because, for him, sexual difference is not significant, or because he wants to eradicate the female body, as Beattie claims,[25] but rather because Balthasar appreciates that the authority that comes from holiness transcends sexual difference.

The fourth inconsistency which is evident in Balthasar's attribution of authority to the saints concerns the consideration of the individual baptized Christian vis-à-vis the extraordinary saint. Balthasar did not consistently emphasize the difference between the two, and did not sufficiently and effectively explain how it is that the member of the *Communio Sanctorum* has more authority than the individual Christian who is holy only through baptism. Balthasar emphasizes that the Holy Spirit dwells in *all* the members of the church.[26] In his *Theo-Logic*, he leaves no doubt that all Christians are equal "on the basis of their human dignity" and "in virtue of their rebirth." They are also equal in their "activity," since all are called to "cooperate in the building up of the Body of Christ in accord with each one's own condition and function."[27] He claims that the ascetic is as much of a witness as the martyr. Those who were later called "martyrs" are not more important than those whose whole life is a daily mortification.[28] He insists that all believers receive their spiritual authority in baptism (and the other sacraments). Consequently, they are all "children of God," "infallibly heard" by God, endowed with the "mind of Christ," able to judge correctly.[29] In the Eucharist, *all* Christ's disciples,

> receive a share in his authority . . . they *all* receive the Holy Spirit who sanctifies them and sends them out into the world (Acts 2:17); from *all* is demanded the witness of their life (to the point

24. Beattie, "Sex, Death and Melodrama," 161–62.

25. Ibid., 170.

26. Balthasar, "Our Shared Responsibility," 143.

27. Balthasar, *The Spirit of Truth (TL3)*, 355. In *Seeing the Form*, Balthasar claims that the "the functional does not jeopardise or abolish the personal, but rather perfects it," and he presents Mary as the perfect example of the application of this principle. Balthasar, *Seeing the Form (TA1)*, 341. He gives Mary as the "perfect example of the application of this principle."

28. Balthasar, *The Spirit of Truth (TL3)*, 409.

29. Ibid., 402.

of martyrdom);[30] *all* must expressly or at least in their disposition preach Christ; *all* have not only the right but, as Christians, a strict duty . . . to forgive their neighbor his sins; *all* can in principle baptize, husbands and wives can give to each other the sacramental blessing of marriage, *all* are authorized to share in the celebration of the Eucharist, and so on (my italics). [31]

The problem here is: How is one to integrate this appreciation for the general with the fact that Balthasar is so scrupulous in his appreciation, praise, and recommendation of some saints more than others? In this regard, we can only say that there is some evidence of contradiction in Balthasar's work. To be fair, it is a contradiction that exists in popular theology as well. A strict separation between the saints and those who surround them (and who may not have achieved the same levels of holiness) would ignore important facets of how the expertise of the saint is enacted. Refusing to acknowledge that some may be closer to God than others would dangerously relativize the expertise of the saint. Majdik and Keith have said that expert authority is not simply something that belongs to the experts: "The bounds of expert authority narrowed to the individual enacting a personal version of expertise defeats the pragmatic function of expertise."[32] However, just as one has to acknowledge that the bounds of expert authority are wider than the expertise of the individual, so also must one acknowledge that individual expertise is necessary in order to preserve the authoritative content of the wider community, to express it, to preserve it, and even to transform it. Something similar must be said for the saints. The authority of the saints cannot be seen apart from the authority of the community, but neither can the authority of the community be understood apart from its representatives. And the real representatives of what the church stands for are the saints, not the members of the Roman curia.

The early Balthasar distinguishes quite clearly between two types of sanctity: "customary" sanctity (by which the Christian fulfills his vocation through the normal, unspectacular cycle of the church's life) and "a special kind of sanctity (by which God singles out some individual for the good of the Church and the community as a model of sanctity)."[33] This would be the "representative" sanctity, "which is much less directly imitable."[34] The latter

30. Balthasar states that "[t]he disciple of Jesus is never asked to do more than give witness." Ibid., 404.

31. Balthasar, "Authority," 133–34.

32. Majdik and Keith, "Expertise as Argument," 376.

33. Balthasar, *Two Sisters*, 24.

34. Ibid., 23, 25.

are, as he describes them, God's great gifts to the Christian community, they are "the great warm centers of light and consolation sunk into the heart of the Church by God."[35] They are the "cornerstones of the Church," the "living interpretations of the Gospel."[36] In his first volume of the *Aesthetics*, Balthasar confirms that "the Catholic Church does not abolish genuine esotericism."[37] It is possible to say that only a small number of people can know and understand certain things. Like Paul before him (1 Cor 3:2), Balthasar distinguishes between the "simple Christians who need material crutches' and 'the advanced and the perfect.'"[38] He maintains that the boundary be drawn between, those who, as qualified witnesses, are mystics by vocation, and, the rest of believers.[39] Balthasar grants that some things may only be "for those who are practiced and experienced in faith and in love's renunciation," and "not be for beginners, nor for those who hesitate in their uncertainty."[40] In his *Explorations*, the saints are the "pillars of the Church" upon which "everything that has universal validity is built up."[41] In *Engagement with God*, in 1971, the saints are "specially chosen individuals,"[42] "individuals who tower above the rest," "the chosen."[43]

Later, Balthasar becomes dissatisfied with some of his early terminology. He still calls some missions "special,"[44] but he claims that he would rather not use the term.[45] How is one to fuse these two Balthasars together? This ambiguity concerning terminology and categorization—which we believe is instigated by Balthasar's desire on one hand to commend the saints as authorities, and on the other to preserve the unity of the church—hinders Balthasar from developing a proper doctrine of the authority of the saints.

Finally, there is yet another inconsistency in Balthasar's attribution of authority to the saints. This is his concentration on the past. Balthasar provides examples indicating how, in the past, some saints have acted as

35. Ibid., 25. One could compare these "representative saints" to Rahner's concept of the saint as "sacrament," as "icon," and as symbol, and to Tracy's concept of the saint as a "classic." See Sullivan, "Saints as the 'Living Gospel,'"6, 9; and Tracy, *The Analogical Imagination*.

36. Balthasar, *Two Sisters*, 24.

37. Balthasar, *Seeing the Form (TA1)*, 33–34.

38. Ibid., 438.

39. Balthasar, *Seeing the Form (TA1)*, 299.

40. Ibid., 259. He refers, here, to those who take the *ekstasis* of love seriously.

41. Balthasar, "The Gospel as Norm," 294.

42. Balthasar, *Engagement with God*, 19.

43. Ibid., 20.

44. Balthasar, *The Christian State of Life*, 465.

45. Ibid., 12.

authorities (e.g. Maximus, Catherine of Siena, and so on), providing support to the Magisterium, challenging the Magisterium or correcting the Magisterium. But Balthasar fails to provide recommendations for the future, directives as to how saints can and ought to behave in times of crisis vis-à-vis the Magisterium, and how the community ought to respond to the saints. As a consequence, Balthasar's reflections often remain vague historical records, rather than clear directives or exhortations for the future.

The above contradictions and incongruities may seem to sometimes dissipate and sometimes sustain what I have been trying to argue concerning the authority to the saints within the church. It is imperative to note, however, that, although Balthasar can be accused of a lack of clarity, of ambiguity, of inconsistency, but my interpretation that Balthasar trusts the saints, and attributes authority to them, though perhaps shaken, still stands. The role of the saints is not restricted to them being an inspiration to Balthasar as a theologian. The saints have an authoritative function, and the authority that is attributed to them has huge similarities with that of the Magisterium.

CRITIQUE 2:

The second critique will deal with the attribution of authority to the saints and with the possible consequences for the church of attributing such an authority. My assumption is that even among those who agree with my reading of Balthasar, there may still be some who disagree with the concept itself, that is, with the attribution of authority to the saints. Perhaps they are afraid that such a theology would lead to division within the church, just as Tertullian's differentiation between "the hierarchical-legal Church of the bishops (*Ecclesia numerus episcoporum*) . . . and the Church of spiritual men" could have done.[46] More than once, Balthasar refers to this chasm which Tertullian saw. Here, the *Ecclesia numerus episcoporum* succeed the apostles in their governmental function. The spiritual men succeed the apostles as "true followers." On his part, Balthasar avoids the distinction found in Tertullian,[47] but that continued to exist in "heretical circle," or "in circles close to heresy" particularly among the Spirituals, also called the Messalians.[48] Balthasar claims that it is also to be found in "those sects pro-

46. Balthasar, *The Office of Peter*, 287.

47. Ibid., 187. See also Balthasar, *The Dramatis Personae: The Action (TD4)*, 453–69.

48. According to Balthasar, it is in the beginning of the second millennium, with the spiritualistic movement, that "there is an open break [between] the hierarchical

fessing to be the 'true unspotted Church,'" who "arrogate to themselves the Church's quality of holiness."[49] Balthasar would never support a "double Church." The question then becomes: how may authority be attributed to the saints while avoiding division within the church and the triumphalism of the few?

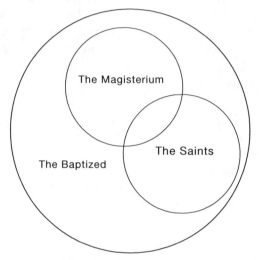

Diagram 10. The Baptized and the saints

Others, yet again, may disagree with the concept of attributing authority to the saints because they simply cannot envision how the saints can be distinguished from the non-saints, how some saints can be recognized as more special. Or perhaps they cannot envision how the category of the saints may, without peril, also incorporate the living saints. Perhaps they cannot foresee how the Magisterium and the saints can conference together, except through written theological debates, and how anybody but the Magisterium can take the final decisions in case of conflict, or whether a generic theology concerning the authority of the saints makes sense. Others will disagree with the concept of attributing authority to the saints because they are aware that there are saints among the members of the Magisterium, just as there are saints among the baptized, and that the two are not homogeneous, and they cannot simply be juxtaposed. Even the suggestion that there could ever be a consultation between the *Communio Sanctorum* and the Magisterium

---

Church that celebrates the liturgy and administers the sacraments" and the person who is genuinely spiritual. There is also a conflict between the spiritual authority and the countless evangelical and charismatic reform movements that were making themselves felt "from below." Balthasar, *The Office of Peter*, 275.

49. Balthasar, *Engagement with God*, 96.

may seem outrageous to some. Since there are members of the Magisterium among the saints, the suggestion that one listen to the saints, rather than the Magisterium, can become a *contradictio in terminis*.

Considering that many of my statements are based on Balthasar's *de facto* practice, and since many of my statements are an expansion of what Balthasar said about the Christian life in general, the details concerning actual processes of consultation, that is, what form such an authority should take if it were approved doctrinally, is not something we can deduce from Balthasar. What I can say is that, despite the perspicacity in some places, where the authenticity and authoritativeness of the saints' being and discourse is concerned, there are still many black holes, the outcome of what Balthasar insinuates, and what I am suggesting in this book, could seem to verge on the bizarre.

Others may disagree with the concept of attributing authority to the saints because they simply cannot envision how the saints can ever speak infallibly, and they argue that, unless the saints can do that, the emphasis on their authority is unnecessary, since they would just be another voice among many. The idea is that, unless we agree that saints can command and can demand obedience, it can be very difficult to argue for their authority. In this regard the distinction which Francis A. Sullivan made between the "*competence* to speak with *authority*," and the "*claim* to speak with *infallibility*" (my emphasis)[50] is useful. The authority that Balthasar would attribute to the saints would seem to be of both the first and the second type, although, with regards to the second, the claim does not come from office but from holiness. *De facto*, we would identify the archetypal figures (such as the Old Testament Prophets) with both the "*competence* to speak with authority" and the "*claim* to speak with infallibility." Adrienne is another example. Her words verge on the infallible for Balthasar. Still, theoretically speaking, Balthasar would then claim that no one "is bound in conscience to have a devotion to some particular saint or believe in certain miracles or private revelations; nor are we bound to accept the words or doctrine of some saint or other as the authentic interpretation of God's revelation."[51]

Strictly speaking, this issue about not being "bound in conscience" cannot be used as an argument against attributing authority to the saints. Today, we are not "bound" to do anything, or to follow anyone. The Spanish Inquisition is long gone, excommunication is out of fashion and, since the development of the doctrine of the Right to Religious Liberty, conscience has taken priority over the Magisterium, so that not even the Magisterium

---

50. Sullivan, *Readings in Church Authority*, 107.
51. Balthasar, *Two Sisters*, 25.

has the right to enforce its beliefs. The teachings of the *Humanae Vitae* are
a case in point. The saints have no power to impose their words or their
doctrine as the authentic interpretation of God's revelation. They cannot
make decisions for others, and they cannot presume that others would obey.
Their authority is limited. In this regard, there are two texts in the Balthasarian corpus which could prove to be helpful. The first one is about the *Pater
Pneumatikos* from the *Aesthetics*, and the second concerns the distinction
between counsel and command from *The Christian State of Life*.

What Balthasar writes about the tradition of the *pater pneumatikos*,
in *The Office of Peter* is critical. Here, it would have been justified for a man
to "give an unconditional command in the name of God," "in an extreme
instance," and "on the basis of a personal authority accepted by the disciple
who has entrusted himself freely to his master." In this context "there is a
personal relationship well founded in human nature." Here, "the one who
obeys can review, judge, ratify or renounce this relationship." In this case,
"his judgment is definitely part of his obedience . . . he is obeying his own
judgment, at least partly, even when something difficult or unexpected is
commanded."[52] Here, Balthasar claims something that is very important:
the authority is not only present in the pater *pneumatikos*, but also in his
disciple.[53]

The second text provides an equation between counsels and commandments. Balthasar insists that only someone who takes justice as his
"standpoint" rather than love distinguishes between the two.[54] According
to Balthasar, counsels should have been enough, and commands are only
necessary because men "no longer possess love."[55] Here, Balthasar portrays
commands and laws as a consequence of sin. He also implies that authority
came in after original sin, and that we would no longer need authority if
there were no sin. On the other hand, he claims that, with pure love, "obligation" is always a "choice."[56] In Balthasar's words, love "needs no other law
than itself; all the laws are subsumed, fulfilled, transcended in the one law

52. Balthasar, *The Office of Peter*, 61–62.

53. The authority of the spiritual director in the Ignatian *Spiritual Exercises*, and
Balthasar's role as Adrienne's spiritual director, also permit the use of commands. The
objective is to remain as unnoticeable as possible, in order that God may be allowed to
shine through.

54. Balthasar, *The Christian State of Life*, 51. In speaking of love it is meaningless
to distinguish between commandment and counsel. See also 49. Balthasar was referring
to the evangelical counsels, but the knowledge that Balthasar equates counsels with
commands has consequences for our study.

55. Ibid., 49.

56. Ibid., 28.

of love."[57] I take this to mean that counsels could be just as demanding as commands, whereas demands made by commands remain a choice. Two implications arise from this. The first is that, whenever orders are about to be given, decisions are about to be made, and obedience is about to be enforced, Christians, including members of the Magisterium, ought *always* (as if it were an imperative) to *take into consideration* what the saints do/did and what they say/said, even if—strictly speaking—it is not obligatory to do so. Secondly, neither the saints nor the Magisterium have any advantage one over the other. The authority of both depends, not only on their existential and epistemological authority, but on the response of those who have come in contact with them. Ultimately, although Balthasar may not be willing to state that the authority of the saints is binding, he does claim their authority in other ways. For example, he says, that the "theological manifestation" which arises out of the "sheer existence" of the saints must "not be neglected" by any of the members of the church.[58] He thus considers the saints' teaching as essential and authoritative, even imperative, where dictates of conscience are concerned.

This brings us to the issue of what form our recognition of the authority of the saints is to take. How is this authority which we concede to the saints to become evident? How are the saints to function authoritatively? In medieval times, the authority of the saints would have taken the form of devotional acts, public honor, shrines, reliquaries, processions bearing their relics, iconography, elaborated tombs, statues, frescoes serving a didactic purpose for the laity. Authoritative saints would have had their name included in the litany of saints, their memory commemorated at the mass or monastic office, their names adopted as patrons by Confraternities, or for "special" situations, elaborate feasts dedicated in their honor, vernacular hagiography reproduced for the use of the Christian. Nowadays, one would expect the authority of the saints to become more evident through a more explicit dependence on their teaching by theologians, through the church's explicit recognition of their contribution, through a deeper appreciation in all Christians for all charisms present in them, through a stronger effort to receive the saints and use them to "fertilize" sanctity.[59] We can use what Balthasar says about the *Pater Pneumatikos*, and in particular about the concept of discipleship, to explain how the recognition of the saint's authority may become evident. Discipleship is more of a *consequence* that comes from attributing authority to the saints, rather than simply an indication that we

57. Balthasar, *The Christian State of Life*, 29.
58. Balthasar, *Two Sisters*, 25.
59. Ibid., 24.

attribute authority to the saints. Balthasar finds nothing inappropriate and incomprehensible in committing oneself to someone, or to the teaching of someone, who appears "to be transparent to God." He insists, however, that "the analogy," or doctrine, only applies "in the real sense . . . to the nature of the saint . . . who, as such, becomes for his disciples a kind of sacrament."[60]

There are others who would disagree with the concept of attributing authority to the saints because they simply cannot envisage a situation where the saints are struggling against the Magisterium. But this fear is unfounded. Within Balthasar's scheme of things, this will never happen. In Balthasar, the saint is not a rebel. Balthasar condemns the tendency to "glorify the saints in the history of the Church as 'avowed nonconformists' and 'potential dissidents.'"[61] Not only does he argue that the authentic saints refused to take a stand against the church, he also claims that they "would refuse to allow anyone to take a stand on their behalf against the Church."[62] While most committed Christians would interpret this as loyalty and commitment, it feeds the imagination of those who see the church as an oppressive and manipulative institution, as patriarchal and dominant, and would easily interpret Balthasar of using the saints to preserve the *status quo*. However, Balthasar is not against *ressourcement* or even *aggiornamento*.[63] In Balthasar's theology, the authority of the saints is grounded in their role of reforming and reanimating the church, in the conviction that this reanimation rarely originates from the hierarchy. It generally comes from the ranks of the nonofficial believers, or from priests "afire with the Spirit."[64] And it is "totally different from skillful organization." For this reason, Balthasar is inclined to suspect "that the great movements and reforms of the Church in the present and the future, will not be initiated by . . . panels and boards but by saints, the ever-unique and solitary ones who, struck by God's lightning, ignite a blaze all around them."[65] It is because of his huge confidence in the saints' competence that Balthasar goes on to write about the collaboration

---

60. Balthasar, *Seeing the Form (TA1)*, 185.

61. Balthasar, *The Office of Peter*, 29.

62. Ibid., 42.

63. In *Razing the Bastions*, Balthasar shows himself to be for *aggiornamento* as well. The two terms (*ressourcement* and *aggiornamento*) are not being used in the sense of discontinuity or continuity, as was done in the postconciliar interpretation debates. Here they became irreconciliable.

64. Balthasar, *The Spirit of Truth (TL3)*, 318.

65. Balthasar, *The Office of Peter*, 40. It is significant that, in Balthasar, "[e]verything which deserves to be called reform again and again in the epochs of Church History has been active, effective exhortation to turn back from the periphery to the centre." Balthasar, *Convergences*, 106.

between the hierarchy and the saints in the reanimation of the church. He writes,

> the charism of great popes and bishops extends to the reanimation . . . of the Church or the diocese as a whole, and for this task they are equipped with the relevant charisms, such as "wisdom," "knowledge," "exhortation," "leadership," and "prophecy." It is mostly not their business to found special "families'" yet there are famous instances where Spirit-inspired communities have been used by them for the great sanctifying and missionary work of the whole Church.[66]

FINAL REMARKS

As has already been said, the authority of the saints already exists *de facto* in Balthasar's work, and probably also in the mind of most Christians and most theologians, even though it has not been developed theologically, and even if there is nothing *de jure* about it: nothing in the canon law, and no official document which expands on it. Steffen Lösel has said that "while current canon law calls and compels the laity to obey the hierarchy, the hierarchy is advised but not required to listen to the laity."[67] My view is that what Lösel has said about the laity, should apply especially to the saints. Their existence, their wisdom, and their ecclesial association, is what grounds their authority. Early on, I quoted Michael Polanyi, stating that "we have no clear knowledge of what our presuppositions are and when we try to formulate them they appear quite unconvincing."[68] We have to acknowledge that the saints *already* have authority, their authority is already presupposed. Balthasar himself may have been aware of this, when he emphasized the expertise of the saints, but did not develop a full argument for their authority. Likewise, the church constantly refers to the writings of the saints without ever having published an official doctrine or a clear theology about the authority of the saints. This is probably why this study of the authority of the saints may seem so outlandish and provocative to some, if not useless and ineffectual. In a sense, our book has dealt with what Balthasar has said about an authority that *should be* attributed, an authority that is deserved, an authority that—although not deliberately demanded in a mandatory way by the saints themselves—is kindled and provoked (unconsciously)

66. Balthasar, *The Spirit of Truth (TL3)*, 318.
67. Lösel, "Conciliar, Not Conciliatory," 43.
68. Polanyi, *Personal Knowledge*, 62.

by them, as well as recognized, promoted, and invoked by us. I wrote this book convinced that the authority of the saints (the "Magisterium of the saints") is an authority that should be explicitly explored, approved, and defined. I wish that Balthasar had made a more explicit effort to formulate the theology of the authority of the saints, but what he has written can help us navigate through such a doctrine.

Although, within the limits required of me, I have tried to provide an argument that is plausible and comprehensive, this book will certainly not answer all the questions. It may even raise more! I would agree with Karen Kilby that "[w]e have not come to the end of exploring what [Balthasar's] work makes possible, of receiving what he has to give, of thinking through where the lines of thought he begins should lead." As Kilby has said, attention to Balthasar "needs to continue."[69] Further research is required on the concept of authority in Balthasar. A more inter-disciplinary analysis of Balthasar's use of the saints would also be helpful. Also useful would be studies that would enable us to assess the influence of particular saints on Balthasar and on the church. One could also compare the *Gegen-Gestalten* (the anti-figures) whom Balthasar used, such as Péguy[70] and Nietzsche,[71] to the saints as depicted in more recent postmodern literature. Also useful would be a comparison of Balthasar's theology of the saints with that of Cardinal Newman, as well as with that of Adrienne von Speyr.

I hope that at least some of the implications of my study for theology and for the church will have become clear through this book. Vatican II affirmed that, in the saints, God "vividly manifests His presence and His face to men. He speaks to us in them."[72] In his interview with Angelo Scola, Balthasar confirms the authority of the saint by stating that

> Nobody will convert to Christ because of a Magisterium, sacraments, a clergy, canon law, apostolic nunciatures or a gigantic ecclesiastical machinery. Conversion will occur when a person encounters a Catholic who communicates the Christian message by his life and thus testifies that there exists not *a* but *the* believable imitation of Christ within the Catholic sphere.[73]

In my introductory chapter, I claimed that there was an important question underlying my argument: does Balthasar merely interpret the saints as a resource for theologians and for the Magisterium? Or should

69. Kilby, *Balthasar*, 167.

70. Kerr, "Forward: Assessing This 'Giddy Synthesis,'" 4.

71. Henrici, "The Philosophy of Hans Urs von Balthasar," 159.

72. *Lumen Gentium*, 50.

73. Scola, *Test Everything*, 18.

we rather interpret Balthasar as saying that the saints are the real authority and that theology and the Magisterium are the mouthpiece of the saints? For Balthasar, the saints are more than just a resource. They are the real witnesses whose testimony requires dynamic paraphrase and vigorous rendition, and that theology and the Magisterium are primarily there to serve them, whereas the saints, aware of their own authority, acknowledge the authority of the Magisterium.[74] Theology and the church must now (more than ever) concentrate on the saints, seek out the saints, recognize them as the authentic authority which they are, listen to them more, and direct others to them, or rather, be mindful about the way in which the Spirit is himself universalizing and publicising them.

Have I misrepresented Balthasar's emphasis on the saints? Overstated the concept of authority in Balthasar? Have I misconstrued Balthasar's use of the saints? Have I developed a doctrine of the authority of the saints where there was none? Am I wrong in having interpreted Balthasar's grounding of the authority of the saints where I did, that is, in their existence, in their wisdom and in their ecclesial association? Evidently, there will always be some difference between how Balthasar meant his texts to be received and how I myself, as the reader, received his texts. It is up to the readers of this book to judge whether Balthasar should be interpreted differently. On my part, I have argued, firstly, for the plausibility of my own analysis of the grounding of the authority of the saints as evident in Balthasar's work, secondly, for the credibility of the assessment of Balthasar vis-à-vis the importance of the saints, thirdly, for the need to use different dimensions in order to analyze the grounding of the authoritativeness of the saints in Balthasar.

Is Balthasar's own theology concerning the authority of the saints flawless? I do not believe that it is flawless, however, I do believe that what I have interpreted as Balthasar's attribution of authority to the saints has immense consequences for theology in general, and for our understanding of the church and of the *Communio Sanctorum*. Have I said all that there is to say about the issue? Certainly not. I have, hopefully, just started a conversation that will keep going.

74. Ibid., 55.

Bibliography

Ackermann, Stephan. "The Church as Person in the Theology of Hans Urs von Balthasar." *Communio International Catholic Review* 29 (2002) 238–49.

Aquinas, Thomas. *Summa contra Gentiles*. Accessed 6/11/2014. www.catholicprimer. org/aquinas/aquinas_summa_contra_gentiles.pdf.

———. "The State of Perfection in General." Question 184. In *Summa Theologiae*. http://www.newadvent.org/summa/3184.htm.

———. "Of the Ministers of the Keys." In Summa Theologiae. Supplement Question 19. http://www.documentacatholicaomnia.eu/03d/1225-1274,_Thomas_Aquinas,_ Summa_Theologiae_%5B1%5D,_EN.pdf.

Austin, Victor Lee. *Up with Authority: Why We Need Authority to Flourish as Human Beings*. London: T. & T. Clark, 2010.

Babini, Ellero. "Jesus Christ: Form and Norm of Man according to Hans Urs von Balthasar." In *Hans Urs von Balthasar: His Life and Work*, edited by David L. Schindler, 221–30. San Francisco: Ignatius, 1991.

Balthasar, Hans Urs von. "The Absences of Jesus." In *New Elucidations*, 46–60. Translated by Sr. Mary Theresilde Skerry. San Francisco: Ignatius, 1986.

———. "Are There Lay People in the Church?" Translated by Sr. Mary Theresilde Skerry. In *New Elucidations*, 168–87. San Francisco: Ignatius, 1986.

———. "Authority." Translated by John Riches. In *Elucidations*, 128–39. San Francisco: Ignatius, 1998.

———. "Catholicism and the Communion of Saints." Translated by Albert K.Wimmer. *Communio International Catholic Review* 15 (1988) 163–68.

———. *The Christian and Anxiety*. Translated by Michael J. Miller. San Francisco: Ignatius, 2000.

———. *The Christian State of Life*. Translated by Sr. Mary Frances McCarthy. San Francisco: Ignatius,1983.

———. "The Church as the Presence of Christ." Translated by Sr. Mary Theresilde Skerry. In *New Elucidations*, 87–103. San Francisco: Ignatius, 1986.

———. "The Communion of Saints." Translated by John Riches. In *Elucidations*, 91–100. San Francisco: Ignatius, 1975.

———. *Convergences: To the Source of the Christian Mystery*. Translated by E. A.Nelson. San Francisco: Ignatius, 1983.

———. *Cosmic Liturgy: The Universe according to Maximus the Confessor*. Translated by Brian E. Daley. San Francisco: Ignatius, 2003.

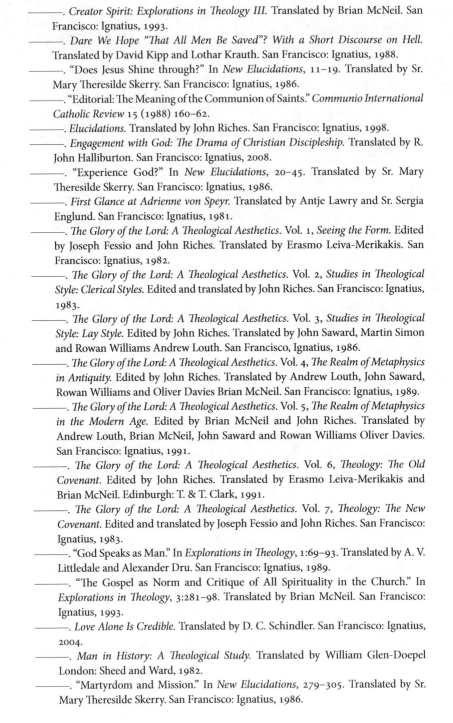

―――. *Creator Spirit: Explorations in Theology III.* Translated by Brian McNeil. San Francisco: Ignatius, 1993.

―――. *Dare We Hope "That All Men Be Saved"? With a Short Discourse on Hell.* Translated by David Kipp and Lothar Krauth. San Francisco: Ignatius, 1988.

―――. "Does Jesus Shine through?" In *New Elucidations*, 11–19. Translated by Sr. Mary Theresilde Skerry. San Francisco: Ignatius, 1986.

―――. "Editorial: The Meaning of the Communion of Saints." *Communio International Catholic Review* 15 (1988) 160–62.

―――. *Elucidations.* Translated by John Riches. San Francisco: Ignatius, 1998.

―――. *Engagement with God: The Drama of Christian Discipleship.* Translated by R. John Halliburton. San Francisco: Ignatius, 2008.

―――. "Experience God?" In *New Elucidations*, 20–45. Translated by Sr. Mary Theresilde Skerry. San Francisco: Ignatius, 1986.

―――. *First Glance at Adrienne von Speyr.* Translated by Antje Lawry and Sr. Sergia Englund. San Francisco: Ignatius, 1981.

―――. *The Glory of the Lord: A Theological Aesthetics.* Vol. 1, *Seeing the Form.* Edited by Joseph Fessio and John Riches. Translated by Erasmo Leiva-Merikakis. San Francisco: Ignatius, 1982.

―――. *The Glory of the Lord: A Theological Aesthetics.* Vol. 2, *Studies in Theological Style: Clerical Styles.* Edited and translated by John Riches. San Francisco: Ignatius, 1983.

―――. *The Glory of the Lord: A Theological Aesthetics.* Vol. 3, *Studies in Theological Style: Lay Style.* Edited by John Riches. Translated by John Saward, Martin Simon and Rowan Williams Andrew Louth. San Francisco, Ignatius, 1986.

―――. *The Glory of the Lord: A Theological Aesthetics.* Vol. 4, *The Realm of Metaphysics in Antiquity.* Edited by John Riches. Translated by Andrew Louth, John Saward, Rowan Williams and Oliver Davies Brian McNeil. San Francisco: Ignatius, 1989.

―――. *The Glory of the Lord: A Theological Aesthetics.* Vol. 5, *The Realm of Metaphysics in the Modern Age.* Edited by Brian McNeil and John Riches. Translated by Andrew Louth, Brian McNeil, John Saward and Rowan Williams Oliver Davies. San Francisco: Ignatius, 1991.

―――. *The Glory of the Lord: A Theological Aesthetics.* Vol. 6, *Theology: The Old Covenant.* Edited by John Riches. Translated by Erasmo Leiva-Merikakis and Brian McNeil. Edinburgh: T. & T. Clark, 1991.

―――. *The Glory of the Lord: A Theological Aesthetics.* Vol. 7, *Theology: The New Covenant.* Edited and translated by Joseph Fessio and John Riches. San Francisco: Ignatius, 1983.

―――. "God Speaks as Man." In *Explorations in Theology*, 1:69–93. Translated by A. V. Littledale and Alexander Dru. San Francisco: Ignatius, 1989.

―――. "The Gospel as Norm and Critique of All Spirituality in the Church." In *Explorations in Theology*, 3:281–98. Translated by Brian McNeil. San Francisco: Ignatius, 1993.

―――. *Love Alone Is Credible.* Translated by D. C. Schindler. San Francisco: Ignatius, 2004.

―――. *Man in History: A Theological Study.* Translated by William Glen-Doepel London: Sheed and Ward, 1982.

―――. "Martyrdom and Mission." In *New Elucidations*, 279–305. Translated by Sr. Mary Theresilde Skerry. San Francisco: Ignatius, 1986.

————. *The Moment of Christian Witness.* Translated by Richard Beckley. San Francisco: Ignatius, 1994.

————. "Movement toward God." In *Explorations in Theology*, 3:15–55. Translated by Brian McNeil. San Francisco: Ignatius, 1993.

————. *Mysterium Paschale: The Mystery of Easter.* Translated by Aidan Nichols. Edinburgh: T. & T. Clark, 1990.

————. *My Work: In Retrospect.* Translated by Brian McNeil et al. Communio. San Francisco: Ignatius, 1993.

————. *New Elucidations.* Translated by Sr. Mary Theresilde Skerry. San Francisco: Ignatius, 1986.

————. "Obedience in the Light of the Gospel." In *New Elucidations*, 228–55. Translated by Sr. Mary Theresilde Skerry. San Francisco: Ignatius, 1986.

————. *The Office of Peter and the Structure of the Church.* Translated by Andrée Emery. San Francisco: Ignatius, 2007.

————. "Our Shared Responsibility." In *Elucidations*, 140–51. Translated by John Riches. San Francisco: Ignatius, 1998.

————. *Our Task: A Report and a Plan.* Communio. Translated by John Saward. San Francisco: Ignatius, 1994.

————. *Prayer.* Translated by Graham Harrison. San Francisco: Ignatius, 1992.

————. *Presence and Thought: Essay on the Religious Philosophy of Gregory of Nyssa.* Communio. Translated by Mark Sebanc. San Francisco: Ignatius, 1995.

————. *Razing the Bastions: On the Church in this Age.* Translated by Brian McNeil. San Francisco: Ignatius, 1993.

————. "Retrieving the Tradition: On the Tasks of Catholic Philosophy in Our Time." *Communio International Catholic Review* 20 (1993) 147–87.

————. *Romano Guardini: Reform from the Source.* Translated by Albert K. Wimmer and D. C. Schindler. Communio. San Francisco: Ignatius, 2010.

————. *Science, Religion and Christianity.* Translated by Hilda Graef. London: Burns & Oates, 1958.

————. *Spirit and Institution.* Vol. 4 of *Explorations in Theology*. Translated by Edward T. Oakes. San Francisco: Ignatius, 1995.

————. *Spouse of the Word.* Vol. 2 of *Explorations in Theology*. Translated by A. V. Littledale. San Francisco: Ignatius, 1989.

————. *Theo-Drama: Theological Dramatic Theory.* Vol. 1, *Prologomena*. Translated by Graham Harrison. San Francisco: Ignatius, 1988.

————. *Theo-Drama: Theological Dramatic Theory.* Vol. 2, *The Dramatis Personae: Man in God*. Translated by Graham Harrison. San Francisco: Ignatius, 1990.

————. *Theo-Drama: Theological Dramatic Theory.* Vol. 3, *The Dramatis Personae: The Person in Christ*. Translated by Graham Harrison. San Francisco: Ignatius, 1992.

————. *Theo-Drama: Theological Dramatic Theory.* Vol. 4, *The Dramatis Personae: The Action*. Translated by Graham Harrison. San Francisco: Ignatius, 1994.

————. *Theo-Drama: Theological Dramatic Theory.* Vol. 5, *The Last Act*. Translated by Graham Harrison. San Francisco: Ignatius, 1998.

————. *Theo-Logic: Theological Logical Theory.* Vol. 1, *Truth of the World*. Translated by Adrian J. Walker. San Francisco: Ignatius, 2000.

————. *Theo-Logic: Theological Logical Theory.* Vol. 2, *Truth of God*. Translated by Adrian J. Walker. San Francisco: Ignatius, 2004.

―――. *Theo-Logic: Theological Logical Theory.* Vol. 3, *The Spirit of Truth.* Translated by Graham Harrison. San Francisco: Ignatius, 2005.

―――. "Theology and Sanctity." In *Explorations in Theology,* 1:181–210. Translated by A. V. Littledale and Alexander Dru. San Francisco, Ignatius Press, 1989.

―――. *A Theology of History.* San Francisco: Ignatius, 1994.

―――. *The Theology of Henri de Lubac: An Overview.* Translated by Joseph Fessio and Michael M.Waldstein. San Francisco: Ignatius, 1991.

―――. *The Theology of Karl Barth: Exposition and Interpretation.* Translated by Edward T. Oakes. San Francisco: Ignatius, 1992.

―――. "Tradition." In *Elucidations,* 114–27. Translated by John Riches. San Francisco: Ignatius, 1998.

―――. *Truth Is Symphonic: Aspects of Christian Pluralism.* San Francisco: Ignatius, 1987.

―――. "Two Modes of Faith." In *Explorations in Theology,* 3:85–102. Translated by Brian McNeil. San Francisco: Ignatius, 1993.

―――. *Two Sisters in the Spirit. Thérèse of Lisieux & Elizabeth of the Trinity.* San Francisco: Ignatius, 1992. *Thérèse von Lisieux* was translated by Donald Nichols and Anne Englund Nash. *Elisabeth von Dijon* was translated by Dennis Martin.

―――. "A Verse of Matthias Claudius." In *Elucidations,* 11–20. Translated by John Riches. 1975. Repr., San Francisco: Ignatius, 1998.

―――. "Who Is the Church?" In *Explorations in Theology,* 2:143–92. Translated by A. V. Littledale. San Francisco: Ignatius, 1989.

―――. *The Word Made Flesh.* Vol. 1 of *Explorations in Theology.* Translated by A. V. Littledale and Alexander Dru. San Francisco: Ignatius, 1989.

―――. "The Word, Scripture, and Tradition." In *Explorations in Theology,* 1:11–26. Translated by A. V. Littledale and Alexander Dru. San Francisco: Ignatius, 1989.

Barth, Karl. *Church Dogmatics.* Vol. 1/1, *The Doctrine of the Word of God: Prolegomena to Church Dogmatics.* Edited by G. W. Bromiley and T. F. Torrance. Translated by G. W. Bromiley. Edinburgh: T. & T. Clark, 1975.

―――. *Church Dogmatics.* Vol. 4/1, *The Doctrine of Reconciliation: The Subject-Matter and Problems of the Doctrine of Reconciliation.* Edited by G. W. Bromiley and T. F. Torrance. Translated by G. W. Bromiley. Edinburgh: T. & T. Clark, 2004.

Barth, Markus. *Der Augenzeuge: eine Untersuchung über die Wahrnehmung des Menschensohnes durch die Apostel.* Evangelischer, 1946.

Barton, Stephen, ed. *Holiness Past and Present.* London: T. & T. Clark, 2003.

Beattie, Tina. *New Catholic Feminism: Theology and Theory.* London: Routledge, 2006.

―――. "Sex, Death and Melodrama: A Feminist Critique of Hans Urs von Balthasar." *The Way* 44, no. 4 (2005) 160–76.

Benedict XVI, Pope. *Deus Caritas Est.* Encyclical promulgated 25 December 2005.

Bingemer, Maria Clara, Andres Torres Queiruga, and Jon Sobrino, eds. *Concilium: Saints and Sanctity Today* 3 (2013).

Blankenhorn, Bernhard. "Balthasar's Method of Divine Naming." *Nova et Vetera* 1, no. 2 (2003) 245–68.

Block, Ed, Jr. "Balthasar's Literary Criticism." In *The Cambridge Companion to Hans urs von Balthasar,* edited by Edward T. Oakes and David Moss, 207–23. Cambridge: Cambridge University Press, 2004.

———. "Hans Urs von Balthasar's Theo-Drama: A Contribution to Dramatic Criticism." In *Glory, Grace and Culture: The Work of Hans Urs von Balthasar*, edited by Ed Block Jr., 175–98. New York: Paulist, 2005.

Block, Ed, Jr., ed. *Glory, Grace and Culture: The Work of Hans Urs von Balthasar*. New York: Paulist, 2005.

Blondel, Maurice. *Action: Essay on a Critique of Life and a Science of Practice*. Translated by Oliva Blanchette. Notre Dame: University of Notre Dame, 1984.

Boersma, Hans. "Sacramental Ontology: Nature and the Supernatural in the Ecclesiology of Henri de Lubac." *New Blackfriars* (2007) 242–73.

———. *Nouvelle Théologie & Sacramental Ontology: A Return to Mystery*. Oxford: Oxford University Press, 2009.

Bramwell, Bevil. "Hans Urs von Balthasar's Theology of Scripture." *New Blackfriars* 86, no. 1003 (2005) 308–22.

Brown, Peter. *The Cult of the Saints: Its Rise and Function in Latin Christianity*. Chicago: University of Chicago Press, 1981.

Brown, Raymond E. *The Churches the Apostles Left Behind*. New York: Paulist, 1984.

Bultmann, Rudolf. "The Concept of Revelation in the NT." In *Existence and Faith: Shorter Writings of Rudolph Bultmann*, 58–91. Translated by Schubert M. Ogden. Fontana Library: Theology and Philosophy. New York: Meridian, 1960.

Bychkov, Oleg V., and James Fodor, eds. *Theological Aesthetics after von Balthasar*. Hampshire, UK: Ashgate, 2008.

Campodonico, Angelo. "Hans Urs von Balthasar's Interpretation of the Philosophy of Thomas Aquinas." *Nova et Vetera*, English edition, 8, no. 1 (2010) 33–53.

Carroll, Anthony J., et al., eds. *Towards a Kenotic Vision of Authority in the Catholic Church*. Washington DC: Council for Research in Values and Philosophy, 2015.

Casarella, Peter J. "The Expression and Form of the Word: Trinitarian Hermeneutics and the Sacramentality of Language in Hans Urs von Balthasar's Theology." In *Glory, Grace and Culture: The Work of Hans Urs von Balthasar*, edited by Ed Block Jr., 37–68. New York: Paulist, 2005.

Castillo, José María. "The History of Canonization in Christianity: Its Real Meaning." In *Saints and Sanctity Today*. Edited by Maria Clara Bingemer, Andres Torres Queiruga, and Jon Sobrino. *Concilium* 3 (2013) 70–77.

Chantraine, Georges. "Exegesis and Contemplation." In *Hans Urs von Balthasar: His Life and Work*, edited by David L.Schindler, 133–47. Communio. San Francisco: Ignatius, 1991.

Cirelli, Anthony. "Re-Assessing The Meaning of Thought: Hans Urs Von Balthasar's Retrieval Of Gregory Of Nyssa." *Heythrop* 50 (2009) 416–24.

Cloud, Christine M. "Embodied Authority in the Spiritual Autobiographies of Four Early Modern Women from Spain and Mexico." PhD diss., Ohio State University, 2006.

Coakley, John Wayland. *Women, Men and Spiritual Power. Female Saints and their Male Collaborators*. New York: Columbia University Press, 2006.

Congar, Yves. "Comment l'Église Sainte doit se renouveler sans cesse." *Irénikon* 34 (1961) 322–45.

Congregation for the Doctrine of the Faith. *Communionis Notio*. Letter to the bishops of the Catholic Church on some aspects of the church understood as communion. Promulgated 28 May 1992.

Conway, Michael A. "A Positive Phenomenology: The Structure Of Maurice Blondel's Early Philosophy." *Heythrop* 47 (2006) 579–600.

Cunningham, Lawrence S. "Current Theology: A Decade of Research on the Saints: 1980–1990." *Theological Studies* 53 (1992) 517–33.

———. *A Brief History of Saints*. Blackwell Brief Histories of Religion. Oxford: Blackwell, 2005.

Daley, Brian E. "Balthasar's Reading of the Church Fathers." In *The Cambridge Companion to Hans Urs von Balthasar*, edited by Edward T. Oakes and David Moss, 187–206. Cambridge: Cambridge University Press, 2004.

———. "Translator's Foreword." In *Cosmic Liturgy Cosmic Liturgy: The Universe according to Maximus the Confessor*, 11–21. San Francisco: Ignatius, 2003.

Dalzell, Thomas G. *The Dramatic Encounter of Divine and Human Freedom in the Theology of Hans Urs von Balthasar*. Studies in the Intercultural History of Christianity 105. Berne: Lang AG, 1997.

Davies, Oliver. "The Theological Aesthetic." In *The Cambridge Companion to Hans Urs von Balthasar*, edited by Edward T. Oakes and David Moss, 131–42. Cambridge: Cambridge University Press, 2004.

———. "Von Balthasar and the Problem of Being." *New Blackfriars* 79, no. 923 (1998) 11–17.

D'Costa, Gavin. "The Communion of Saints and Other Religions: On Saintly Wives in Hinduism and Catholicism." In *Holiness Past and Present*, edited by Stephen C. Barton, 421–40. London: T. & T. Clark, 2003.

Deane-Drummond, Celia. "The Breadth of Glory: A Trinitarian Eschatology for the Earth through Critical Engagement with Hans Urs von Balthasar." *International Journal of Systematic Theology* 12, no. 1 (2010) 46–64.

De Maeseneer, Yves. "Review Symposium." *Horizons: The Journal of the College Theology Society* 40, no. 1 (2013) 100–106.

Denzinger, Henricus, and Adolphus Schönmetzer. *Enchiridion Symbolorum Definitionum et Declarationum de Rebus Fidei Et Morum*. http://patristica.net/denzinger/#n200. Accessed 20 March 2017.

De Witte, Pieter. "The Church as *simul justus et peccator*? Ecumenical Challenges for Roman Catholic Ecclesiology." CTSA Proceedings 66 (2011) 96–97.

Dickens, William Thomas. *Hans Urs von Balthasar's Theological Aesthetics: A Model for Post-Critical Biblical Interpretation*. Notre Dame: University of Notre Dame Press, 2003.

Dickinson, Colby. "Jean Genet versus Saint Genet: Searching for Redemption among the 'Unredeemable.'" In *The Postmodern Saints of France. Refiguring "the Holy" in Contemporary French Philosophy*, edited by Colby Dickinson, 13–24. London: Bloomsbury, 2013.

Dickinson, Colby, ed. *The Postmodern Saints of France. Refiguring "the Holy" in Contemporary French Philosophy*. London : Bloomsbury, 2013.

Dillon, Janette. "Holy Women and Their Confessors or Confessors and Their Holy Women? Margery Kempe and Continental Tradition." In *Prophets abroad: The Reception of Continental Holy Women in Late-Medieval England*, edited by Rosalynn Voaden, 115–40. Cambridge: Brewer, 1996.

Dulles, Avery. "*Successio apostolorum—Successio prophetarum—Successio doctorum*." *Concilium* 148, no. 8 (1981) 61–67.

————. "Teaching Authority in the Church." In *Church and Society: the Laurence J. McGinley Lectures, 1988–2007*, 16–26, New York: Province of the Society of Jesus: 2008.

Dupré, Louis. "The Glory of the Lord: Hans Urs von Balthasar's Theological Aesthetic." In *Hans Urs Balthasar: His Life and Work*, edited by David L. Schindler, 183–206. San Francisco: Ignatius, 1991.

————. "Seeking Christian Interiority: An Interview with Louis Dupré." *The Christian Century* 114, no. 21 (1997) 654–60.

————. "Symbolic Variety and Cultural Integration." *Issues in Integrative Studies* 24 (2006) 173–82.

Endean, Philip. "Von Balthasar, Rahner, and the Commissar." *New Blackfriars* 79, no. 923 (1998) 33–38. Accessed 27/2/2017. http://www.theway.org.uk/endeanweb/vonbrc.pdf.

Eno, Robert B. "Authority and Conflict in the Early Church." *Église et Théologie* 7, no. 1 (1976) 41–60.

Fahey, Michael A. "Church." In *Systematic Theology: Roman Catholic Perspectives*, edited by Francis Schüssler Fiorenza and John P. Galvin 315–72. 2nd ed. Minneapolis: Fortress, 2011.

Føllesdall, Dagfinn. "Phenomenology." In *A Companion to Metaphysics*, edited by Jaegwon Kim, Ernest Sosa, and Gary S.Rosenkrantz, 483–84. Oxford: Wiley-Blackwell, 2009.

Francis, Pope. *Lumen Fidei*. Encyclical promulgated 29 June 2013.

Gardner, Lucy. "Balthasar and the Figure of Mary." In *The Cambridge Companion to Hans Urs von Balthasar*, edited by Edward T. Oakes and David Moss, 64–78. Cambridge: Cambridge University Press, 2004.

Gardner, Lucy, et al, eds. *Balthasar at the End of Modernity*. Edinburgh: T. & T. Clark, 1999.

Geanakoplos, Deno J. "Some Aspects of the Influence of the Byzantine Maximos the Confessor on the Theology of East and West." *Church History* 38, no. 2 (1969) 150–63.

General Convention of the Episcopal Church. "Holy Women and Holy Men: Celebrating the Saints." Document approved in 2009. New York: Church, 2010.

Goldberg, Michael. *Theology and Narrative: A Critical Introduction*. Eugene, OR: Wipf and Stock, 2001.

Goulding, Gill K. "Hans Urs von Balthasar's Theology of Vocation." In *The Disciples' Call: Theologies of Vocation from Scripture to the Present Day*, edited by Christopher Jamison, 115–38. London: Bloomsbury, 2013.

Groppe, Elizabeth Teresa. *Yves Congar's Theology of the Holy Spirit*. AAR. New York: Oxford University Press, 2004.

Harrison, Victoria. *The Apologetics of Human Holiness: Von Balthasar's Christocentric Philosophical Anthropology*. Dordrecht: Kluwer Academic, 2000.

————. "*Homo Orans*: Von Balthasar's Christocentric Philosophical Anthropology." *Heythrop* 40, no. 3 (1999) 280–300.

Hayward, J. E. S. "Lamennais and the Religion of Social Consensus." *Archives de Sociologie des Religions* 21 (1966) 37–46.

Healy, Nicholas J. *The Eschatology of Hans Urs von Balthasar: Being as Communion*. Oxford Theological Monographs. Oxford: Oxford University Press, 2005.

Healy, Nicholas M. *Church, World and the Christian Life: Practical-Prophetic Ecclesiology*. Cambridge Studies in Christian Doctrine. Cambridge: Cambridge University Press, 2000.

Heffernan, Thomas J. *Sacred Biography: Saints and Their Biographers in the Middle Ages*. New York: Oxford University Press, 1988.

Hegel, Georg Wilhelm Friedrich. *Introduction to the Philosophy of History: With Selections from the Philosophy of Right*. Translated by Leo Rauch. Indianapolis: Hackett, 1988.

Heidegger, Martin. *Being and Time*. Translated by Joan Stambaugh. Albany: SUNY, 2010.

Hellemans, Staf, "*The Magisterium*: Conjunctions and Disjunctions in Modernity: A Historical-Sociological Analysis." In *Towards a Kenotic Vision of Authority in the Catholic Church*, edited by Anthony J. Carroll et al., 55–72. Washington, DC: Council for Research in Values and Philosophy, 2015.

Henrici, Peter. "Hans Urs von Balthasar: A Sketch of His Life." In *Hans Urs von Balthasar: His Life and Work*, edited by David L. Schindler, 7–44. San Francisco: Ignatius, 1991.

———. "The Philosophy of Hans Urs von Balthasar." In *Hans Urs von Balthasar: His Life and Work*, edited by David L. Schindler, 149–67. San Francisco: Ignatius, 1991.

Holland, Scott. *How Do Stories Save Us? An Essay on the Question with the Theological Hermeneutics of David Tracy in View*. Louvain Theological & Pastoral Monographs 35. Louvain: Peeters, 2006.

Hoose, Bernard, ed. *Authority in the Roman Catholic Church: Theory and Practice*. Aldershot, UK: Ashgate, 2002.

Hopgood, James F., ed. *The Making of Saints: Contesting Sacred Ground*. Tuscaloosa: University of Alabama Press, 2005.

Howell, A. C. "Res and verba: Words and things." *ELH* 13, no. 2 (1946) 131–42.

Howsare, Rodney A. *Balthasar: A Guide for the Perplexed*. London: T. & T. Clark, 2009.

———. *Hans Urs von Balthasar and Protestantism: The Ecumenical Implications of His Theological Style*. London: T. & T. Clark, 2005.

Hunsinger, George. "Postliberal Theology." In *The Cambridge Companion to Postmodern Theology*, edited by Kevin J. Vanhoozer, 42–57. Cambridge: Cambridge University Press, 2003.

Husserl, Edmund. "Philosophy as Rigorous Science." In *Phenomenology and the Crisis of Philosophy*, 71–147. Translated by Quentin Lauer. New York: Harper & Row, 1965.

Jantzen, Grace M. *Power, Gender and Christian Mysticism*. Cambridge: Cambridge University Press, 1995.

Johnson, Elizabeth A. *Friends of God and Prophets: A Feminist Theological Reading of the Communion of Saints*. London: Continuum, 2005.

Jung, Carl Gustav. *The Symbolic Life: Miscellaneous Writings*. Vol. 18. Edited and translated by Gerhard Adler and R. F. C. Hull. Princeton: Princeton University Press, 2014.

Kemp, Eric Waldram. *Canonization and Authority in the Western Church*. London: Oxford University Press, 1948.

Kerlin, Michael J. "Maurice Blondel: Philosophy, Prayer and The Mystical." 2005. Accessed 27/7/2016. http://www.aarmysticism.org/documents/Kerlin.pdf.

Kerr, Fergus. "Balthasar and Metaphysics." In *The Cambridge Companion to Hans urs von Balthasar,* edited by Edward T. Oakes and David Moss, 224–38. Cambridge: Cambridge University Press, 2004.

———. "Forward: Assessing this 'Giddy Synthesis.'" In *Balthasar at the End of Modernity,* edited by Lucy Gardner et al., 1–13. Edinburgh: T. & T. Clark, 1999.

Kilby, Karen. *Balthasar: A (Very) Critical Introduction).* Grand Rapids: Eerdmans, 2012.

Kim, Eunsoo. "Time, Eternity, and the Trinity: A Trinitarian Analogical Understanding of Time and Eternity." PhD diss., Trinity Evangelical Divinity School, 2006.

Küng, Hans. *The Incarnation of God: An Introduction to Hegel's Theological Thought as Prolegomena to a Future Christology.* Translated by J. R. Stephenson. New York: Crossroad, 1987.

Laberthonnière, Lucien. *La notion Chrétienne de l'Autorité: Contribution au Rétablissement de l'Unanimité Chrétienne.* Oevres de Laberthonniére Publiés par les Soins di Louis Canet. Paris: Librarie Philosophique J. Vrin, 1955.

Lakeland, Paul F. "I Want to Be in That Number: Desire, Inclusivity, and the Church." CTSA Proceedings 66 (2011) 16–28. Accessed 27/7/2016. http://digitalcommons. fairfield.edu/cgi/viewcontent.cgi?article=1094&context=religiousstudies-facultypubs.

Latourelle, Réne, and Rino Fisichella, eds. *Dictionary of Fundamental Theology.* New York: Crossroad, 2000.

Leo XIII, Pope. *Aeterni Patris.* Encyclical promulgated 4 August 1879.

Lindbeck, George. *The Nature of Doctrine: Religion and Theology in a Postliberal Age.* Philadelphia: Westminster, 1984.

Loome, Thomas Michael. "Revelation as Experience. An Unpublished Lecture of George Tyrrell." *Heythrop* 12 (1971) 117–49.

Lösel, Steffen. "Unapocalyptic Theology: History and Eschatology in Balthasar's Theo-Drama." *Modern Theology* 17, no. 2 (2001) 201–25.

———. "Conciliar, Not Conciliatory: Hans Urs von Balthasar's Ecclesiological Synthesis of Vatican II." *Modern Theology,* 24, no. 1 (2008) 23–49.

Löser, Werner. "Hans Urs von Balthasar and Ignatius Loyola." *Way* 44, no. 4 (2005) 115–30.

———. "The Ignatian Exercises in the Work of Hans Urs von Balthasar." In *Hans Urs von Balthasar: His Life and Work,* edited by David L. Schindler. 103–20. Communio. San Francisco: Ignatius, 1991.

Loughlin, Gerard, ed. *Queer Theology: Rethinking the Western Body.* Oxford: Blackwell 2007.

Louth, Andrew. "The Ecclesiology of Saint Maximos the Confessor." *International Journal for the Study of the Christian Church* 4, no. 2 (2004) 109–20.

Lubac, Henri de. *Catholicism: Christ and the Common Destiny of Man.* Translated by Lancelot C. Sheppard. London: Burns & Oates, 1962.

———. *The Mystery of the Supernatural.* Translated by Rosemary Sheed. New York: Crossroad, 1998.

Lüning, Peter. "Facing the Crucified: The Dialectics of the Analogy in an Ignatian Theology of the Cross." *Heythrop* 50 (2009) 425–47.

MacIntyre, Alisdair. *After Virtue.* 3rd ed. London: Duckworth, 2007.

———. *Whose Justice? Which Rationality?* London: Duckworth, 1988.

Maggiolini, Alesandro. "Magisterial Teaching on Experience in the Twentieth Century: From the Modernist Crisis to the Second Vatican Council." *Communio*

International Catholic Review 23, no. 2 (1996). Accessed 6/11/2014. http://www.ewtn.com/library/THEOLOGY/MT20THCN.htm.

Majdik, Zoltan P., and William M. Keith. "Expertise as Argument: Authority, Democracy, and Problem-Solving." *Argumentation* 25 (2011) 371–84.

Mannion, Gerard, et al., eds. *Readings in Church Authority: Gifts and Challenges for Contemporary Catholicism*. Aldershot, UK: Ashgate, 2003.

Mannion, Gerard. *Ecclesiology and Postmodernity: Questions for the Church in Our Time*. Collegeville, MN: Liturgical, 2007.

Maritain, Jacques. *The Degrees of Knowledge*. Translated by Bernard Wall and Margot Robert Adamson. Notre Dame: University of Notre Dame, 2011.

Matzko, David Matthew. "Postmodernism, Saints and Scoundrels." *Modern Theology* 9, no. 1 (1993) 19–36.

Matzko McCarthy, David. "Desirous Saints." In *Queer Theology: Rethinking the Western Body*, edited by Gerard Loughlin, 305–12. Oxford: Blackwell, 2007.

McClendon, James William. *Biography as Theology. How Life Stories can Remake Today's Theology*. Philadelphia: Trinity, 1974.

McDade, John. "Von Balthasar and the Office of Peter in the Church." *Way* 44, no. 4 (2005) 97–114.

McDonagh, Enda. "The Theology of Vocation." *Furrow* 21, no. 5 (1970) 292–97.

McGinn, Bernard. "Evil-Sounding, Rash, and Suspect of Heresy: Tensions between Mysticism and Magisterium in the History of the Church." *Catholic Historical Review* 90 (2004) 193–212.

———. *The Presence of God: A History of Western Christian Mysticism*. Vol. 1, *The Foundations of Mysticism: Origins to the Fifth Century*. New York: Crossroad, 1991.

———. *The Presence of God: A History of Western Christian Mysticism*. Vol. 2, *The Growth of Mysticism: Gregory the Great Through the 12th Century*. New York: Crossroad, 1996.

———. *The Presence of God: A History of Western Christian Mysticism*. Vol. 3, *The Flowering of Mysticism: Men and Women in the New Mysticism: 1200–1350*. New York: Crossroad, 1998.

———. *The Presence of God: A History of Western Christian Mysticism*. Vol. 4, *The Harvest of Mysticism in Medieval Germany*. New York: Crossroad, 2005.

McInroy, Mark. *Balthasar on the Spiritual Senses, Perceiving Splendour*. Oxford: Oxford University Press, 2013.

McIntosh, Mark A. *Mystical Theology: The Integrity of Spirituality and Theology. Challenges in Contemporary Theology*. Oxford: Blackwell, 1998.

———. *Christology from within: Spirituality and the Incarnation in Hans Urs von Balthasar*. Notre Dame: University of Notre Dame, 1996.

McLoughlin, David. "Communio Models of Church: Rhetoric or Reality?" In *Authority in the Roman Catholic Church: Theory and Practice*, edited by Bernard Hoose, 181–90. Aldershot, UK: Ashgate, 2002.

McPartlan, Paul. "Who Is the Church? Zizoulas and von Balthasar on the Church's Identity." *Ecclesiology* 4 (2008) 271–88.

Médaille John C. "The Daring Hope of Hans Urs von Balthasar." Accessed 27/2/2017. https://www.academia.edu/6094884/The_Daring_Hope_of_Hans_Urs_Von_Balthasar.

Meilaender, Gilbert C., Jr. *The Theory and Practice of Virtue*. Notre Dame: University of Notre Dame Press, 1988.

Merleau-Ponty, Maurice. *Phenomenology of Perception.* Translated by Colin Smith. London: Routledge, 1962.

Minnis, Alastair J., and Rosalynn Voaden, eds. *Medieval Holy Women in the Christian Tradition c.1100–c.1500.* Turnhout: Brepols 2010.

Mueller, Joseph G. "Christian and Jewish Tradition behind Tyconius's Doctrine of the Church as Corpus Bipertitum." *Theological Studies* 73, no. 2 (2012) 286–317

Möhler, Johann Adam. *Unity in the Church: Or, The Principle of Catholicism: Presented in the Spirit of the Church Fathers of the First Three Centuries.* Translated by Peter C. Erb. Washington, DC: Catholic University of America Press, 1996.

Molinari, Paul. *Saints: Their Place in the Church.* New York: Sheed and Ward, 1965.

Mongrain, Kevin. "Review Symposium." *Horizons: The Journal of the College Theology Society* 40, no. 1 (2013) 96–100.

Mooney, Catherine M. "Voice, Gender and the Portrayal of Sanctity." In *Gendered Voices: Medieval Saints and their interpreters,* edited by Catherine M. Mooney, 1–15. Philadelphia: University of Pennsylvania Press, 1999.

Moss, David. "The Saints." In *The Cambridge Companion to Hans urs von Balthasar,* edited by Edward T. Oakes and David Moss 79–92. Cambridge: Cambridge University Press, 2004.

Mouroux, Jean. *The Christian Experience: An Introduction to a Theology.* Translated by George Lamb. London: Sheed and Ward, 1955.

Muers, Rachel. "A Queer Theology: Hans Urs von Balthasar." In *Queer Theology: Rethinking the Western Body,* edited by Gerard Loughlin, 200–212. Oxford: Blackwell, 2007.

Murphy, Michael P. *A Theology of Criticism: Balthasar, Postmodernism, and the Catholic Imagination: Balthasar, Postmodernism, and the Catholic Imagination.* Oxford: Oxford University Press, 2008.

Navone, John. *Seeking God in Story.* Order of St Benedict. Collegeville, MN: Liturgical, 1990.

Newman, Card. Henry. "Preface to the Third Edition." In *Lectures on the Prophetical Office of the Church, Via Media,* 1. Accessed 27/2/2017. http://newmanreader.org/works/viamedia/volume1/preface3.html.

Nichols, Aidan. *A Key to Balthasar: Hans Urs von Balthasar on Beauty, Goodness, and Truth.* London: Darton, Longman and Todd, 2011.

———. "Balthasar's Aims in the 'Theological Aesthetics.'" In *Glory, Grace, and Culture: The Work of Hans Urs von Balthasar,* edited by Ed Block Jr., 107–26. New York: Paulist, 2005.

———. *Divine Fruitfulness: A Guide through Balthasar's Theology beyond the Trilogy.* London: T. & T. Clark, 2007.

———. *No Bloodless Myth: A Guide through Balthasar's Dramatics.* Edinburgh: T. & T. Clark, 2000.

———. *Say It Is Pentecost: A Guide through Balthasar's Logic.* Edinburgh: T. & T. Clark, 2001.

———. "Theo-Logic." In *The Cambridge Companion to Hans urs von Balthasar,* edited by Edward T. Oakes and David Moss, 158–71. Cambridge: Cambridge University Press, 2004.

———. *The Word Has Been Abroad: A Guide through Balthasar's Aesthetics.* Edinburgh: T. & T. Clark, 1998.

Nietzsche, Friedrich. *Beyond Good and Evil*. Translated by Helen Zimmern. New York: Prometheus, 1989. Accessed 27/07/2016. http://www.gutenberg.org/files/4363/4363-h/4363-h.htm.

Nussberger, Danielle. "Saint as Theological Wellspring: Hans Urs von Balthasar's Hermeneutic of the Saint in a Christological and Trinitarian Key." PhD diss., University of Notre Dame, 2007.

————. "Theologians and Saints: The Drama of Iconic Reflections." CTSA Proceedings 66 (2011) 155–56.

————. "Review Symposium." *Horizons: The Journal of the College Theology Society*, 40, no. 1 (2013) 91–96.

Oakes, Edward T. "Balthasar's Critique of the Historical-Critical Method." In *Glory Grace and Culture: The Work of Hans Urs von Balthasar*, edited by Ed Block Jr., 150–74. New York: Paulist, 2005.

Oakes, Edward T., and David Moss, eds. *Cambridge Companion to Hans Urs von Balthasar*. Cambridge: Cambridge University Press, 2004.

Ouellet, Mark. "Foundations of Christian Ethics." In *Hans Urs Balthasar. His Life and Work*, edited by David L. Schindler, 231–50. San Francisco: Ignatius, 1991.

O'Donaghue, Noel Dermot. "A Theology of Beauty." In *The Analogy of Beauty: The Theology of Hans Urs von* Balthasar, edited by John Riches, 1–10. Edinburgh: T. & T. Clark, 1986.

O'Donnell, James J. "The Authority of Augustine." Accessed 27/07/2016. http://faculty.georgetown.edu/jod/augustine/augauth.html.

O'Donnell, John. *Hans Urs von Balthasar*. London: Chapman, 1992.

————. "Hans Urs von Balthasar: The Form of His Theology." In *Hans Urs Balthasar. His Life and Work*, edited by David L. Schindler, 207–20. San Francisco: Ignatius, 1991.

O'Hanlon, Gerard. *The Immutability of God in the Theology of Hans Urs von Balthasar*. Cambridge: Cambridge University Press, 1990.

O'Loughlin, Thomas. "The Credibility of the Catholic Church as Public Actor." *New Blackfriars* 94 (2013) 129–47.

Olsen, Cyrus P. "Remaining in Christ: A Paradox at the Heart of Hans Urs von Balthasar's Theology." *Logos: A Journal of Catholic Thought and Culture* 13, no. 3 (2010) 52–76.

Olsen, Glenn W. "The Theologian and the Magisterium: The Ancient and Medieval Background of a Contemporary Controversy." *Communio: International Catholic Review* 7, no. 4 (1980) 292–319.

O'Meara, Thomas F. *Theology of Ministry*. Completely rev. ed. Mahwah, NJ: Paulist, 1999.

O'Regan, Cyril. "Review of *Theology and the Drama of History* by Ben Quash." *Modern Theology* 23, no. 2 (2007) 293–96.

Padgett, Alan G. "What Is Biblical Equality?" *Priscilla Papers Academic Journal* 16, no. 3 (2002). Accessed 27/2/2017. http://www.cbeinternational.org/sites/default/files/pp163_5wibe.pdf

Palakeel, Joseph. *The Use of Analogy in Theological Discourse: An Investigation in Ecumenical Perspective*. Rome: Gregorian Biblical, 1995.

Paul VI, Pope. *Ecclesiam Suam*. Encyclical promulgated 6 August, 1964.

————. *Evangelii Nuntiandi*. Apostolic Exhortation. 8 December 1975.

Peterson, Janine Larmon. *Contested Sanctity: Disputed Saints, Inquisitors, and Communal Identity in Northern Italy, 1250–1400*. Bloomington: Indiana University Press, 2006.

Philipon, Marie Michel. *Sainte Thérèse de Lisieux*. Paris: Desclée, 1946.

———. *The Spiritual Doctrine of Sister Elizabeth of the Trinity*. Translated by a Benedictine of Stanbrook Abbey. Westminster, MD: Newman, 1947.

Pieper, Josef, *The Four Cardinal Virtues*. Indiana: University of Notre Dame Press, 1966.

Pitstick, Alyssa, Lyra. *Light in Darkness: Hans Urs von Balthasar and the Catholic Doctrine of Christ's Descent into Hell*. Cambridge: Eerdmans, 2007.

Pius X, Pope. *Pascendi Dominici Gregis*. Encyclical promulgated 8 September 1907.

Pius XI, Pope. *Studiorum Duce*. Encyclical promulgated 29 June 1923.

Pius XII, Pope. *Humani Generis*. Encyclical promulgated 12 August 1950.

———. *Mystici Corporis Christi*. Encyclical promulgated 29 June 1943.

Polanyi, Michael. *Personal Knowledge: Towards a Post-critical Philosophy*. Corrected ed. London: Routledge, 1962.

Pontifical Council for Promoting Christian Unity (PCPCU) and the Lutheran World Federation. *Joint Lutheran-Roman Catholic Declaration on the Doctrine of Justification by Faith* (JDDJ). Signed on Reformation Day, 31 October 1999.

Potworowski, Christophe. "An Exploration of the Notion of Objectivity in Hans Urs von Balthasar." In *Glory, Grace, and Culture: The Work of Hans Urs von Balthasar*, edited by Ed Block Jr., 69–87. New York: Paulist, 2005.

Quash, Ben. "Drama and the Ends of Modernity." In *Balthasar at the End of Modernity*, edited by Lucy Gardner et al., 139–72. Edinburgh: T. & T. Clark, 1999.

———. "Hans Urs von Balthasar." In *The Modern Theologians. An Introduction To Christian Theology since 1918*, edited by David F.Ford with Rachel Muers, 106–23. 3rd ed. Oxford: Blackwell, 2005.

———. *Theology and the Drama of History*. Cambridge Studies in Christian Doctrine. Cambridge: Cambridge University Press, 2005.

Rahner, Karl. *The Dynamic Element in the Church*. Translated by W. J. O'Hara. New York: Herder and Herder, 1964.

Rahner, Karl. "The Relation between Theology and Popular Religion." Translated by Joseph Donceel. In *Theological Investigations*, 22:140–47. New York: Crossroad, 1991.

Ratzinger, Joseph. *Joseph Ratzinger in Communio, 1, The Unity of the Church*. Ressourcement, Retrieval & Renewal in Catholic Thought. Cambridge: Eerdmans, 2010.

———. "Christian Universalism: On Two Collections of Papers by Hans Urs von Balthasar." In *Joseph Ratzinger in Communio, 1, The Unity of the Church*, 131–143. Ressourcement, Retrieval & Renewal in Catholic Thought. Cambridge: Eerdmans, 2010.

Raven, Bertram H. "The Bases of Power and the Power/Interaction Model of Interpersonal Influence." *Analyses of Social Issues and Public Policy* 8, no. 1 (2008) 1–22.

———. "Kurt Lewin Address: Influence, Power, Religion, and the Mechanisms of Social Control." *Journal of Social Issues* 55, no. 1 (1999) 161–86.

Riches, John. "Balthasar and the Analysis of Faith." In *The Analogy of Beauty: The Theology of Hans Urs von Balthasar*, edited by John Riches, 35–59. Edinburgh: T. & T. Clark, 1986.

————. "Von Balthasar as Biblical Theologian and Exegete." *New Blackfriars* 923 (1998) 38–45.

Ridderbos, Herman. *Paul: An Outline of His Theology.* Grand Rapids: Eerdmans, 1975.

Rieff, Philip. *Charisma: The Gift of Grace, and How It Has Been Taken Away from Us.* New York: Pantheon, 2007.

Robinson, Dominic. *Understanding the "Imago Dei": The Thought of Barth, von Balthasar and Moltmann.* Farnham, UK: Ashgate, 2011.

Rogers, Eugene F. "Bodies Demand Language: Thomas Aquinas." In *Queer Theology: Rethinking the Western Body,* edited by Gerard Loughlin, 176–87. Oxford: Blackwell, 2007.

Roten, Johann. "The Two Halves of the Moon: Marian Anthropological Dimensions in the Common Mission of Adrienne von Speyr and Hans Urs von Balthasar." In *Hans Urs von Balthasar: His Life and Work,* edited by David L. Schindler, 65–86. Communio. San Francisco: Ignatius, 1991.

Rousselot, Pierre. *The Eyes of Faith.* Translated by Joseph Donceel. New York: Fordham University Press, 1990.

Rush, Ormond. *The Eyes of Faith: The Sense of the Faithful and the Church's Reception of Revelation.* Washington, DC: Catholic University of America Press, 2009.

Sachs, Randy. "The Pneumatology and Spirituality of Hans Urs von Balthasar." CTA Proceedings 40 (1985), 192–93. Accessed 27/2/2017. https://ejournals.bc.edu/ojs/index.php/ctsa/article/viewFile/3310/2923

Saward, John. "Mary and Peter in the Christological Constellation: Balthasar's Ecclesiology." In *The Analogy of Beauty: The Theology of Hans Urs von Balthasar,* edited by John Riches, 105–33. Edinburgh: T. & T. Clark, 1986.

Schindler, David C. *Hans Urs von Balthasar and the Dramatic Structure of Truth: A Philosophical Investigation.* New York: Fordham University Press, 2004.

————. "Towards a Non-Possessive Concept of Knowledge: On the Relation between Reason and Love in Aquinas and Balthasar." *Modern Theology* 22, no. 24 (2006) 577–607.

————. "Hans Urs Balthasar, Metaphysics, and the Problem of Onto-Theology." *Analecta Hermeneutica* 1 (2009) 102–13.

Schindler, David L., ed. *Hans Urs Balthasar: His Life and Work.* Communio. San Francisco: Ignatius, 1991.

————. "Experience as a Theological Category: Hans Urs von Balthasar." CTSA Proceedings 47 (1992) 109–11.

————. *Love Alone Is Credible, Hans Urs von Balthasar as Interpreter of the Catholic Tradition.* Grand Rapids: Eerdmans, 2008.

————. "The Significance of Hans Urs von Balthasar." In *Glory, Grace and Culture,* edited by Ed Block Jr., 16–36. New York: Paulist, 2005.

Schillebeeckx, Edward. "The Christian Community and Its Office-Bearers." *Concilium* 133: *The Right of a Community to a Priest,* edited by Edward Schillebeeckx and J. B. Metz, 95–133. New York: Seabury, 1980.

————. *Ministry: Leadership in the Community of Jesus Christ.* New York: Crossroad, 1981.

Schönborn, Christoph. "Hans Urs von Balthasar's Contribution to Ecumenism." In *Hans Urs von Balthasar: His Life and Work* edited by David L. Schindler, 251–63. San Francisco: Ignatius, 1991.

Schüssler Fiorenza, Francis, and John P. Galvin, eds. *Systematic Theology: Roman Catholic Perspectives*. 2nd ed. Minneapolis: Fortress, 2011.

Scola, Angelo, "Christian Experience and Theology." Translated by Adrian Walker, *Communio: International Catholic Review* 13, no. 2 (1996) 203–6. Accessed 27/2/2017. http://www.ewtn.com/library/THEOLOGY/EXTHEO.htm.

———. *Hans Urs von Balthasar: A Theological Style, Retrieval & Renewal in Catholic Thought*. Grand Rapids: Eerdmans, 1995.

———. *Test Everything: Hold Fast to What Is Good. An Interview with Hans Urs von Balthasar*. San Francisco: Ignatius, 1989.

Secomb, Meredith Anne. "Hearing the Word of God: Toward a Theological Phenomenology of Vocation." PhD diss., Australian Catholic University, 2010. Accessed 20/11/2014. http://dlibrary.acu.edu.au/digitaltheses/public/adt-acuvp266.24022011/02whole.pdf.

Sharman, Scott. "Ecumenical Hagiography: Ecclesiologies of Roman Catholic and Anglican 'Saint-Making.'" CTSA Proceedings 66 (2011) 96–97.

Sherry, Patrick. "Philosophy and the Saints." *Heythrop* 18 (1977) 23–37.

Sherwood, Polycarp. "Survey of Recent Work on St Maximus the Confessor." *Traditio* 20 (1964) 428–37.

Sicari, Antonio. "Hans Urs von Balthasar: Theology and Holiness." In *Hans Urs von Balthasar: His Life and Work*, edited by David L. Schindler, 121–32. San Francisco: Ignatius, 1991.

Simon, Martin. "Identity and Analogy: Balthasar's Hölderlin and Hamann." In *The Analogy of Beauty: The Theology of Hans Urs Von Balthasar*, edited by John Riches, 77–104. Edinburgh: T. & T. Clark, 1986.

Simon, Yves. *A General Theory of Authority*. Notre Dame: University of Notre Dame Press, 1962.

Speyr, Adrienne von. *Book of All Saints*. Translated by D. C. Schindler. San Francisco: Ignatius, 2008.

Stagaman, David J. *Authority within the Church*. Collegeville, MN: Order of St Benedict, 1999.

Steck, Christopher. *The Ethical Thought in Hans Urs von Balthasar*. New York: Crossroad, 2001.

———. "Studying Holy Lives: A Methodological Necessity for the Christian Ethicist?" *Josephinum Journal of Theology* 12, no. 1 (2005) 68–86. Accessed 27/2/2017. http://www.pcj.edu/files/2014/1339/4583/steck12-1.pdf.

Stuart, Elizabeth. "Sacramental Flesh." In *Queer Theology: Rethinking the Western Body*, edited by Gerard Loughlin, 65–75. Oxford: Blackwell, 2007.

Štrukelj, Anton. *Teologia e Santita' a Partire da Hans Urs von Balthasar*. Translated by Ellero Babini et al. Milan: San Paolo, 2010.

Sullivan, Patricia A. "Saints as the 'Living Gospel': Von Balthasar's Revealers of the Revealer, Rahner's Mediators of the Mediator." *Heythrop* 52 (2011) 1–16.

Sullivan, Francis A. *Magisterium: Teaching Authority in the Catholic Church*. Mahwah, NJ: Paulist, 1983.

Sutton, Matthew Lewis. "Hans Urs von Balthasar and Adrienne von Speyr's Ecclesial Relationship." *New Blackfriars* 94, no. 1049 (2013) 50–63.

Swain, Scott and Michael Allen. "The Obedience of the Eternal Son." *International Journal of Systematic Theology* 15, no. 2 (2013) 114–34.

Tillard, Jean-Marie Roger. *Church of Churches: The Ecclesiology of Communion.* Translated by R. C. de Peaux. Collegeville, MN: Liturgical, 1992.

Tilley, Maureen A. "One Wholly Catholic: Saints and Sanctity in the Post-Apostolic Church." CTSA Proceedings 66 (2011) 1–15. Accessed 28/11/2014. http://www. ctsa-online.org/Convention%202011/0001–0015.pdf.

Tourenne, Yves. "Foreword." In *The Christian and Anxiety*, 11–29. San Francisco, Ignatius, 2000.

Tracy, David. *The Analogical Imagination: Christian Theology and the Culture of Pluralism.* New York: Crossroad, 1981.

Vatican Council II. *Dei Filius.* Dogmatic Constitution. 24 April 1870.

———. *Dei Verbum,* Dogmatic Constitution. 18 November 1965.

———. *Lumen Gentium,* Dogmatic Constitution. 24 November 1964.

Viladesau, Richard. "The Beauty of the Cross." In *Theological Aesthetics after von Balthasar,* edited by Oleg V. Bychkov and James Fodor, 135–52. Hampshire, UK: Ashgate, 2008.

Voaden, Rosalynn, ed. *Prophets abroad: The Reception of Continental Holy Women in Late-Medieval England.* Cambridge: D. S. Brewer, 1996.

———. "All Girls Together: Community, Gender and Vision at Helfta." In *Medievel Women in Their Communities,* edited by Diane Watt, 72–91. Toronto: University of Toronto Press, 1997.

Vogel, Jeffrey A. "The Unselfing Activity of the Holy Spirit in the Theology of Hans Urs Balthasar." *Logos: A Journal of Catholic Thought and Culture* 10, no. 4 (2007) 16–34.

Wainwright, Geoffrey. "Eschatology." In *The Cambridge Companion to Hans Urs von Balthasar,* edited by Edward T. Oakes and David Moss, 113–27. Cambridge: Cambridge University Press, 2004.

Watson, Claire Louise. "The Authority of Saints and their Makers in Old English Hagiography." PhD diss., University of Leicester, 2004.

Weber, Max. *The Protestant Ethic and the Spirit of Capitalism.* Translated by Talcott Parsons, New York: Dover, 2003.

———. *Theory of Social and Economic Organization.* Translated by A. R. Anderson and Talcott Parsons. New York: Free, 1947.

Weinstein, Donald, and Rudolph M. Bell. *Saints and Society: The Two Worlds of Western Christendom, 1000–1700.* Chicago: University of Chicago Press, 1982.

Wheeler, Michael, "Martin Heidegger." *Stanford Encyclopedia of Philosophy.* Edited by Edward N. Zalta. Fall 2015 ed. Accessed 28/11/2014. http://plato.stanford.edu/ archives/fall2015/entries/heidegger/.

Wigley, Stephen. *Balthasar's Trilogy.* Readers' Guides. London: T. & T. Clark, 2010.

Williams, Rowan. "Theological Integrity." In *On Christian Theology,* 3–15. Challenges in Contemporary Theology. Oxford: Blackwell, 2000.

Woodward, Kenneth L. *Making Saints: Inside the Vatican: Who Becomes a Saint, Who Doesn't, and Why.* New York: Touchstone, 1996.

Wyschogrod, Edith. *Saints and Postmodernism: Revisioning Moral Philosophy.* Religion and Postmodernism Series. London: Chatto & Windus, 1990.

Yeago, David S. "Literature in the Drama of Nature and Grace: Hans Urs von Balthasar's Paradigm for a Theology of Culture." In *Glory, Grace and Culture: The Work of Hans Urs von Balthasar,* edited by Ed Block Jr., 88–106. New York: Paulist, 2005.

Yenson, Mark Leslie. *Existence as Prayer: The Consciousness of Christ in the Theology of Hans Urs von Balthasar.* PhD diss., University of St. Michael's College, Toronto, 2010.